5 skills companies seek

The method that landed a job for 70 percent of
50+ job seekers

10 rules that put you on the road to a successful
career change

The sure-fire résumé that employers don't ignore

6 letter-writing rules you should never break

The best way to evaluate your goals and research the
market

The single most important ingredient for success

CRACKING THE
OVER-50
JOB MARKET

"You made a smart choice buying J. Robert Connor's
wonderful book, *Cracking the Over-50 Job Market*. That
tells me you're anxious to get yourself a good job, and
you'll use Bob's excellent advice to guide you through
the process, step by step. Then all you need to do is
believe you can get what you want—and you will."

—From the Foreword by Robert Half

J. ROBERT CONNOR is the author of *A Job with a Future
in Automotive Mechanics* and co-author of *The National Job-
Finding Guide*. An editor of various business magazines for
thirty-five years, he served as editor-in-chief of *Graduating
Engineer* and *Business Week Careers*. Now freelancing and
working on a new magazine, he lives in Huntington,
New York.

CRACKING THE

OVER-50

JOB MARKET

J. Robert Connor

A PLUME BOOK

PLUME
Published by the Penguin Group
Penguin Books USA Inc., 375 Hudson Street,
New York, New York 10014, U.S.A.
Penguin Books Ltd, 27 Wrights Lane,
London W8 5TZ, England
Penguin Books Australia Ltd, Ringwood,
Victoria, Australia
Penguin Books Canada Ltd, 10 Alcorn Avenue,
Toronto, Ontario, Canada M4V 3B2
Penguin Books (N.Z.) Ltd, 182–190 Wairau Road,
Auckland 10, New Zealand

Penguin Books Ltd, Registered Offices:
Harmondsworth, Middlesex, England

First published by Plume, an imprint of New American Library,
a division of Penguin Books USA Inc.

First Printing, June, 1992
10 9 8 7 6 5 4 3 2

 REGISTERED TRADEMARK—MARCA REGISTRADA

LIBRARY OF CONGRESS CATALOGING IN PUBLICATION DATA

Connor, J. Robert.
    Cracking the over-50 job market / J. Robert Connor.
        p. cm.
    Includes bibliographical references and index.
    ISBN 0-452-26835-4
    1. Job hunting. 2. Middle aged persons—Employment. I. Title.
    II. Title: Cracking the over-fifty job market.
    HF5382.7.C66 1992
    650.14'0844—dc20   91-33362
                                                              CIP

PRINTED IN THE UNITED STATES OF AMERICA
Set in New Baskerville
Designed by Leonard Telesca

BOOKS ARE AVAILABLE AT QUANTITY DISCOUNTS WHEN USED TO PROMOTE PRODUCTS OR
SERVICES. FOR INFORMATION PLEASE WRITE TO PREMIUM MARKETING DIVISION, PENGUIN
BOOKS USA INC., 375 HUDSON STREET, NEW YORK, NEW YORK 10014.

DEDICATED TO
Robert Brian Connor
"The angel has passed"

Contents

Acknowledgments

It would be impossible to thank all the kind, cooperative, friendly, and wonderful people—most of whom I've never met—who graciously gave me their time and expertise for this book. I'm indebted to you all and I thank you. Special thanks to my wife, Marie L. Connor, Ph.D., for her invaluable editing help, who also spent many hours putting together the survey chapter. In addition, my special thanks to Hugh Rawson, my editor, and the individuals and companies listed below. This book could not have been written without your help.

Willard Anderson, ITT
American Association of Retired Persons
American Society for Training & Development
Avon Products, Inc.
Nella G. Barkley, Chrystal-Barkley Association
Robert Brocksbank, Council on Career Development for
    Minorities
Shirley Brussel, ABLE
Vera Burger
Bureau of Labor Statistics
Bill Bygrave, Boston College
Sharon Cantor, Manpower Temporary Services
Catalyst
William L. Caudell, Talent Tree Personnel Services
Letitia Chamberlain, New York University
Bud Clarke, Clark-Thompson
Richard Clarke, Richard Clarke Associates
James Cabrera, Drake Beam & Morin Inc.
James E. Challenger, Challenger, Gray & Christmas Inc.
Jim Crisman, Dobisky Associates
Lois Davis

Dr. Sandra Davis
Floyd Dickens, 21st Century Management Services Inc.
Frank Dobisky, Dobisky Associates
Patricia Eidson
Employment Management Association
Erdlen Bogard Group
John L. Estrada, Amoco Corporation
Forty Plus
Marcia Fox, Ph.D., Drake Beam Morin, Inc.
Marjorie Freedland, Deutsch, Shea & Evans Inc.
Carolyn Fryer, Kelly Services Inc.
Cathy Fyock, Innovative Management Concepts
Robert Half, Robert Half International
Dick Hamel
Institute for Educational Leadership
Dr. Bailey Jackson, University of Massachusetts
Tom Jackson, Equinox Corporation
Barbara Stark Jordan
Dr. Thomas S. Law, St. Paul's College
Chris Mackaronis, AARP
Joseph R. Mancuso, Center for Entrepreneurial
    Management
Dr. David McClelland, Boston University
John McLain Dobisky Associates
Minority Business Development Agency
Moe Mozier
National Council on Aging
Office of Personnel Management/Federal Job Information/
    Testing Offices
Sharon Perkins, Director of Senior Employment, New York
    City
Mike Prelee, station WNEW, New York City
Frank Reilly
Bob Rheinhart, Retiree Skills, Inc.
Frank Ross
Samuel Sacco, National Association of Temporary Services
Service Corps of Retired Executives (SCORE)

Donald Sexton, Ohio State University
Hugh Sharp
Davis Small, University of Houston
Small Business Administration
Rick Spahn, Goodrich & Sherwood Company
State Job Centers
John Stodden, Ph.D.
Alexander J. Sussman
The Conference Board
Dr. R. Roosevelt Thomas, Jr., Morehouse College
Al Thompson
John Thompson, IMCOR
Dr. Martha Turnage, Ohio University
U.S. Department of Labor
Joyce Welsh, National Council on Aging, Inc.
Kate Wendleton, The Five O'Clock Club
General Charles Williams, New York City School Construc-
   tion Authority
Workforce 2000/The Hudson Institute Inc.
Dr. Neil Yeager, University of Massachusetts-Amherst
Janet Zoebel, National Urban League, Inc.

Foreword

The young have the energy to gain experience. The old have the knowledge to use it. Both are necessary.

Do you remember how hard it was for you to find your first job? "They won't hire me because I don't have the experience. It's a vicious cycle. I'll never find a job." But you did find a job. It may have taken you many months because you believed no one would hire a beginner; or, on the other hand, perhaps it only took a couple of weeks because you knew you'd overcome the problem.

You might have *too-timed* yourself *too* many times in your career. First you thought you were *too* young, now maybe you think you're too *old*. Remember when you were 40, and you worried you'd had *too* many jobs, that you were a job-jumper? Or maybe you'd had *too* few jobs—you were in a rut—not enough diversification? You may have thought you were *too* fat or *too* thin; *too* short or *too* tall: But now you're *too* old!

And if you believe that—you are!

There's something wrong with all of us when it comes to getting any job. Understand what's wrong with you, but don't become paranoid over it. Balance your thinking with what's *right* about you. I'm sure you'll find there's much more right than wrong.

Prove to those who interview you that any preconceived ideas about people your age are wrong. Prove it by casually working an appropriate anecdote into the conversation. "By the way, Mr. Jones, I enjoy work, I'm energetic and healthy. Last year, for that matter, I worked seventy-five hours in one week in order to get important reports on the controller's desk." In one sentence you've counteracted any doubts the interviewer may have about your health, energy, willingness, and loyalty—based on your age.

You made a smart choice buying J. Robert Connor's wonderful book *Cracking the Over-50 Job Market*. That tells me you're anxious to get yourself a good job, and you'll use Bob's excellent advice to guide you through the process, step by step. Then all you need to do is believe you can get what you want—and you will.

Robert Half
Founder, Robert Half International, Inc.

CHAPTER 1

Ability Is Ageless

Several years ago a job seeker wrote a letter to *The New York Times* complaining about the manatory retirement age of 70. He said, "At age 73, I voluntarily retired. After a year of frustrating idleness, I determined to seek employment that could utilize my background in sales, sales promotion, advertising, and management. I was one-hundred percent able mentally and physically, but I was consistently and regretfully turned down because of my age.

"In desperation, I revised my résumé, taking 11 years off my age. Within two months I had a job. Seven years later, even though I had received merit increases and additional responsibilities every year, I was mandatorily retired at age 70—I was 81 but as able physically and mentally as when I was hired."

An inspiring—and sad—story of an older able worker forced out of a job because of age. Contrary to the so-called golden years concept, current statistics show that approximately half of today's retirees 55 years old or more are not happy living in the world of retirement. And why should they be? They are members of the "new young," healthy, vigorous professionals—with skills they are eager to use in full- or part-time employment, skills honed during difficult times. Individ-

**1988 Census Bureau Figures:
50-plus Population in the United States
(Thousands)**

	Men	Women
Ages 50–54	5,511	5,866
55–59	5,121	5,605
60–64	5,079	5,788
65–69	4,631	5,538
70–74	3,464	4,549
75–79	2,385	3,648
80–84	1,306	2,422

Census Bureau figures show the current 50-plus population in the United States. Men and women in this population seeking employment make it a significant potential work force.

uals such as the letter writer and countless others like him have already demonstrated that ability is ageless. Companies currently employing mature professionals 50 years or older have discovered that, like fine wine, they get better with age. This is also borne out by a number of recent studies that show mature workers bring much-needed skills to the corporate workplace.

It's Not Easy

Despite changing attitudes by many corporations and individuals in the business world, discrimination against older people in the workplace does exist, especially against minorities and women. Be prepared for it. The older professional worker may find it especially difficult to find a job, but it is by no means impossible. It helps a great deal to know what you want to do. If you've been out of the job market for some time—as a woman returning to the workplace after many years, or a retired person reentering the job market—planning, patience, and persistence will be the keys that unlock the door to your new career. If ability is ageless, a good attitude is contagious. A positive attitude is a must for a job seeker at any age.

Prized Abilities: Know-how and Experience

You may not be aware of it, but you do have choices, and your abilities and years of invaluable on-the-job experience are prized in the corporate world. Don't underestimate yourself or be too bashful to talk about your skills. Even the loss of a job is not the end of the world for the 50-plus professional. It can be the beginning of an exciting new adventure.

When he lost his job, Hugh Sharp, 60, was not ready to retire, but he was prepared to do something about it. It took Sharp less than three months to find a new job after he lost his old one because of a major company cutback. How he did it is a classic example of being prepared and a case study of how to find a job. It involved planning his campaign and marketing his skills.

Sharp, a trim man who exudes energy with his can-do attitude, says, "When you lose your job, don't waste time being bitter. It is not productive and it colors your outlook. It also comes through in interviews."

He also recommends treating the job hunt as "an adventure and learning experience." Don't turn down a good job in another part of the country, he says. "You may wind up renting a place and keeping your house for a couple of years but you are not locked in. Don't take away your flexibility."

When Sharp was let go he was vice-president of product planning and development of the Sweet's Group at McGraw-Hill Inc., an international publishing company headquartered in New York City. Sharp holds a chemical engineering degree from Villanova University and had completed courses in management at New York University. He had risen through the ranks at McGraw-Hill during his 37-year-career and was responsible for planning and developing new business that produced about 15 percent of his unit's annual revenues. He also developed growth strategies for the unit and found and recommended acquisitions. In addition, Sharp's past experience in sales, marketing, and editorial positions contributed to his reputation as one of the most savvy and successful executives in the company.

Sharp is a man who plans for all eventualities. For example, every year he made an appointment with the company's pension department to check out what he would receive in pension and savings if he retired. He says, "I believe anyone who assumes that his or her job is assured or safe in the climate we've worked in in recent years is crazy. It's important to know where you stand financially, to keep your résumé up to date, and to review it every year."

When the ax fell, Sharp was shocked, but not surprised, he says. Over the years he made a habit of keeping track of people and had assembled a data base of professionals he had encountered in the information and construction industries. When he was told in January of 1990 that his job was being eliminated and that he had three months before being terminated, he was able to sit down, "and in a few minutes" go over his résumé, edit it, and print it out because he had kept it current. In addition, he had the use of his office for the three months, including his secretary's services, telephone, computer, and printer. He went to the office every day, at 8:30 A.M., as if still employed, to conduct his job-finding campaign.

Preparation Pays. Sharp feels it is a waste of valuable time to begin putting a résumé together when you really need it, which is why he always kept his up to date. "You have to have a marketing plan and make a sale," he says. "If you are not sufficiently disciplined for a job search, why should an employer trust you to have the discipline necessary to be a good manager?

"I worked this like a job, like a marketing assignment, including a well-thought-out marketing plan," says Sharp. He went on interviews as if they were sales calls. He even kept a speaking engagement that he had agreed to before he was let go.

The next step, says Sharp, was to assemble three mailing lists. The first one—about 120 names—listed professionals he knew from different companies who might have jobs he could fill. He wrote each person a letter, saying that due to a recent reorganization his job was being eliminated, then briefly reviewed his background, and said he would call about a week later on a specific day to see if there was a mutual interest for further discussion. He eliminated 30 names from his list and sent out 90 letters.

The second list was comprised of people who could possibly suggest a number of contacts. He called them, talked to them about his situation, and sent them his résumé.

The third group was composed of people who had no jobs to offer. Sharp wrote each one a farewell letter, saying he was leaving and wanted to stay in touch. He also told them how much he enjoyed meeting and working with such great people and hoped their paths would cross again.

In all, says Sharp, 50 people—about 10 percent of those he contacted—requested résumés, told him to stay in touch, or telephoned. Many said they would be glad to provide a reference. They were all very nice, says Sharp.

Another ploy Sharp used was to write a consultant friend and request that he send a letter introducing Sharp to someone he knew. Sharp claims that many consultants do this, and that it can be very useful strategy.

Lightning Strikes. During his search Sharp's interviews resulted in seven consulting assignments, but he decided he would be happier in a full-time job. Near the end of his job quest, Sharp had nine job possibilities of which, he said, "six were a lot of smoke or things I'm really not interested in. The remaining three were fairly solid."

But on March 30 lightning struck. Sharp accepted a job as vice-president and general manager at R. S. Means, a publisher of construction and cost information in Kingston, Massachusetts.

Sharp landed the job he wanted two and a half months after he began his search. Obviously, being prepared pays.

Job Fairs for Mature Workers

In today's changing economy and workplace nothing is sacred or secure. You can't predict what will happen so you must be prepared for any eventuality or opportunity, whether you are working or looking for a job. For example, the job fair is an avenue to explore. Today many progressive companies recognize the talents of the 50-plus professional and actively recruit through annual job fairs in New York, Boston, Chicago, and Los Angeles, and other cities. In New York City, for example, the Ability is Ageless Fair—targeted to the mature worker 55 years and older—has become an annual event. It draws more than 4,500 seekers of jobs, and representatives from more than 100 companies provide information about their organizations and discuss employment and other opportunities with the mature workers.

The exhibitors include retail stores, banks, law firms, publishing houses, insurance companies, and agencies for temporary employment. In addition to the employer booths, the fair features a Resource and Employment Information Center staffed by experienced employment interviewers from the New York State Department of Labor, where the attendees receive listings of specific jobs offered by the exhibitors as well as many small businesses that do not have booths at the fair. Fair-goers are also given in-depth employment interviews to discuss job openings at the various booths and job listings posted by the New York State Department of Labor.

Sixty-five-year-old Ed Selder, who attended a recent fair, says, "I went to the fair and was amazed at the variety of exhibitors and how many different skills and trades were covered." Asked "What can you do? What skills do you have?" Selder replied that he had said, " 'Using the phone.' I've had some 40 years of experience as a fund-raiser, and have used the phone quite a bit to raise money. I filled out an application that was screened by the very able people who worked there. I was sent to an employer in my field. They needed someone for one campaign and they hired me. I have found that it was very fruitful for me to have gone there and I'm very grateful to them."

Workshops That Really Help. Attendees also have access to free workshops on such subjects as résumé writing and job interviews, part-time and temporary job opportunities, job trends, networking, time management, employer perceptions of the overqualified mature labor force, and alternatives to retirement. There is even a workshop for bilingual Spanish/English job seekers—the Busqueda de Empleo.

Sharon Perkins, Director of the Senior Employment Divisions of the New York City Department for the Aging that runs the job fairs, cites two reasons mature people want to work. "One is financial, they may not have financial security," she says. "The second reason is that some mature workers would like to develop other interests. Sometimes they want part-time jobs because they may be looking for second-career opportunities or they are trying something new. Perhaps for a number of years they have been in a particular type of profession. Now they want to change careers."

Frank Ross was more than willing to try something new and change careers. Ross, 67, spent 32 years in the brokerage business in New York City, the last 15 years in the back office of Merrill Lynch working with government securities. Then the company instituted a personnel reduction plan in an effort to thin its ranks and reduce expenses. "There was an option," says Ross, "retirement or taking the chance of being fired."

Starting a New Life and Career

It was a difficult time for Ross. His wife had passed away two months before, and now, suddenly, he faced retirement.

He recalled going to the office at 7:00 A.M. on that fateful day and heading home to Staten Island at 9:00.

"I was retired, it was that quick," says Ross. "But it was okay for me. The company kept me on the payroll, with full benefits, for almost eight months."

Ross was not expecting retirement and had not given any thought to what he might do. But then his son, John (Ross has five sons) called from Sacramento, California, and said, "Would you like to come and work with me?" Ross had no pangs about moving but had one more problem to consider before making a decision. His 90-year-old father was in a nursing home and Ross felt "apprehensive" about leaving him. He went to see his father and talked to him about the possibility of going to California.

"Go to California and enjoy yourself" was his father's response. So Ross moved to Sacramento to work with his son, who owns and operates Eagle Press, which does commercial and direct mail printing. Ross gets along well with his son and enjoys working with the "very nice" people who staff the business. The senior Ross says he's learning the printing business and "doing a little bit of everything." He works five days a week from 7:00 A.M. to 4:00 P.M.

"Home," says Ross, "is a condo in Sacramento, a beautiful place to live with everything you could possibly want: a swimming pool, tennis court, bicycles one can borrow, and a laundry." As for New York, "I truly don't miss it," says Ross.

California living agrees with Ross. He says, "I truly love Sacramento. It's a laid-back and beautiful city." He also enjoys seeing seven of his nine grandchildren regularly, but misses the two that are back East.

"All my life I said I would never retire," says Ross. "You can't turn off the motor and sit down. I'm glad I didn't. I get up in the morning, shower and shave, and have a place to go. I don't have time to sit around. I enjoy the discipline of working. I feel that I am not stagnating by getting up every morning and going out to face the world. I think too many people in my age group, when they hit 65, start turning down their engines. I don't feel that way. I want to keep on going as much as I possibly can.

"I'm very happy I made the move and I'm grateful to my son for suggesting that I move to California."

Ability Is Ageless

Many people who attain the age of 50 or more years have a tendency to put themselves down, to develop a defeatist attitude that they can't compete with younger people or do a good job. You've heard them say, "I'm too old for that," or "I can't get a new job at my age. Who would hire me?"

This attitude is disturbing because many of us don't always appreciate, or fail to understand, the many valuable talents we've nurtured and the experience we've acquired over the years. More and more the talents of older workers are being recognized in both the private and public sector. For example, a recent *Wall Street Journal* poll found that 84 percent of personnel managers felt that older workers are more productive than their younger counterparts. And President Bush, in his 1988 inaugural address, speaking of a new kind of activism, noted the importance of older workers when he said, "And I am speaking of a new engagement in the lives of others—a new activism, hands-on and involved, that gets the job done. We must bring in the generations, harnessing the unused talent of the elderly and the unfocused energy of the young. For not only is leadership passed from generation to generation, so is stewardship. And the generation born after the Second World War has come of age."

That ability is ageless is not a glib phrase but a proven fact. "Chronological age has nothing to do with one's functional capacity," says Joyce Welsh, director of corporate employment programs at the National Council on Aging, Inc., in Washington, D.C., a private nonprofit organization working to meet the current and changing needs of older persons, and to tap the abilities they can offer to the nation. Since 1950 NOCA has served as a resource for program development, research, training, technical assistance, and publications on all aspects of aging. "Intellectual capacity does not begin to diminish until well into the 70s," she says. "And in many individuals it does not diminish."

You Remain What You Are. NOCA studies show that age does not significantly alter the ability of older workers in such areas as speed, attentiveness to detail, stamina, and accuracy. "In some areas," according to the studies, "such as attentiveness, which requires concentration and accuracy, there is a general increase in performance as workers age."

The study also states that older workers have "fewer accidents on the job than their younger associates," fewer sick days. The ability to learn new things has also been demonstrated, says NOCA, citing cases where older workers in companies adapted to new procedures as competently as their younger counterparts. The study also showed that basic personalities do not change. For example, a flexible personality remains flexible in old age, whereas a rigid personality will become more so in later years.

Older Workers: Human Resources

Companies in the vanguard of hiring experienced older workers include such well-known names as Chase Manhattan Bank, Grumman Corporation, Polaroid, Levi Strauss, Travelers Insurance Companies, Wal-Mart Stores Inc., and Xerox Corporation.

One of the best-known is the Travelers Insurance Companies' Retiree Job Bank, which the Hartford, Connecticut–based company created in 1980 through its Older Americans Program. A primary goal of the Older Americans Program is to increase economic security of older people through extended employment, according to the company. It offers part-time employment to retirees and meets the Travelers' needs for experienced and reliable temporary workers. The in-house temporary service program is called Trav Temps.

The Travelers abolished mandatory retirement and altered its pension plan to permit retirees to work up to 960 hours a year without jeopardizing their retirement benefits.

Job Bank. The Job Bank was opened in 1981 to the Travelers' retirees. In 1985 when demand for retirees for supervisors grew beyond the pool's capacity, the company began recruiting retirees from other area companies through an "unretirement" campaign, which matches retirees' skills and schedules with temporary openings. Retirees fill in during absences, and delays in hiring full-time personnel, and for special projects. Retirees are paid on skill level, experience, and job performance. In 1990 the program was expanded to include homemakers and students.

Approximately 750 retirees are registered in the Job Bank. In a typical week, 250 retirees are working at the company. They earn more through the retiree Job Bank than through outside temporary employment services. The Job Bank can often accommodate retirees' schedules through flexible hours. Computer training opportunities are offered to retirees to help keep their skills current with business needs.

By decreasing the costly use of temporary employment agencies, the Travelers saves an estimated $4 million each year. The company also gains from the experience and knowledge retirees bring to the jobs they perform for the company.

"Buying 32 Years of My Experience"

When Bernard Chiccione, 61, of Massapequa, New York, went back to work it was because he was a "little bored." Says Chiccione, "There is so much you can do, time hangs heavy on your hands."

Travelers asked him to come back, he says. "It's a mutual thing. They have a program that they set up if there is a need for what you have done in the past. I only want to work a couple of days a week, so I decided to go back. Travelers has afforded an opportunity to many people. I wouldn't have gone back if I couldn't have contributed."

Chiccione works two days a week as a commercial casualty property underwriter. He says, "Travelers Insurance is buying thirty-two years of experience."

Job banks are expected to increase in number in the 1990s, according to a recent report—"Job Banks for Retirees"—issued by the Conference Board. Companies like Grumman, Varian, and Wells Fargo use the services of retirees to fill niches in their work force. Check with large companies in your area to see if they have job banks or special programs that utilize the talents of older workers.

Sam Walton, founder and chairman of Arkansas-based Wal-Mart Stores Inc., a huge national discount department store, accepting an award for his company's older worker and recruitment policies, said, "Wal-Mart has found the older worker to be an experienced and dependable resource with strong moral and work ethics that have proven invaluable. We will continue to depend on them as an important part of our future growth."

Jan Moen, an economist with the Federal Reserve Bank of Atlanta, notes that companies like Xerox are using older workers who have retired, keeping them around on a part-time basis or encouraging them to stay on longer to use their skills and pass them on to younger people. "They are reliable workers," he says, "with good attendance records who get their work done well and on time. Older workers do not lose their ability."

The United States has long been wasting one of its greatest national resources, the 50-plus mature workers with gray hair and fire in the furnace. But today Uncle Sam, together with many forward-looking organizations like those mentioned previously, is looking at people like you—a potent professional work force that can help solve the growing shortage of skilled workers who will be required to keep the country competitive in the global marketplace.

Recent government studies commissioned by former Labor

Secretary Ann McLaughlin pointed out that employers increasingly will have to tap into the pool of older workers to overcome major shortages. Retaining and retraining older workers for highly skilled jobs is critically important, according to the report.

Patricia Eidson, 58, who now lives in Norman, Oklahoma, changed her life 11 years ago when her husband died suddenly at age 50. Eidsons' Architect was the name of their company in Manhattan, Kansas. Since that time Eidson has gotten her degree and is now a consultant on interior design and interior architecture. She is also a licensed architect and an associate professor at the University of Oklahoma in the College of Architecture, Interior Design Division.

In the interim, in addition to getting her degree, she has taught at the University of Massachusetts, the University of Cincinnati, and the University of Hawaii. After her husband died, she said, "It's rebuilding your life. It's like starting over again at 30. I don't think of myself as special nor really of the 'late-in-life' career person, yet I know I am."

Renewal

Sometimes it isn't necessary to change jobs or career to find that elusive something so many of us seek at some point in our working lives. That's why it is important to look within and know what it is you want in both your work and personal life. Barbara Stark Jordan did and found what she wanted where she worked, and it changed her life.

Jordan, 52, who was born and raised in the San Francisco–Oakland Bay area, works at Wells Fargo Bank in San Francisco, where she is assistant vice-president and manager of furniture services and warehousing. She started with the bank in 1975 and administers a staff of four project managers and eight warehousemen, and manages two warehouses filled with what she called "excess product."

When Jordan joined Wells Fargo, she learned that the company had a personal growth program that offered any employee with 10 years on the job the opportunity to take a three-month paid leave to "do something you want to pursue in life you can't do because of having to work a forty-hour week," says Jordan.

Three Goals. "I wanted to do something for myself," she says. "I was tired, overweight, and out of shape." She applied to Wells Fargo for her personal growth leave and it was granted. Because she had vacation time coming, she tied it into her leave, which gave her four months off with pay. She began her leave with three goals in mind: to get down to her college weight; to place fifth or better in the World Masters Swimming Championships in Brisbane, Australia (she placed fifth on the U.S. Olympic Team in Helsinki in 1952); and swim within 30 percent of her 1:16.8 Olympic time for the 100-meter backstroke.

Off she went to Walnut Creek, California, to train with the Walnut Creek Masters—"about 250 persons 19 to 90 years old," she says. For three months Jordan swam twice a day, lifted weights, jogged, and watched her diet. She worked 10 hours a day and lost 35 pounds, slimming down to her Olympic weight. "It was physically tough but not as mentally tough as working in the bank," she says.

Jordan spent a week and a half in Brisbane and, lo and behold, won four first places—in the 100- (1.28.1) and 200-meter backstroke and on two relay teams. When Jordan returned from Brisbane she was "athletically in shape" and determined to stay that way. She claims she has as much or more stamina than peers in their thirties. She swims every morning for an hour and fifteen minutes at the Piedmont Swim Club and is at work at the bank by 8:00 A.M. She also swims in the evening with the Masters at Walnut Creek three times a week.

Staying Active. She now keeps active competitively, swimming at Masters Championship meets in various parts of the country. "This experience has given me a good feeling about Wells Fargo, and it has made me a better employee," she says.

"I've met a brand-new group of healthy people at Walnut Creek who are stimulating to be around. There is no distinction of age, which is quite remarkable." Jordan not only achieved her three goals but renewed her business and personal life in the process.

As you can see, there are various ways to realize one's goals. Knowing what you want and planning to achieve it can smooth the road ahead. Sometimes fate or luck or both play a part. But the new young achieve success by following their instincts, by traveling new roads, and by not being afraid to take risks.

These examples of successful 50-plus professionals emphasize the importance of controlling your destiny. You must decide what you want to do with your life and career. What kind of job do you want? A full-time job, a part-time job, or one that lets you work two or three days a week? We can't promise you a job or get you a job, but we can point you in the right direction and tell you what to do, what problems you'll face and how to handle them, what companies are seeking in the employees they hire, and start you on an exciting life and career adventure.

CHAPTER 2

The Job Opportunity Outlook

There are three things to consider before making a career decision and plunging into the job market. The first one is to understand the current workplace. The second is to know what skills companies seek in the employees they hire, and the third is to know what kinds of jobs offer the best opportunities in this decade.

Make it your business to know what is going on in the work world. This will make it easier for you to plan for your future and select an appropriate career path in terms of the work you'll do, job satisfaction, and compensation.

Business Week magazine has underscored the desperate demand for skilled labor in the United States and the need for "Human Capital" (Sept. 19, 1988, p. 100–108). As you step into the job market, concentrate on the unique skills, experience, and human capital you offer a would-be employer. Companies are changing their attitudes and becoming more realistic in terms of hiring employees. For example, many companies offer valued professional female employees the opportunity to work two or three days a week or to create their own hours. This permits them to pursue their careers and still have time to care for their families. Flextime, where employees choose the hours they want to work, is another option offered by a growing number of companies. Many employers use temporary help services during seasonal periods when work loads are unusually heavy.

The Knowledgeable Worker

In this decade the emphasis on education will continue. The industrialization of U.S. plants will increase the use of robots, which means that more highly skilled, but fewer workers will be employed in such facilities. Jobs for those with lower skills will be reduced. The use of computers will continue to increase, making it possible for companies to hire fewer people to perform more work. Computer literacy is a must in today's work world. This is the decade of the knowledgeable worker.

In view of the changes taking place, there are both advantages and disadvantages for the over-50 job seeker. One advantage is that the labor shortage is here to stay, and as time goes on, more and more companies will be forced to consider hiring both older workers and minorities to solve their full- and part-time employment needs. The mature worker also brings specific skills and experience to the workplace, attributes that are not always easy to find in younger employees. Progressive companies are devising ways to retrain and employ such people.

The disadvantages include convincing an interviewer, who may be half your age, that you are qualified for the job. This will require confidence and flexibility on your part, and the ability to create comfortable rapport with the interviewer.

Diversity in the Workplace. Multicultural management is another consideration for today's professionals, especially for those age 50 or older who are returning to the job market. A scant 20 years ago, corporate corridors were inhabited almost exclusively by white American males. Today women and minorities—blacks, Asians, and Hispanics—are well represented in America's corporations.

"Multicultural management," says Floyd Dickens, president and chief executive officer of 21st Century Management Services Inc. of Cincinnati, Ohio, a management consulting firm, "is really the art and science of managing people from different cultures as opposed to centering just on white culture. It is important because you can't manage all people the same way."

Opportunities. The changes taking place in the work world open the doors of opportunity to the 50-plus professional seeking employment, retirees returning to the job market, or homemakers reentering the workplace. Take advantage of the opportunities they offer in terms of your experience and know-how.

Five Skills Companies Seek

When you are hired for a job, your expertise is usually taken for granted. You are expected to be knowledgeable in your field; that's why you were hired. But there are also important attributes that compaines seek in employees, and these attributes are just as important to your career success as the experience and knowledge you bring to the job. They include the following:

Communication Skills. Word skills can help you get a job and solidify your position on the job. Communicating includes writing memos, proposals, and letters that are clear and grammatical. It is the ability to give a speech, address a meeting, or explain a technical subject clearly and concisely. It is a technique to sell a manager or peer a new idea. An often overlooked communication skill is listening. Learning to listen can help pave the road to success.

Creative/Innovative Skills. Today more than ever, companies are seeking ways to compete more effectively in the marketplace, reduce costs, improve productivity, and develop new strategies that will increase profits. The creative person is one who can handle several projects at once and improve them as they develop.

Interpersonal Skills. The ability to get along with peers and superiors and clients, to work with a group or on a team is essential in today's workplace. Many innovative organizations use the team approach to research and solve problems and speed products to market. This is a concept that will continue to grow.

Leadership Skills. There are never enough leaders to deal with the problems and challenges facing organizations today. True leaders have a vision of where they want to go. They know they can't do the job alone and delegate responsibility to subordinates. Leaders bring diverse groups of people together and encourage and inspire them to work toward an objective. Men and women who have leadership skills are prized in the corporate world.

Problem-Solving Skills. Finding new ways to do things and correcting problems before they get out of hand can save companies time and money and make a difference between profit and loss. The problem-solver can help an organization compete more effectively by improving productivity and reducing costs.

Jobs with a Future

The United States is expected to add about 18 million jobs by the year 2000, about 1,000,500 a year. If you know what you want to do and where you want to work, you are ahead of the game. If you are still uncertain about what to do, look at the jobs that offer the best opportunities, keeping in mind that new and exciting occupations, jobs that don't exist today, will be created as we move toward the twenty-first century.

Service-Producing Industries. The growth of the service-producing sector creates an image of a work force dominated by cashiers, retail sales workers, and waiters. In addition to such jobs, the service sector will also generate jobs for financial managers, engineers, electrical and electronics technicians, nurses, and many other managerial, professional, and technical workers. Environmental management and conservation of oil and gas are vital industries that will continue to grow.

According to *Workforce 2000*, a report from the Hudson Institute, "The new jobs in service industries will demand much higher skill levels than the jobs today. Very few new jobs will be created for those who cannot read, follow directions, and use mathematics. Ironically, the demographic trends in the work force, coupled with the higher skill requirements of the economy, will lead to both higher and lower employment: more joblessness among the least-skilled and more jobs among the educationally advantaged."

John Stodden, Ph.D. economist and career expert, says, "There is a tremendous surge in the services sector, which is highly labor intensive and increases the need for workers— knowledgeable workers. In this kind of variable, dynamic, and tricky economy, you need people who know what they're doing. Let's just say it, you need graybeards. You don't need wet noses. There's a premium of wisdom over enthusiasm here; people who know the ropes, who can find markets, develop products. The economy is too topsy-turvy to babysit youngsters until they learn what's going on. I think that falls right into the lap of the over-50 target audience."

The service industry is projected to account for almost 50 percent of all new jobs by the year 2000. These jobs will be in small companies as well as large corporations, in all levels of government, and in such diverse industries as banking, data processing, hospitals, and management consulting.

Health Care. This field will continue to be one of the most important groups of industries in terms of job creation. New technology and a growing and aging population will increase the demand for health services. Because of the growth of health care, seven of the ten fastest-growing occupations between now and 2000 will be health related.

Business Services. Personnel supply services, which include temporary help agencies, the largest industry in this group, will continue to grow. Business services also include the fastest-growing industry in the economy—computer and data processing services. This industry is predicted to grow five times faster than than the average for all industries. Research, management, and consulting are other business services areas that will boom, though not as quickly as computer and personnel supply services.

Education. There is a need in both the public and private sector for teachers, teacher's aides, counselors, technicians, and administrative aides. There is a shortage of skilled technical workers and engineers, professionals needed to create, plan, and develop tomorrow's new products. Approximately half of the Ph.D.'s teaching in colleges and universities are foreign born. And Ph.D. minorities, desperately needed on U.S. engineering college campuses, comprise 1.7 percent of those holding this degree; over all, only 5.6 percent of Ph.D.'s are minorities. In addition to a growing need for Ph.D.'s to teach at the college level, many college professors will be retiring during the 1990s. Result: Approximately 500,000 college teaching vacancies will occur in this decade.

Retail Trade. The food service industry will be among the fastest-growing industries and will employ the most workers in this area. An increasing number of jobs are also projected in grocery, department, and other types of stores.

U.S. Government. Uncle Sam is the country's largest employer, with jobs ranging from secretaries to doctors and engineers and everything in between. There will also be a broad range of jobs in state and local governments.

Goods-Producing Industries

This group includes the areas of construction, manufacturing, mining, and agriculture. Employment in agricultural jobs will continue to decline, except for strong growth in the agricultural services industry. Mining will remain the same and construction will increase, depending on economic conditions. Although manufacturing employment will decline because of productivity gains resulting from new technology, the number of managerial, professional, and technical positions in this industry will increase.

There will be a strong demand by many companies for executive, administrative, and managerial expertise. In addition to technicians, marketing, sales, and financial professionals will be needed to operate and program technical equipment and assist engineers and scientists.

These are only a few of the many jobs available to the 50-plus professional. If you are a retiree who has been itching to rejoin the work force, you are not alone. A recent survey conducted by AARP (American Association of Retired Persons) revealed that one-third of retirees would prefer to work. Other polls report 51 percent of all workers surveyed would like to work past age 65. In addition, many workers who retire early by choice or termination soon discover that they are unhappy about not having a place of work to go to every morning. They miss the day-to-day contact with people and the feeling of accomplishment.

Keep in mind that companies seek people with common sense, who are capable of planning for both the short and long term, who can make critical decisions, and can adapt to change.

Alan Pifer, chairman of the Southport Institute for Policy Analysis, a nonprofit organization that conducts analytical studies of federal social policies and population aging, advocates continual education and retraining throughout one's life. "It would be nice if a lot of people could be repotted," he says.

If the statement reads . . .	Employment is projected to . . .
Much faster than average	Increase 31% or more
Faster than average	Increase 20% to 30%
About as fast as average	Increase 11% to 19%

Here is your chance to start anew. The chart that follows was compiled by the Bureau of Labor Statistics on the job outlook between now and the year 2000. It shows the employment opportunities available in your field, or it can help you choose a new career path. Many employers in the various industries have part-time jobs in your field, if you don't want to work full-time. It is important to note that in most occupations, openings resulting from replacement needs are more numerous than those stemming from increased demand. Thus even occupations that are not expected to grow, or those in decline, provide opportunities for employment.

More detailed information is provided in *Occupational Projections and Training Data*, Bureau of Labor Statistics Bulletin 2351, and in *Outlook 2000*, BLS Statistics Bulletin 2352.

SMALL INCREASE

Occupation	Reason for changes in staffing pattern	Projected change in total employment
Economists	Changes in business practices	Faster than average
Hosts/Hostesses, restaurant/lounge/ coffee shop	Changes in business practices	Much faster than average

SMALL INCREASE (cont.)

Occupation	Reason for changes in staffing pattern	Projected change in total employment
Personnel, training and labor relations managers and specialists	Changes in business practices	Faster than average
Teachers, secondary school	Demographic trends	About as fast as average

MODERATE INCREASE

Occupation	Reason for changes in staffing pattern	Projected change in total employment
Administrative service managers	Changes in business practices	More slowly than average
Counselors	Changes in business practices	Faster than average
Food service and lodging managers	Changes in business practices	Faster than average
Human services workers	Other	Much faster than average
Property and real estate managers	Changes in business practices	About as fast as average
Securities and financial services sales workers	Changes in business practices	Much faster than average

SIGNIFICANT INCREASE

Occupation	Reason for changes in staffing pattern	Projected change in total employment
Computer programmers	Growing use of computers	Much faster than average
Computer systems analysts	Growing use of computer	Much faster than average
Management analysts and consultants	Changes in business practices	Much faster than average
Operations research analysts	Change in business practices	Much faster than average

CHAPTER 3

Deciding What You Want to Do

Benjamin Franklin is reputed to have said, "There is nothing wrong with retirement as long as it doesn't interfere with your work"—wise words from a sage of another era, as many of today's displaced professionals have discovered.

At this point in your career, you should have a good idea of what you want to do. If you don't, it's time to make some important decisions. What kind of work do you want? Do you want to work full-time, part-time, or perhaps three days a week? What kind of lifestyle do you prefer? Do you plan to relocate to another part of the country?

Are you an achiever? Are you interested in making money? Do you want power? Are you interested in art and in self-expression? Do you want to serve humanity? Are you a creative person who wants to deal in the realm of ideas?

These are questions that require a great deal of thought, time, and effort if you expect to achieve your goals. But the most important question of all is what do you want to do? If you are uncertain at the moment, don't worry. It is perfectly normal at this stage of your life to flounder a bit. You wouldn't be human if you didn't. But giving serious consideration to your future is important because you don't want to waste time going down the wrong road and having to retrace your steps later. The best course of action is to set realistic goals as to what you want to do and the kind of company you want to join. Then plan and execute your job campaign, because nothing will happen unless you make it happen.

If you are still undecided about what to do, *Career Design*, developed by the Crystal-Barkley Corporation, may help. It is an easy-to-use, self-paced software program that covers every aspect of the career and job search. It can help you decide what to do, how to do it, and where to do it. According to Eric O. Sandburg, the co-author of *Career Design*, it is the software's ability to help the user deal immediately with a broad range of career issues that makes it so appealing. This varies from identifying what skills and aptitudes a person has to showing how to develop multiple and appealing job choices. Paramount among these issues is deciding what career to pursue.

Don't Procrastinate.

Don't let uncertainty about what you want to do turn into procrastination where you do nothing and thus waste valuable time. It is important—and good self-discipline—to do something constructive every day, whether it be putting your thoughts on paper, making phone calls to contacts and setting up appointments, or writing letters and sending out résumés. You want to build momentum and sustain it until you achieve your goal.

In making your career decision, "You must have a clear sense of direction, and be able to articulate what that direction is," says Wayne Carlisle, director of placement and career services at Wichita State University.

Put Your Thoughts on Paper. It's important to put your thoughts and ideas in writing. Often we have good ideas, but forget them because we failed to write them down. Listing your goals will serve as a reminder that you are waging a job-hunting campaign to market and sell your services, and will also serve as a guide to your course of action.

Targeting Industries and Companies. When it comes to deciding what you want to do, a good strategy is to look for companies that are growing and prospering in your area. They can be small or large companies, although the smaller ones are likely to offer more opportunities. How do you find such companies? Construction companies, banks, insurance companies, and real estate agencies are good sources of information. Write managers and executives in such companies and then call to arrange to talk with them, preferably face-to-face rather than on the telephone. When you meet with such individuals, don't ask for a job. Request information about potential businesses in the area that may need your expertise. Talking to executives in different industries will provide both information and potential contacts.

From our experience, you'll find most executives you contact both friendly and helpful. And you may even get a job offer or a referral as you conduct your interviews and meet new contacts. This kind of research may also help you find a different kind of job that could prove more challenging than you anticipated.

Don't overlook pockets of the economy that may be in the throes of a recession. In such cases the professional sector of such companies may be in a down cycle but still need employees. In many instances the average job seeker won't consider such companies, even though there may be good openings for the savvy job hunter. You can find such companies by reading newspapers and magazines, and by watching business news and TV broadcasts. Don't overlook word-of-mouth contacts through your network.

Don't discount working for the U.S. government. Uncle Sam hires more than 100,000 professionals a year, and you won't have to worry about discrimination—due to race, religion, color, or age—if you are a minority. The government also uses temporary employment services for its seasonal needs.

Transferring Your Skills. Whether you are returning to the workplace, changing jobs, or switching careers, you'll be using the skills and experience you gained in previous jobs. These skills are transferable to different jobs, companies, and industries. Professionals don't suddenly lose these skills because they were fired or laid off the day before yesterday. Unfortunately, many professionals who are suddenly terminated put themselves down psychologically, forgetting that they are the same persons who were successfully working on the job only a week ago. For example, if you are a financial person, your expertise can be used in virtually any company or industry that requires fiscal know-how—that's common sense. Don't overlook the many skills you can bring to a new job and a new industry.

Self-assessment. This is the key to your job campaign, which consists of two parts: the plan and its execution. Knowing what you want to do is half the battle. The other half is the execution of your plan and finding the job you want.

Now let's look at you and your particular situation. Which one of the following categories best describes your situation?

- You've recently been fired
- You believe you are a victim of discrimination
- You are a victim of a merger or acquisition
- You are forced to take early retirement or made the mistake of retiring too soon
- You are a college-educated homemaker, or widow, or divorcée who raised a family and wants to resume a career
- You need help in getting started

Fired!

There are a number of reasons why professionals are terminated in today's turbulent job market. They include corporate downsizing, acquisitions, company mergers, and layoffs due to budget cuts. Today it is not uncommon for entire departments to be wiped out in an eyeblink. Perhaps the worst-case scenario is being fired because of personality conflicts.

When a person is fired, it can be a traumatic experience at any age. One's self-esteem often takes a nosedive. Suddenly one's neat and organized little world comes apart. The amenities one takes for granted in his or her working life disappear. For example, the comfortable office cocoon that confers a measure of dignity, identity, and importance evaporates. The convenient office telephone and fax machine are no longer available. The daily camaraderie of fellow workers is lost. Even the convenience of a nearby bathroom is gone. Suddenly you are a man or woman without a company.

What Do I Do? The first step is to tell your family and friends, and broadcast to the world that you are looking for a new job. The worst thing you can do is not tell your family at a time when you desperately need their support and all the help you can get.

This is also the time to take a close look at your finances, plan a budget, and reduce costs until you find a new job. Put any termination pay into an interest-bearing account so that funds are available when you need them. If you walk out with a large lump-sum payment from a company savings plan that has not been taxed, you have 60 days to roll it over into another nontaxable account. A good tax adviser or financial expert should be consulted about the best way to invest this money. If you go beyond 60 days, Uncle Sam will demand his tax bite from your lump-sum payment.

Today there is no longer the stigma attached to getting fired that there was a few short years ago. In fact, being fired can often be a blessing in disguise, and it rarely has anything to do with your competence. It does force you to take a hard look at yourself and decide what you really want to do. John J. Davis, president of J. Davis & Associates, a New York City–based executive search firm, agrees. He says, "Many people need to be prodded into changing their lives. Few people embrace change with open arms. That's why millions of people remain in boring jobs—for a weekly paycheck and security. Getting fired could be just what the doctor ordered, if you seize the opportunity and strategically pursue a better job than the one you lost."

Lost-Job Trauma. Some people are psychologically devastated when they are terminated. A person may go through several stages, beginning with refusing to believe what happened. You can't accept the company's violation of your trust and loyalty, says career counselor Alexander J. Sussman. You begin to internalize and lose your sense of reality and perspective.

The second stage is anger—you become vindictive and want to get even. This is destructive because it immobilizes you.

Stage three, especially if you were not expecting termination, is the feeling that "I may not be able to get a job again." You begin to question your capabilities. If this lack of confidence persists, it will increase the time it takes to find another job.

The next step is to plan your future, and the sooner you stop brooding and move to this stage, the better. An optimistic attitude and persistence are essential for a successful job hunt. Treat the job search as a job in itself, which it is.

The Best Medicine—Action. The best medicine and the key to success is action, preparing cover letters, writing résumés, and making contacts, including family, friends, business acquaintances, managers in professional associations, and executives in the company that terminated you. Don't be afraid to ask for their help. These steps are all part of the marketing plan necessary to find another job. You can't afford to be bashful when seeking employment.

Don't go into the job fray by yourself, says career counselor Sussman. Too many people feel that being fired is a black mark against them. They're embarrassed, and tend to withdraw from their friends and families at a time when they badly need their help and understanding. Family support is essential if you are to succeed in your job quest. Life should continue as normally as possible under the circumstances, which can be difficult.

Once you begin to mount an effective job campaign, the negative things that bothered you in the first three stages will begin to diminish in intensity. Looking for a job is challenging, because you are working on a representation of yourself. Whether or not you get a job rests solely on your shoulders. It is one of the few times you control your destiny, says Sussman. It can be a very rewarding experience.

Don't Burn Your Bridges Behind You. Difficult as it may be never leave a job in anger no matter how wronged you feel. You want your former employer to give you a good reference. Talk with your boss and other executives in the company to discuss severance pay and the use of a temporary office with a telephone and someone to take messages. If you can keep your secretary, so much the better. Also request outplacement, with expenses paid by the company. And make sure that your boss is willing to give you a good recommendation.

Some companies do not want terminated employees coming into the office, and the terminated employee also may feel uncomfortable about the situation.

So don't hesitate to ask for such help. Also arrange to have your boss corroborate your version of the reason you left the company. If you do have to tell a would-be employer that you were fired, do it honestly and without rancor. Don't criticize your company or individuals with whom you formerly worked. If you bad-mouth your former company or boss, an interviewer will think you'll do the same to his or her company. It's even possible that your former company may want to hire you at a later date because of your expertise. Executives don't enjoy firing people; they realize that finding a job in today's market can be difficult, and they don't want to create a bad reputation for themselves or their companies. Don't burn your bridges behind you—build them. "Firing or termination is never a personal failure, but a circumstance," says Sussman.

You Believe You Are a Victim of Discrimination.

As a person who is 50-plus years old you may feel that you were fired without cause because of your age. You must also be prepared to encounter discrimination when you look for a job. Much of it is subtle, sometimes it is overt, and most of the time you won't know whether or not you were the victim of discrimination.

Denise Loftus, manager of the Workforce Education Worker Equity Department for AARP says many people believe they are victims of discrimination when, indeed, poor job performance may be part of the problem. That does not mean there is no age discrimination, she says, but it's often subtle and very hard to prove. A complaint to the Equal Employment Opportunity Commission (EEOC) can drag on and there are limitations to what can be accomplished; each state has different rules on the subject.

Chris Mackaronis, an attorney, and the AARP Manager of Avocacy Programs, says that if somebody wants to find out about your age, he or she can unless the résumé you submit is carefully written. Many older workers are told that they are overqualified for a job. This is not a legitimate business decision but a pretext for age discrimination. AARP gets hundreds of complaint letters on this subject, says Mackaronis.

Should You Sue? Most experts agree that in the majority of cases it is not worthwhile to pursue a discrimination lawsuit. The reasons: It is time-consuming, costly (both psychologically and financially), and legally difficult to prove your case. The likelihood of litigation success may not be more than 50-50, according to Mackaronis. Under such circumstances it is better to move on, expending your energies in targeting companies that can use the skills you offer.

You Are a Victim of a Merger or Acquisition.

If you are an employee who was suddenly let go or working in a department that was fired en masse, you are not alone. These are common occurrences in today's workplace. When you hear rumors about possible reorganization or upheavals it is wise to prepare for any eventuality. Barring that, it is a good time to evaluate what you want to do. Oftentimes circumstances beyond our control force us to do things we had only thought—or dreamed—about.

That's what happened to Al Thompson, who was forced out of his job at age 61. "It wasn't a happy time," he said. Thompson had worked 40 years as a steamship broker, 17 years with Funch Edye, a subsidiary of the Cunard Lines, and 23 years with American and Overseas Charting. His job was to charter freighters that hauled such cargos as scrap metal, coal, and grain to all parts of the world. He negotiated the rates and terms for each deal via telephone, telex, and fax.

"Your word was your bond in this profession," says Thompson. Once the charter arrangements were concluded, the ship was loaded and sailed. Thompson had a long and successful career as a maritime broker and claims that he liked his work.

"But then the market began to have its ups and downs for five years, and the company wasn't making any money," he says. "The company was in the red, and salaries had to be cut."

Finally, it became obvious that two brokers in the four-man company had to go, says Thompson, who had a 10 percent interest in the company. He volunteered, telling his partners, "If things don't go well, I'll go." Things didn't get better and Thompson was out.

"It was a difficult time," said Thompson. "For the first month out of work I made a lot of calls. I was mixed up. I lost my sense of humor, and walked to the mail box every day." But the mail didn't bring any job offers.

Thompson was out of work for about six months when he got a telephone call from Tom Hall, a friend and former maritime steamship broker who had suffered the same fate as Thompson. Hall had bought a travel agency franchise—Uniglobe Custom Travel in Wantagh, Long Island, in New York. Would Thompson like to work with him?

"Hall heard I was looking for a job," says Thompson, "and contacted me. He knew I knew a lot of people in the steamship business, all potential clients." So Thompson went into the travel business.

Hall specialized in maritime business travel and virtually all of his clients are steamship brokers. "They were all brokers I did business with," says Thompson. "I visited them and gave presentations on how we could help them with their travel plans. The business travel also led to vacation travel. Now I make reservations all over the world for tickets, hotels, and cars."

When Thompson started he was given a two-day seminar on selling. He also had to master a word processor, which is vital in his new career. He learned on the job, he says, and his knowledge of ports throughout the world was a big help. Now he is familiar with "inland cities," he says. The only problem Thompson encountered when he started was giving business presentations, but he's overcome that hurdle. In the beginning, he was reluctant to call on former colleagues, but he soon found them friendly and polite. "They always say 'thank you,'" says Thompson, "and recommend new customers."

Thompson, in his mid-sixties, has been working at Uniglobe Custom Travel for several years. He is a widower, married for the past 13 years to his second wife, Barbara, who helps him with his work. Thompson says he loves his work and doesn't consider himself a salesperson. He says, "I am a businessman in travel."

Forced or Early Retirement

Being forced into early retirement can be traumatic for a successful, hard-working professional. But it happens. Again, request as much help from the company as you can in the way of severance, an office, outplacement, secretarial help, and references before you begin your job quest. When you settle on your priorities, jump back into the job market as fast as you can.

Things can be more difficult for the man or woman who decided to call it a career and retire early only to realize it was a mistake. The reason: A year or two may have slipped by without your having practiced your skills.

The moral: If you are recently retired, keep your options open by doing volunteer work or taking on part-time or temporary jobs. Even though you feel you may never want to work again, you may change your mind and decide to return to work sometime in the future. By keeping active, it will make the job hunt easier if and when you decide to return to the work force on a full- or part-time basis.

Women Returning to the Work Force

The college-educated woman coming back to the job market faces a different problem, depending on her circumstances. She may have been a homemaker, active in the community, done volunteer work, raised a family, helped her husband manage a business, and now wants to pursue her own career. Or she may suddenly find herself divorced or widowed. Too often this accomplished individual comes into the workplace with low self-esteem, unaware of the many talents she possesses that are valued in the corporate world.

Homemakers often fail to recognize the many salable skills (including interpersonal skills) they have acquired and practiced over the years. These are the talents that frequently spell success in business. They include raising children, administering family affairs, solving problems, handling the family's finances, doing volunteer work and other extracurricular activities, and helping their husbands in business or running a small business of their own.

Vera Burger is a prime example of a woman whose many and varied volunteer activities served as springboard to a business career. Burger, now in her early sixties, had to be coaxed into the real estate business. Today she owns and operates Vera Burger Realtors agency in Longmeadow, Massachusetts. She and her 20-person staff do business in the Springfield area and outlying districts.

Burger, a trim soft-spoken woman, mother of four (and grandmother of four), came to Longmeadow via Czechoslovakia, where she was born; London, where she graduated from a Church of England prep school and subsequently majored in economics and business at the City of London College; and then Toronto, Canada, where she took courses in personnel administration and psychology at the Ryerson Institute of Technology.

But it was in London that she began the volunteer work that was to prove so valuable later on. As a student there, she became active in the Young People's Christian Student Association. Later she became president of the YWCA (Young Women's Christian Association). She was also active in her church, the United Way, the Red Cross, and other organizations. When she moved to Toronto, she continued her activities in the YWCA.

In 1959 Burger and her family moved to Springfield, Massachusetts, where she became active in the local YWCA. One of the programs she is proud to have started is PAGE (Pregnant Adolescent Girls Education), a marketing program that gave young pregnant women an opportunity to continue their educations instead of being expelled, as they were in the

1960s. "We had to storm the citadel," says Burger, "to prove to the city the school program would save money and keep the pregnant women off the welfare rolls. That program is still going."

The PAGE program was also responsible for Burger moving into real estate. She had given a talk at the Rotary Club in Springfield in exchange for a $1,000 donation for PAGE. Later the president of the Rotary Club, and a realtor, invited Burger to his office and suggested that she consider going into the real estate profession, and in two or three years open her own business. "That was like someone suggesting that I go to the moon," says Burger.

"This old gentleman had a small real estate agency and was a true philanthropist," she says. "I didn't want to do anything about it but he called me and persevered, and talked to my husband. With my husband's encouragement I decided to take the real estate course, even though I wasn't that excited about it. I never liked selling. But fate wanted me to do it so I worked for him for two years. When he retired and went to Arizona, I embarked on my own company. If it wasn't for the support of my husband I never would have done it. I've never regretted it."

Recently Burger celebrated 20 years in the business. "It was a true blessing," she says, "because in 1978 my husband ended his career due to health problems, so it was vital for me to be in the job market, earning enough money to help educate my children."

Burger is active in her realtor association; she was elected Realtor of the Year in 1982 and president in 1983. She also serves on two national committees. "I learned to be flexible and happy," says Burger. "I'm happy to have had the opportunities I've had and grateful for some of my accomplishments. It's important to like yourself, to have confidence in a plan that you outline for yourself. The fifties are extremely important years and if you are fortunate enough to enjoy good health and energy, then it is incumbent upon you to remain active."

Dr. Martha Turnage, vice-president for university relations at Ohio University, points out that one of the mistakes women make is to expect more than they should as widows or divorcées. For example, they don't inherit the social position that they enjoyed as part of a couple; it may have been due to the husband's status in the community as a business and professional leader. Many times wives of prominent men can't understand why they are not invited to functions. They expect to be accorded the same kind of preferential treatment their husbands received. When they start looking for jobs they discover they must get along without any help.

These are the realities job-hunting women face when they return to the workplace. As one of these women you have many talents to offer would-be employers, but you must be able to articulate your skills and convince an employer that you will be an asset to the company.

When you make up your mind what you want to do, go for it with confidence; look the interviewer in the eye and tell her or him the many things you've done and what you can do to help the company. A positive attitude will go a long way toward helping you achieve your goals. You might also consider temporary employment services to get started. This will give you the opportunity to work with different companies and help you decide which career path is right for you.

You Need Help in Getting Started

Job seekers who get good professional career counseling are more successful at finding jobs than those who don't. It's wise to check out a counselor before your first visit. Get recommendations from colleges and universities in your area. One reliable way to get good advice is to visit major universities in your area that are involved in continuing education—the University of California–Los Angeles and New York University are good examples. Many major universities and two-year colleges will provide counseling and assistance, often at no charge. And many schools have special programs or offer discounts to 50-plus students. Investigate the schools in your area. Counselors in such institutions can help you clarify your goals, recommend courses that will be helpful, and start you on the right career path at no cost, or at least at a reasonable cost.

Ohio University's Dr. Turnage made a careful assessment of her skills and abilities when she made a job change. She says she paid $1,000 to a career counselor and claims it is "one of the best investments I've ever made."

Dr. Turnage says she engaged in a series of sessions with her counselor and kept saying, "But I don't do this well." Finally, her counselor said, "Has anyone ever given you a raise for what you don't do well?"

She finally realized that she had to sell herself, that she couldn't be defensive. Turnage says that you can't be looking for someone to praise you or pat you on the back.

"We're in competition with people in the job market," she says. "We've got to show that we have the assets, the life experiences we can bring to the job."

New York University's Center for Career and Life Planning in Manhattan is run by the school of continuing education. Its over-50 population, according to director Letitia Chamberlain, has recently increased 12 percent and is still growing, especially for retirees and women.

"Many of those who come in don't know what they need to know," says Chamberlain. "Many people sell themselves short. They don't know how to go about getting a job, they've never written a résumé, and they don't know how to use contacts. They need help."

One of the first things Chamberlain does is work with her clients to help them overcome any negative feelings, focus on specifics, articulate what is important, and encourage them to think about "What can I do to shape my future?"

CHAPTER 4

Switching Careers: How to Do It

Many people "hit the career wall" around age 46. One day they look up and say, "Hey, I don't like what I'm doing." More often than not such people have enjoyed successful careers and above-average incomes. But they suddenly realize they are not doing what they want, and that something is missing in their lives. In short, they're not happy. Suddenly, for the first time, they begin to think seriously about their careers, their lifestyles, and what they would really like to do with their remaining work lives.

This is often the catalyst that makes a person think about switching careers and changing lifestyles. The two go hand-in-hand. You've heard the stories of the stockbroker and his wife who left the financial world to run a country inn, or the corporate executive who gave up a good salary and all the perks to become a teacher.

Unfortunately, few of us gave much thought to our careers when we were starting out. Unless we were lucky, we didn't have the foresight, the discipline, or the know-how to think about and select careers for the long term that are attuned to our talents and things we like to do. This is borne out by the Rockford Institute, a career consulting organization, that reports, "More than 50 percent of working professionals say they may have picked the wrong career direction. Often they feel stuck with the choices they have made and don't know how to go about choosing a new career path."

What Do We Mean by Switching Careers?

According to the Bureau of Labor Statistics, approximately 10 percent of the work force change careers each year. That is a small percentage considering the size of our working population. Many people are deceived by the term "switching careers." The fact is very few people actually change careers in the sense that they perform work that is completely different from what they did in the past. For example, an editor may move into public relations or advertising, or become a speech writer, but that person is still employing the skills that made him or her successful in the first place.

A financial person is another example of a professional who can move into a new industry and function successfully because of his or her skills. This is true of virtually every profession. The problem in switching to a different industry is to convince the company interviewer that based on your knowledge, experience, and know-how, you can do the job. That is why it is so important to make the right choice to avoid wasting a lot of time and effort and temporarily derailing your career before getting back on the right track.

Stay Fluid

When I was introduced to a famous broadcaster while attending college, I asked his advice about my career.

"Stay fluid," he said.

I've never forgotten his advice, but it wasn't until a few years later that I gave serious thought to what those two wise words really meant. They mean taking advantage of opportunities that beckon—opportunities that you may not recognize at first. You have to learn to look for them, which involves a willingness on your part to accept challenges and try something new. They mean listening to the grapevine in both your professional and private life and being aware of what is taking place around you.

Sometimes a chance comment by a friend or business acquaintance can help you recognize a trend or trigger an idea that can assist you in your job hunt. This takes practice, but if you make a disciplined effort to look for opportunities at every turn, it becomes a habit. It all adds up to being creative and energetic, which can help you get a job or start you off on a new and exciting career path.

Amherst's Neil Yeager, manager of adult career transitions at the University of Massachusetts–Amherst, tells of a man who decided he wanted to try something new after being forced out of a job he had held for 20 years, because his manufacturing company had relocated to the Far East. He put his résumé together, sent it out, and received two job offers, both of which he turned down.

Twenty years ago he would have accepted one of those jobs, because he had young children and mortgage payments to meet, says Yeager. Now his kids are grown and he doesn't want the corporate grind anymore. He wants to make an impact on other people's lives, something he says he had never been able to do when he was in the rat race.

He decided to teach math and accepted a teaching job at half his former salary. He likes the contributions he makes and the satisfaction he gets from his new job.

Do Something You Enjoy

It is no secret that professionals who work at something they enjoy have the most success. That is why it is vital to make the right decision whether you reenter the corporate world or go into business for yourself. Dr. Sandra Davis, a consulting psychologist at MDA Consulting Group in Minneapolis, Minnesota, offers this advice: "When deciding what you want to do, consider the skills you like to use, skills that in the past you felt best about, that contributed the most to what you were doing, and that were fun to do. The elements: 'Is this something I really enjoy doing? Is it worthwhile?' " If the answer is yes, then chances are good that you are starting out on the right path.

A Banker Goes to the Zoo

Let's look at the experience of Frank Reilly and his unusual career switch. "They made me an offer I couldn't refuse" is Reilly's explanation for his sudden transition from senior vice-president in the corporate corridors of the Chase Manhattan Bank in New York City to assistant director of the Baltimore Zoo. "It was something I never expected," says Reilly.

Fate intervened recently when the bank offered a number of employees the option of voluntary retirement and said, "Look, this is it. You have until the end of November to make your decision, and one week to revoke that decision, and it's effective December 31."

Reilly says, "I had no plans to do this. I was extremely happy and pleased with my career. It was a circumstance, not something I had been anticipating, or planning. The bank never had, based on my 30-year career, a voluntary retirement program."

Reilly decided to take the money and run. He had been working for Chase Manhattan for 30 years. "I was basically for two-thirds of the time a domestic officer, and one-third international. Most of my career revolved around lending as a credit officer or as a manager of credit officers."

Reilly, a thoughtful man, had no specific job in mind. But about that time the board of trustees of the Baltimore Zoo commissioned an executive recruiter to find candidates for the job of assistant director. The recruiter happened to call the Chase Manhattan human resources department at the time the bank announced its early retirement program. "By fortunate happenstance," says Reilly, "the recruiter spoke to a friend of mine in human resources who knew I was retiring. My friend called me and my first reaction was one of great mirth, but the more I thought about it, the more I thought it was something to look into."

Reilly left the bank at the end of December and was interviewed for the job at the end of January. "I went quietly mad for that one month I wasn't working," says Reilly. "I dismantled my snowblower and put it back together again. I cleaned the cellar. I took walks. I read books. I tried cross-country skiing. There's a certain franticness to show you are truly happy with your leisure."

Define Your Objectives

When Reilly decided to leave the bank, he had four basic objectives for a new job. In his words:

1. I wanted to do something I enjoy.
2. I wanted to do something I was good at, administering, and developing.
3. I wanted to get paid for it. By pay I mean had I elected to go to school, I would have gone for credits as opposed to audit.
4. Lastly, and this is the one I had the most difficulty with, I wanted to grow at whatever I was going to do.

"This job fulfilled these objectives," says Reilly, who began working at the Baltimore Zoo in February 1988. He says his title of assistant director actually means business manager. The zoo is run by the Maryland Zoological Society. Basically it is 160 acres in the city of Baltimore, with about 45 acres under exhibit. Reilly is responsible for all aspects of administration.

"Reporting to me," he says, "are the bird department, the mammal department, veterinarian—we have a large hospital—horticulture, finance, and construction. We're the third oldest zoo in the United States. We have a staff of approximately 120 people, and we have an annual budget of about $5 million."

Reilly likes his new job and claims it's challenging. "Zoo people are dramatically different," he says. "They have more common sense than they have a right to have. They are very pragmatic. They couldn't care less where you come from as opposed to what you can do to make the zoo, or their jobs, function smoothly. It's very much 'prove yourself and you are accepted.' The work is such and the staffing so thin that people have to have a camaraderie and common interest to make the place work. It doesn't lend itself to any sort of pulling or tugging."

Reflecting on his past, Reilly says, "One of the questions I wanted answered was as a senior vice-president had I become such a specialist that I required a sophisticated infrastructure to support me? Or could I operate in a minimum infrastructure and be a generalist?

"I was intrigued by that, and whether or not I had been such a unique specialist at Chase. Whether or not I could adapt to a more rough-and-tumble environment that had none of the cultural accoutrements that I had been working with for more than 30 years. It was a sense of whether or not you can make it in a different league.

"The essence of staying young is the ability to change. That's the key. If you want to take your experience of 30 years, you really have to adapt it to today. It is not something that comes without change.

"You are going to do something. Do something that is pleasant and fulfilling. You've got to stay active. I don't think you can make a total career change to one of leisure after going to New York every day. It would not be a satisfying change.

"I learned more about biology and zoology than I ever thought existed. It's a whole new world that I was exposed to, having been in finance. I'm intrigued by these people who do so well, devote their time to the care of animals and conservation, which I am appalled I never had a sense of before coming here. You have to do something that permits you to grow, which makes you expand, makes you feel valuable."

Opening Up a New World

Reilly is a good example of a versatile job hunter not sure what he wanted to do but with specific needs his future career had to fulfill. He worked to achieve them, and adapted to change along the way. The result: success—and a satisfying new career.

Making a drastic switch in careers can be difficult, and it is not something that everyone is equipped to do, from both career and psychological standpoints, because it requires change. Admittedly, the process is more common today because of mergers and acquisitions, and because we live in a complex and changing society. This has resulted in professionals in a variety of fields being forced into the ranks of the unemployed and having to look for new careers to survive.

The secret to a successful career change is to know what you want to do, the kind of a company you want to work for, and whether the company's needs and culture match your skills and personality.

How Long Will It Take?

Changing careers usually takes four to six months, and sometimes longer. You may be a lucky exception to the rule, but it is wise to plan for the long term. If you find and embark on a new career early on, so much the better.

Start by putting your ideas and goals on paper. Look at your career change as a long-term business plan that will require periodic updates, reevaluation, and changes. Pursue your campaign as if you were running a business, because you are. Your new career will impact on both your business and personal life, so it's important to make the right choice.

To help you get started, here are 10 rules that will put you on the road to a successful career change.

Rule 1. Be Certain You Really Want to Change Careers

Before you make any career-change decisions be certain you really want to do it. If you are unhappy in your present job, it could be your attitude, your boss, the work you do, the fact that you feel unappreciated, or that you don't fit in with the corporate culture. Ask yourself if you are dissatisfied with your career or with your job. Sometimes it's easier to look within a company. For example, can you find satisfaction in a similar job in your field? If so, it may be easier to search for one within your company before looking outside.

In short, if you are unhappy with your circumstances, look within yourself for specific reasons why, and make certain that it is your career you are dissatisfied with and not something else, before making a hasty decision you may later regret.

Some questions to consider when making your decision:

Can you afford—or are you willing—to take a salary cut to start over? If so, will this have an adverse affect on your family or your lifestyle?

What will you have to give up, and what will you gain by making a career change? Will it be worth the sacrifice you may have to make?

Do you have the discipline, the patience, and the persistence required to take an entry-level job, if necessary, and begin working your way up the corporate ladder?

Neil Yeager, manager of adult career transitions at the University of Massachusetts-Amherst, says it is becoming less difficult to switch careers and somewhat easier to move from one industry to another. He says, "People are not staying in their jobs as long, and many of them have been forced out of their positions because of mergers and acquisitions. Because of this, many of them end up pursuing work in new fields. This kind of economy fosters change."

The norms have changed, says Yeager. "It used to be 30

years and a watch with one company. Today it's three to five years and then moving on. The result: Companies are getting used to hiring people from other fields. A good example is in technical fields where people often move to different companies, thus increasing work force mobility."

One more avenue to consider is professional counseling. Speaking with someone who can draw you out, make you articulate your goals, and play devil's advocate, can be revealing and help you reach a decision.

Rule 2. Prepare Properly

What do you have to offer that will make a company want to hire you? What skills can you bring to the workplace that will make you a valuable employee? Do you have expertise in a specific industry? Do you have unusually good interpersonal skills that enable you to motivate others? This requires a detailed self-analysis on your part, a difficult but necessary exercise to determine your personality, and your likes, dislikes, and weaknesses. Knowing your interests and what you want before you start will make the transition easier.

Do you have marketable skills that you can't use on your present job that can be transferred to another company?

Are you willing to risk changing careers—and failing? If you do fail, do you have a backup plan? If not, do you have the psychological stamina to leave failure behind and pursue something new?

Have you diligently researched your target field in terms of the kind of work you want to do and the companies that may employ a person of your talents?

Nella G. Barkley, president of New York City–based Crystal-Barkley Association, specializing in Life/Work consulting, leads her clients through a process that recounts their life histories. The result: They identify 100 or more qualities that relate to their working and nonworking lives.

"What you find," says Barkley, "is that they sometimes deliver a relatively pedestrian performance in their firms but hit home runs in overseeing United Way campaigns in their offices or working in political campaigns. They discover that some of their most important skills are used outside of the workplace."

These skills are just as important as your on-the-job skills, because they can be invaluable in helping you change careers. Barkley emphasizes that when you are looking for a job or seriously thinking about changing careers, you have to act like an entrepreneur, taking matters into your own hands and considering what you have to offer.

For example, she points out that a person over 50 brings experience and judgment to the marketplace, two "priceless commodities" that can help you compete in the job market.

Rule 3. Define Your Objectives

What kind of job do you want when you change careers? Do you want to stay in the same industry, which can be an advantage because of your knowledge and contacts? Or do you want to do something completely different?

For example, a fund-raiser who has dealt with people on the telephone or face-to-face should be able to make a relatively easy transition to telemarketing, a booming profession today. An English teacher, on the other hand, would have a difficult time teaching a computer science course without expensive and additional time-consuming training.

Another important aspect to consider is your lifestyle. The over-50 professional is more selective about his or her career, and lifestyle is a major consideration. What you valued at 50-plus is different from what you consider important at age 35 or 40. That's why it's helpful to put your objectives on paper. It gives you a balance sheet and forces you to think realistically about what you want to do.

This is the time to daydream and outline the kinds of jobs you'd like. For example, would you prefer working in a large or small company? Do you enjoy working with people on a team? Do you prefer supervision or are you more comfortable working on your own? Perhaps you would be better in an entrepreneurial enterprise, running your own business.

Rule 4. Consider Long-Range Goals

Although it may seem irrelevant to talk about long-range goals at this point, it is not. Consider that at 50 years of age you have at least another 20 years of your work life if you continue in your chosen profession until you are 70 or beyond. Even if you are 60, you have 10 years or more to go if you're not planning to retire in the near future. Another point to consider is that people are healthier and living longer, and they can make important contributions in the job market.

With the changing demographics, a smaller work force, and the growing need for trained employees, the opportunities for the 50-plus professional should blossom in this decade. Even though companies are running lean today they can't always hire employees with the skills they need. The result is that many more companies are hiring mature workers on either a full- or part-time basis, which gives the person who wants to switch careers more options in the marketplace. Thus it becomes important not only to pursue that new career, but to choose a company that can use your talents, one that offers on-the-job training, and provides the opportunity to learn new skills.

Consequently you should be searching for potential companies that value and seek the talents of the 50-plus worker in or near your community. Target such companies, research them, and approach them with specific contributions you can make to their businesses. The result can be a career change and the job of your choice.

Rule 5. Know Where to Get Help

When switching careers it is essential that you get some help along the way. Change is stressful to many people, especially when it affects one's career. Our work life is important because it gives us a certain prestige and perquisites, a place to go every day, and a standing in the community.

Where does a career switcher get help? The best starting point is to talk to family, friends, and people where you work or have worked. Don't hesitate to talk to former employers and peers, especially human resource professionals.

As mentioned in the preceding chapter, an excellent way to get career-changing information is to visit colleges and universities in your area, including community colleges. Today many colleges have specific courses designed for the 50-plus person who wants to change careers. Talk to the career counselors in such schools. Look upon the cost, if any, as an investment in your future.

"Counseling," according to Drake Beam Morin's James Cabrera, "is utilizing a body of knowledge. It's making a calculated, educated decision as opposed to a gut decision. This doesn't preclude what some great entrepreneurs have established by following their gut feelings. But then there are many more prospective entrepreneurs that never made it than succeeded.

"It's an educated decision. A person gets all the facts. It is easy to relate to others in such circumstances but difficult when one deals with his or her career. If you weren't facing a problem-solving situation you would go through a step-by-step analysis of all alternatives, all the risks involved before you made a calculated decision. When one is involved in something as important as one's career, it is imperative to go through the same process.

"You are in a sense an entrepreneur. Your product is yourself. You have to see who will buy it at what price. And to do this you must have the facts—about yourself."

One caution: There are good counselors and bad counselors wherever you go. Listen carefully to what they say, but remember that you are the one who must make the final decision. Common sense is the critical factor here.

Another information source on changing careers is the professional counselor who charges a fee for services rendered. Good professional counseling can pay big dividends when it comes to career-making decisions. But be wary of those who charge high prices and promise you the moon. Get recommendations from friends and check with the Better Business Bureau in your area for those counselors that may have had complaints filed against them.

Don't forget networking, which is one of the best ways to find a new job or career situation. Many companies have difficulty finding competent people to fill specific jobs. The more people who know you are looking for a job the better your chances of finding what you want.

Rule 6. Retrain

Retraining may be necessary to help you launch a new career, depending on your circumstances. For example, if you've been out of the workplace for a number of years, moving into a brand-new field may require that you take some refresher courses to get started. In some cases, depending on your field, extensive instruction may be necessary, especially if you are the victim of a permanent downsizing.

That's what happened to Dick Hamel, 60, a highly skilled industrial engineer currently hard at work designing trade-show exhibits for his new company, Innovative Designs & Concepts in Freeport, Long Island. A talented man, Hamel recently lost his job at the Grumman Corporation. He was one of approximately 2,500 employees let go because of a canceled military contract. To make matters worse, Hamel had recently helped design a complex $11.5 million system for painting aircraft for his company and was noted for his efficient and creative factory designs.

"I was never out of work before and it really bothered me," says Hamel. "Any job change prior to that was my decision. My prospects didn't look too rosy. It was a traumatic thing to go through."

To help the aircraft manufacturer's "displaced workers," the town of Oyster Bay on Long Island received a $1 million grant to retrain Grumman employees who had lost their jobs. "The school was in Amityville," says Hamel. "I went to the interview with the town to see if I had the smarts to be funded. I was accepted." The government-funded program paid for his books and $6,000 tuition for a 1,000-hour course in technical drafting.

Sowing the Seeds of Success. At that time the annual nationwide Drafting & Design Association contest was taking place. "I had not done any architectural renderings since 1947," he said, "but I finished my course about a month early, because each student worked on an individual basis. So I began to do some renderings. In 25 hours I produced an architectural rendering of the building. It won the first-place prize from more than 400 entries from schools and colleges all over the country."

Hamel got his job when a co-worker who had taken the drafting course suggested that Innovative Concepts & Designs call the school for a position they wanted to fill. "I went there, applied, and got the job," says Hamel. "When I went to the job interview I took the rendering along, which influenced the company in hiring me."

Hamel likes his new job. He says, "It's gotten more interesting because it is more artistic."

Adaptive and Functional Skills. Remember that you, too, bring professional experience to the work force, plus the proven skills developed over your 50-plus career lifetime. So don't sell your talents short. Also remember that your skills are portable and adaptable to any job you take.

Career counselors call these skills adaptive and functional. Adaptive skills can be termed as self-management, which a person uses to function in the workplace environment. These include such personality characteristics as assertiveness, creativity, emotional stability, initiative, resourcefulness, to name a few.

Functional skills—our transferable skills—relate to how individuals function at work. This includes dealing with people and performing specific tasks. The key is to take these adaptive and functional skills and transfer them to your new career.

Rule 7. Sell Your Skills

Switching careers requires that you sell your skills to a potential employer. What do you have to sell? As a 50-plus professional, you have a lot to offer. For example, you bring to the company considering hiring you four vital skills that are increasingly scarce in today's labor market: experience, common sense, the ability to solve problems, and interpersonal skills acquired during a working career of 30 years or more.

Obviously many people have similar skills to a greater or lesser degree. What you must do is convince the people who interview you that you are the man or woman for the job, something that is easier said than done.

Experience. This is a special commodity in the job market. You either have it or you don't. It is not something you can buy or suddenly acquire, and it is one of your strongest selling points. You've been tested by fire. You've accomplished tasks under pressures that would have some managers biting their fingernails.

When you sit down to talk with a would-be employer, stress your experience and give specific examples of what you've done in specific situations. Relate these experiences in terms that will impress the interviewer and make this person feel that you would be an asset to the company.

Common Sense. As any manager is quick to tell you, common sense is not so common. Emphasize this trait when talking with interviewers and detail how your good judgment saved the day on more than one occasion in your career. Here you can stress how you saved your company money, prevented a bad decision, rescued a failing sales effort, or improved a new product to mention a few examples. Be prepared to back up your statements by saying, "You can check with my previous boss, Mr. Jones, about this matter." This adds credibility to your claims, and it also permits your would-be employer to verify that what you've said is true. This is, after all, common sense.

Problem-Solving Skills. All companies seek problem-solvers—perceptive employees who can spot problems before they get out of hand, derail them, and solve them are worth their weight in gold in the corporate marketplace. This is a skill you can sell to a potential employer.

Another talent to merchandise is the fact that you can handle several assignments at the same time. Today companies are operating as lean as they've ever been to maintain their bottom lines. If you are the type of person who can efficiently juggle several assignments at once and complete them on time, sell this talent hard to your would-be employer.

Interpersonal Skills. These are sought after by employers everywhere. You can demonstrate yours during the interview by creating an image of a positive, experienced professional, confident and comfortable as you sit in the office and talk with the interviewer about your accomplishments and what you can contribute to his or her company.

Here you sell your ability to motivate people, to improve their performance, to work well in a team effort or as a team manager, to handle difficult employees. Again, use specific examples from your past experience to demonstrate the valuable talents you can bring to the interviewer's company.

Rule 8. Select the Right Work Environment

It's important to work for a company in which you fit in with the corporate culture and enjoy the people with whom you work. Although this is something that doesn't come with a guarantee, you should get a sense of the corporate climate during your interviews.

Some other company assets to consider: Does the company have a fair employment policy? For example, does it treat women and minority employees fairly, pay equal salaries for equal work, and promote individuals on their merits? Does the company offer additional training to help employees improve skills?

These are questions that should be answered before accepting employment with a company.

Rule 9. Enjoy What You Do

If you don't enjoy your work, all the time and effort you've invested in switching careers is wasted because it will adversely affect your private as well as your business life. Nicholas Lore, director of the Rockford Institute, a career consulting company in Washington, D.C., says, "Take your innate abilities, couple them with your interests, and you obtain a natural confidence that gives you a distinct advantage over your future. You can more easily join the growing number of people who don't think of their work as work, but as pleasure."

That statement neatly sums up the importance of enjoying what you do.

Rule 10. Integrate Your Lifestyle with Your Work Life

At this juncture in your career your professional and personal lives should be in harmony, because they are interrelated. For example, if you are unhappy and are having problems on the job, these problems will affect your personal life as well. Life isn't perfect, but we do have some control over events that occur. That is why it is so important to strive for the right job when you make a career change. It can go a long way toward helping you achieve a satisfying lifestyle.

Compensation. Money is another vital consideration when switching careers, and can present problems, depending on your particular needs. Here is what University of Massachusetts–Amherst Neil Yeager has to say on the subject:

"When changing careers, it is sometimes easier to take a pay cut by taking a job with the potential to rise to your former level. Many over-50 people today don't want to be dependent on a job for all their income. In such cases they may be willing to take a cut in salary."

Yeager also points out that there are not that many plum jobs available today. "Sometimes," he says, "you may have to settle for less. If you are not willing to take less money, you may be unemployable. For example, you may have to take $50,000 rather than $70,000. It's a tradeoff. Are you willing to be unemployed for a year instead of finding something in six months at a lower income? Money is one of the toughest questions you have to deal with.

"On the other hand, it is a myth that you need to accept low pay. Many people switch careers with the wrong mentality, because they have unique qualities that can help them achieve higher levels."

And a greater number of new jobs will be created in the 1990s by smaller firms, not by Fortune 500 companies, says Yeager, with obvious advantages for the over-50 career changer.

Moe Mozier had a long, successful, and peripatetic career in the restaurant business that permitted him to switch to commercial real estate where he handles hospitality sales.

Mozier, now in his late fifties, was attending premedical school at the University of New Hampshire, paying his way by working in restaurants, cleaning pots and pans, washing dishes, waiting on tables, all "general gamut restaurant jobs," he says. During this time Mozier's education was interrupted by the Korean War.

When he returned he decided to postpone his premed studies and work for a year. He taught fifth grade and coached three sports at Cardinal Cushing Academy outside of Newburyport, Massachusetts. At the end of the year he had bought a car and a sports coat and had less money than when he started. He went to work for an insurance company in Vermont and stayed four years. He woke up one morning and decided he didn't want to continue working in insurance, even though he had been promoted to state manager.

It was back to the restaurant business. Over the years Mozier has held a variety of jobs in this business as a consultant, manager, and owner, which eventually landed him in Keene, New Hampshire, where he purchased an old building that had been built by Henry David Thoreau's grandfather. Mozier remodeled it and turned it into a restaurant. It grossed more than $2 million before he sold it for $1.65 million.

This became Mozier's stepping-stone to his new career. During this period Mozier had been named "restauranteur of the year" in New Hampshire. He also served as president of the New Hampshire Hospitality Association, where he is still on the board of directors.

What made him sell his restaurant and leave the business? Mozier says, "The labor shortage had become acute." In previous years, he said, he had a huge labor pool consisting of young, motivated people in their twenties. Today, says Mozier, there is a lack of young motivated people and it is difficult to find competent help in the restaurant business.

The result: Mozier went into a new occupation—commercial real estate. In 1989 he got his real estate license and went to work for Curran-Fosket & Company in Keene, where he is responsible for hospitality sales. According to Mozier, "They are two capable and versatile realtors who specialize in commercial real estate. There are eight people in the office. We have more than $50 million in listings, including $13 million in restaurants."

Mozier claims that "Although the commercial realty market at this time is at an all-time low, we're experiencing what we feel is a comfortable success. I'm anxious to see what good times are, because there are still people who want to own restaurants.

"Ninety-two percent of people who start a restaurant—not a chain—for the first time fail within the first five years," he says. "No other occupation has a mortality rate like that."

Mozier says he relies on his expertise, contacts, and knowledge acquired from owning and managing restaurants over the years. He puts in long hours working as a commercial realtor, but likes being an "independent contractor." He says, "You never become a success working a forty-hour week."

Mozier claims he was burned out in the restaurant business and revitalized by commercial real estate. The contacts he made during the years in the restaurant business served as a springboard for his new career. Married, with two grown children—a daughter and son—Mozier says he still has a lot to learn about "this complicated business, including developing more contacts." When he does, he plans to take some time to "slack off."

That's one successful account of switching careers. It's not something that everyone can and should do. But if it is your choice, know what you want to do, put your plan on paper, and go for it!

The responsibility for deciding what you want to do—whether it's looking for a new job or switching careers—rests squarely on your shoulders. No one else can make the decision for you. You can solicit advice and help from friends and relatives and even pay a professional career counselor to help, but eventually you have to make the decision that will affect the rest of your life. The time to start is now.

CHAPTER 5

How to Get Started

At this point you should have a better idea of what you want to do and where you want to go. As you begin your quest, don't worry about your age; concentrate on getting the job. Robert Half, chairman of Robert Half International, says, "If you believe you are too old, you have a problem. You will make it happen that you don't get the job."

A positive attitude is crucial to your conducting a successful job campaign. You may get lucky and strike pay dirt when you are depressed, but the odds are against it. Today's job market competition is too tough. If you are depressed, anxious, and lack confidence, you telegraph these negative feelings to the interviewers and those you meet. Your attitude should be such that if the interviewer asks you to move the building two inches to the left during lunch hour, your answer is a cheery "No problem." Company managers seek competent, confident, can-do people who perform well on the job.

If you're depressed because you've recently been fired or are the victim of a merger or acquisition, remember that you are the same person you were before this happened, with all the skills and experience you've acquired during the course of your career. You don't suddenly lose a lifetime's experience

61

overnight because of a circumstance. Too many job hunters forget this after the traumatic experience of losing their jobs.

What You Should Know

As you begin your job search, keep the following facts and statistics in mind:

- Jobs change in both good times and bad.
- Approximately 20 percent of jobs in the United States change hands every year.
- The average job opening is usually known in an organization from two to ten weeks before it is advertised.
- There is no shortage of jobs. Companies are always seeking competent professionals. That means you.
- The hidden job market consists of approximately 80 percent of the jobs in the United States that are never advertised.
- A job is an opportunity for you to help a company accomplish a task or solve a problem.

These fascinating facts reveal that there is a job waiting for you. Jobs are always available for competent, well-trained professionals. It may not be easy to locate the one you want, but it is up to you to find the right one and nail it down. Remember that job hunting is a time-consuming, full-time endeavor that requires you to do something every day. Whether you are unemployed, looking for a new job, reentering the job market, or researching a career change, invest your time in setting up a workplace to plan, organize, and execute your job campaign.

Conduct your job search as you would a professional business—keeping records, including expenses, dates, and the name, address, and telephone number of every person with whom you've interviewed or talked with on the telephone.

The Job Campaign Planner featured in this chapter will help you set up an easy-to-use campaign-at-a-glance chart.

Plan Your Finances for the Duration. The next step is to plan your campaign on a week-by-week basis. You'll be writing letters, making telephone calls, and then following up.

It's also necessary at this point to consider finances. Looking for a job when you are unemployed is difficult enough in itself. If money is tight, it can be devastating to one's family and self-esteem, especially when the main breadwinner is out of work.

If you've walked out of your company with a pension and lump-sum payment, it is not the time to take a vacation and lament your state of unemployment. Instead start an action plan that will get you back into the ranks of the employed as quickly as possible.

Register for unemployment insurance immediately. Sit down with your family and plan an austerity budget until you get back into the work force. Include all members of the family in this meeting, explaining what changes will have to be made while you are looking for a job. During this period also plan for periods of relaxation and time spent with the family. Try to keep your life as normal as possible under the circumstances. Maintain your standards on a business and personal basis.

If money is a serious problem, consider signing up with a temporary agency until you can find the job you want. A temporary position can often lead to full-time employment. Many temporary employment agencies now hire 50-plus professionals to fill their job assignments.

If your are reentering the job market, the same rules apply. Job hunting requires expenditures for letterheads, stamps, envelopes, telephone calls, carfare, lunches, train or bus fare, your automobile—27.5 cents per mile when you use it in your job search plus parking fees—and the appropriate clothes and dry-cleaning necessary to present a professional image during interviews. Keep daily records of everything you spend; most of these costs are tax deductible.

Four Rules to Follow

At this stage there are four must-do things critical to your job quest. Although they are basic, many job seekers overlook them.

Advertise Your Availability. Tell everyone you know or meet that you are looking for a job. You can't afford to be bashful. The more people who know you are seeking employment, the better your chances of getting a job. That means family, friends, relatives, neighbors, acquaintances, people you've worked with in the past, and people you meet. The more job seeds you sow, the better your chances of having one sprout. You'll be surprised at the number of leads you'll get by asking people about potential jobs, even those you talk to for the first time. Often a secretary or a manager you speak with on the phone will mention a company looking for people to hire. Sometimes a secretary will provide information that leads you to a potential employment opportunity. But you have to ask: "Do you know anyone in the construction business looking for an estimator? I'm currently looking for such a job." This kind of communication is called *networking* and is a proven way to find job leads.

Avoid Self-pity. Begin looking for a new job immediately. If you start feeling sorry for yourself and sit around waiting for the phone to ring, you'll waste valuable time. You should do something every day to find a new job. If you are rejected for a job you wanted, don't waste time blaming yourself about what you may or may not have done wrong. You don't know the company politics of the office and the turf battles that may have been taking place behind the scenes. Instead of negative "what if" self-criticism, concentrate on your campaign and the next interview.

Maintain a Regular Schedule. This is important because it requires discipline on your part. That means you should be at your workplace desk or table at 8:30 or 9:00 every morning, as you would if you were still at the office, working until 4:30 or 5:00, with a break for lunch. Maintaining a regular schedule is psychologically important, because even if you have a bad day, you'll know you've made an effort and did something positive. Every day is a fresh start. Remember that job hunting is a difficult and tedious process that involves rejection. But the more negative responses you get, the better your chances of getting a positive reply and finding a job. Perseverance is essential.

Stay Away from Alcohol. Enticing though it may be to have a drink in the afternoon, if it becomes a habit and one drink turns into two or more, alcohol can inhibit or destroy your motivation and your chances of getting a job. Alcohol can be a serious problem for some job hunters, and it can wreak havoc with both marriage and career.

Now it's time to get to work. Plan and organize your work week so that you are doing something every day, with some time off to relax for a few hours on weekends. A good part of your time will be spent researching contacts and companies, writing letters, sending out résumés, then following up with telephone calls to arrange interviews.

Valuable Information Sources

In addition to doing work at home and at the library, there will be days when you are going on interviews, meeting people, and making luncheon appointments. That's why it's important to plan your work week in advance. On some days you'll be working at home and other days you're keeping appointments. Planning your week will help you run a coordinated business campaign, and ensure that you won't forget appointments.

Read your daily newspaper for information about companies in your industry and executives you can write to about possible employment. Read magazines such as *Business Week*, *Forbes*, *Fortune*, and *Inc*. *The Wall Street Journal* is also a valuable source of information, as is the *National Employment Weekly*, which contains help-wanted advertisements and short, practical articles on how to get a job. Chances are good that your library subscribes to these publications.

Trade journals that are available at your local library are also excellent sources of information about specific industries. A good place to look for information about industries or companies is in industry associations. *The Encyclopedia of Associations* lists virtually every association of any importance in the United States. It contains association names, contacts, and telephone numbers. A letter or telephone call to a staff member or director of an association will bring you contacts and information.

Another excellent source is *Standard & Poor's*. This book is published in several volumes and lists executives' names, and the addresses and telephone numbers of companies throughout the United States. In addition, there is a brief synopsis of what business the company is in, including information about its sales and income.

Once you have decided what companies you'd like to contact for potential employment, you can research specific ones in the library. Many different books summarize information about specific industries. For example, *Stardard Rate & Data* lists all the consumer and trade magazines in the United States in separate volumes. In the front of each volume is an alphabetized list of every magazine mentioned, by category. Turn to the category you're interested in to find the name and address of each company, telephone number, list of executives, a synopsis of the material published, frequency of publication, and the circulation and advertising rates. If special issues are published, they are also listed.

A list of multiple publishers, those that produce several magazines, is also available. You don't have to be a writer, editor, or publisher to use such a book in your job hunt. Occupations such as accountants and auditors, business managers, circulation personnel, engineers, computer professionals, public relations and promotion experts, salespersons, human resource professionals, lawyers, nurses, and doctors are employed in many of these businesses.

Talk to the librarian and ask for resource books geared to your specific needs. You'll be amazed at the number and variety of books that can provide information and help in your job hunt.

Software Resources

If you have a computer with a modem, you can research companies through data bases from the comfort of your home. A data base is available for virtually every subject you can imagine. Here is a brief description of four major companies that offer a great variety of helpful data base information about companies and people:

Dialog. The data base on this system contain more than 175 million records of directory listings for companies, associations, and famous people, in-depth financial statements for companies, citations with bibliographic information, and complete texts of journal articles, and many more subjects.

Dow Jones News/Retrieval. This online source is designed for business and financial professionals, as well as for serious personal investors. This data base contains up-to-the-minute news about companies, markets, and investments. Stock quotes and detailed financial information are available on thousands of companies.

LEXIS/NEXIS. This online service provides in-depth information on specialized subjects in business and industry. LEXIS contains legal research material, whereas NEXIS contains news and business information. Clients can subscribe to each one independently.

Standard & Poor's Business Information Online. This data base features information on more than 45,000 companies, virtually all publicly and privately owned companies with sales of $1 million or more, or more than 50 employees. The data base also contains biographical information about approximately 70,000 top-level executives in U.S. business.

These data bases are updated periodically with information about industry trends and specific facts about a company's executive organization and finances. There is usually an initiation fee to sign up, and charges for obtaining online information are reasonable. For a job seeker researching a specific company, a computer with a modem can be a helpful and timesaving resource.

You may on occasion use a fax machine to send a letter or résumé prior to an interview or to supply information afterward. Use every resource that is available.

Your Job Search Planner

The next step is to plan your job hunt. That's where our Job Search Planner with its campaign-at-a-glance chart can be helpful. To conduct a successful job-finding campaign, you have to be organized. Keep a record of the many people you contact. Job hunters who maintain good records, who follow up with letters, phone calls, and thank-you notes, get the most responses.

In addition to your Job Search Planner, keep a diary of detailed notes of every person you talk to, your impression of the company and its personnel, and what was said on the telephone and at interviews. Such notes can be helpful when making follow-up telephone calls and writing letters and thank-you notes.

Using your Job Search Planner and the chart in this chapter in conjunction with your dairy will help avoid mixups when making or keeping appointments, and help you remember them. You will also make yourself more competitive in the marketplace, because most people look for a job in a haphazard way. If you rely solely on your memory, you may forget or overlook important details.

If you have a computer, you can use it to set up your Job Search Planner and print out weekly records to keep your campaign up to date.

How to Use the Job Search Planner. This is a practical and professional system that permits you to chart a day-by-day record of the job hunt. Looking for a job requires that you do something every day. This means tracking down contacts, writing letters, making telephone calls, setting up information interviews, following up, and keeping an eagle eye out when reading newspapers or magazines for information and contacts that may be helpful to you.

Start to organize your job hunt with a legal-size, lined yellow pad. With a ruler, make four vertical columns labeled, in order, Company, Address, Contact, Telephone Number. Take this pad to the library when researching companies and clearly pencil in the required information in each of the columns. This will be your working contact list. You'll also include the names of contacts you obtain from friends and business acquaintances. Obviously, not all the contacts will be helpful. For those that are, transfer the information to your Job Search Planner, which will be your active contact list.

Plan to organize your campaign by setting aside some time each day to do the many chores that are required in a job-hunting campaign. As you can see, your Job Search Planner chart is divided into sections. The first section is headed Company & Contact. Here you keep a record of the name of the person you talk to or interview, the name of his or her company, and the date.

The next three columns are headed Preparation, Interview, and Result.

Preparation. The first section requires research in order to get the information you need. You've got to research the companies, target those that interest you, and then get the names of the executives, including titles and addresses, through a telephone call or a current reference book in the library. This section also has space for information interviews, should you feel them necessary, and dates you mailed out cover letters and résumés. The dates are important, because if you don't get an answer within a week or two, you can make a follow-up call to find out if your letter and résumé were delivered. By keeping meticulous records, you'll be able to follow every lead and know when someone has not replied to your letter or phone call. You can also see what methods work best for you.

If you plan to do information interviews, now is the time to schedule them. As you progress during this part of your job search, keep your day-to-day records, including the date, and jot down your impressions in the diary. As you'll note in the Preparation section, there is space to write in the dates you mailed your cover letters and résumés and made follow-up telephone calls.

Interview. This section is designed to record your interviews, appointments, and your assessments, which you record in your diary for future use. A reminder for thank-you notes, and your follow-up telephone calls is included. Don't overlook any of these steps. The thank-you note, for example, is often forgotten or overlooked by job hunters. It's a way of expressing your appreciation for the time the interviewer or executive spent with you, reaffirming your interest in the job and the company, and mentioning something that may have been overlooked during the interview. The follow-up letter also permits you to introduce new ideas that occurred to you after the interview and to highlight the skills and talents you can bring to the company.

Remember, the more interviews you get, the better your

chances of clinching the job. Don't be discouraged by rejections. They are part of the job hunt.

Result. The Result category is where you hit pay dirt. You have your second or third interviews, you get out your thank-you notes, and keep in touch with would-be employers by telephone. The payoff is the job offer and acceptance.

That's the way the Job Search Planner works. Using it in conjunction with your diary/notebook on a daily basis will give you a "bottom line" for your campaign. You will know at every stage of the search precisely where you are, and what contacts you still have to make.

A job campaign is like wheel that never stops turning. If you keep up with it on a daily basis, it is easy to stay current. If you get too far behind, you may never catch up. That is why it is so important to run your job-hunting campaign like a business. If you know what you want, have a plan, and execute it in a professional manner, you will greatly increase your chances of success.

There are also psychological benefits. By keeping daily records and planning your weekly chores ahead of time, you'll be in control of your program. You'll also know what has to be done, and where you have to do more work.

If you run a haphazard campaign, you'll risk missing or mixing up interview dates, possibly fail to follow up by telephone or letter, diminish your chances of getting a job. You might get lucky and hit the job jackpot, but luck usually is the companion of hard work.

Also keep in mind there is no single best way to get a job. The secret is to keep plugging away every day. Try to be innovative. What can you do to outshine your unknown competition? You can incorporate ideas and suggestions in your letters to interviewers. For example, if you are a salesperson, you might suggest a technique to increase sales. Depending on the field you're in, think of ideas that might help the company. True, there is an element of risk in making such suggestions, but if you do your homework about the company, you have the opportunity to enhance your image and present something different and creative. Be willing to take a chance.

Try to keep a positive attitude at all times—that's important. You'll have your low days when you think you'll never get a job. Then there will be days when you have a good interview and your spirits soar and all will seem right with the world. Job hunting requires hard work, effort, and consistency, and it is important to keep at it until you succeed.

Here are three vital rules to remember as you begin your job quest: Be yourself, do something every day, and believe in yourself. If you follow these three simple rules, success will ultimately seek you out.

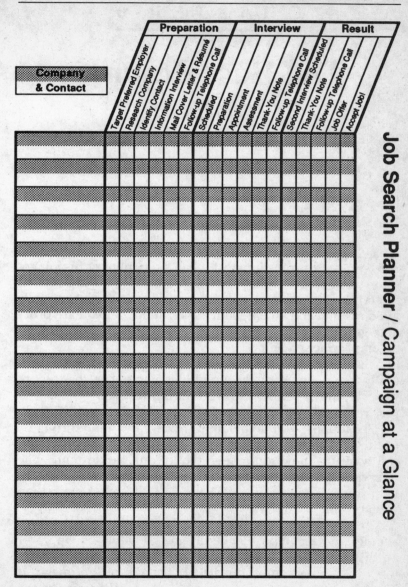

Company & Contact	Preparation								Interview							Result		
	Target Preferred Employer	Research Company	Identify Contact	Information Interview	Mail Cover Letter & Résumé	Follow-up Telephone Call	Scheduled	Preparation	Appointment	Assessment	Thank-You Note	Follow-up Telephone Call	Second Interview Scheduled	Thank-You Note	Follow-up Telephone Call	Job Offer	Accept Job!

Job Search Planner / Campaign at a Glance

CHAPTER 6

The Best Résumé for You

A 51-year-old professional who had suddenly lost his job got some good advice from a seasoned counselor during his first interview. The counselor told him, "You've got an unusually good résumé and an excellent background, but you are probably going to get a job through your contacts, not through an employment agency."

As it turned out, the counselor was right. The man eventually found a new job through his contacts. The chances are you will, too. Then why do you need a résumé?

A résumé is still required for most job situations. For example, suppose you do get an interview and a job through a friend or business acquaintance. The person who hires you will want to know something about your background. The interviewer will use the résumé to trigger questions that can help you nail down the job. That's why it is important to keep your résumé up to date.

A résumé is a unique document, because it highlights your abilities and accomplishments. It gives a would-be employer an organized and detailed picture of you in terms of your work life and accomplishments. It also creates an image. If it's neat, well written, and precise, it simplifies the interviewer's job, which is a plus for you. Busy managers can't waste time reading poorly written, long-winded résumés that don't describe the talents and accomplishments of the person seeking employment.

Don't submit a picture with your résumé. The law prohibits discrimination against job hunters over 40 on the basis of age, ethnic background, sex, and religion. Your health, height, weight, and marital status should not be included because they are not relevant. A photo is not necessary and could work against the over-50 job hunter.

Don't include your salary range on your résumé, because you may eliminate yourself from an interview by specifying a salary that is too high or too low. Salary is usually discussed after several interviews, when the employer is ready to hire.

The Best Résumé for You

Most résumés are scanned for a few seconds before they are rejected or tossed into the wastebasket. For the 50-plus professional seeking employment, a selling résumé is vital. It is the visa that lets you cross the first barrier in the job market—getting the interview.

James Cabrera of Drake Beam Morin, Inc., a counseling and outplacement company headquartered in New York City, succinctly sums up the subject: "Treat a résumé as bait. It's not going to get you a job. The only thing it does is get you an interview. So it should be written in such a way as to say who you are, what you've done, and with whom. It should highlight your accomplishments and achievements."

Its value to employers is "What can he or she do for us?" The answer to this question in too many cases is "Nothing." The reason? Employers say that most of the résumés they receive do not sell the talents of the persons who submit them, which means if you write an above-average résumé, you greatly increase your chances of getting called in for the interview.

When you contact a potential employer, you want to make an impression on the person in the company who will evaluate your potential. You want that person to remember you. A good way to accomplish this is to first send an introductory letter to your contact, briefly outlining your career plans, saying a résumé will follow. A few days later, send a résumé with a cover letter, which should always accompany a résumé. If you do get the interview with this person, your third letter— a thank-you note for the time he or she spent with you— should make an impression, which will make it easier for you to follow up with a telephone call to inquire about your prospects.

Hurdling the Age Barrier

The first obstacle to be overcome is the age barrier. As we've mentioned earlier, you are entering a tough and competitive job market. You don't want to submit a résumé and have it tossed aside because a prejudiced interviewer takes a quick look and rules you out because of your age. One way to prevent this is to highlight the last 20 years of your experience to the present, using dates for the different positions you've held. Another method is to use the functional or targeted résumé, with or without dates, depending on how you decide to present your résumé material. This way you don't immediately reveal your age, but present a résumé that portrays an experienced professional to a potential employer.

On the other hand, don't be gun-shy about your age. Some companies will not judge you by age, but by what you can do for the company. Some of these companies are listed in Chapter 12, "Companies That Hire 50-Plus Professionals."

How to Handle Time Gaps

Time gaps in a résumé can present problems for 50-plus professionals because they require explanations. Be prepared to answer such questions so you can concentrate on selling your experience. You want to spend your time talking to the interviewer about the expertise you can bring to the company.

The best way to deal with the time-gap question is with candor. You may even be able to turn the time-gap into an advantage. For example, you may have been fired because of an acquisition or merger, or because your company was cutting back and your department was eliminated. You could say then that you took some time off to decide what you wanted to do with your career. Upheavals in the American workplace have caused the displacement of many workers. Job loss no longer carries the stigma of being fired.

Or you might say: "I took early retirement because my company encouraged it, but I found it was a mistake. I was doing the best, most productive work of my life and decided to get back in the job market."

Another good explanation for the time gap is that you were not happy with your job and considering a career change. You returned to school to take some courses to see if you were on the right track.

These are honest, rational, and reasonable explanations for a time gap, especially for an older professional. So don't be uncomfortable when you are asked for an explanation—be prepared. If you have the talents an employer seeks, the chances are good that you will be considered for the job.

Reentering the Job Market

What if you've been out of the job market for a while? Perhaps you are a widow or a homemaker who has raised a family and now want to get back into the work force. Or perhaps you are retired and have discovered you would rather get back to work. How do you prepare your résumé?

Many women returning to the job market underrate their skills and abilities. That's why it is so important to sit down with a blank sheet of paper and list your interests, skills, and accomplishments. This requires discipline and time, and may take a few hours or several days before you come up with a good list, but the results will be worth the effort. One way to get started is to ask your children. They'll get you off to a good start. Once you begin committing your thoughts to paper you'll be surprised at how much information you'll uncover.

When you begin to commit this information to paper, don't be modest. You want your résumé to flaunt your talents. This is not the time to underestimate your abilities. For example, if you have had a variety of unrelated work experiences, include them. You can mold the facts into a selling résumé. You must create a career profile of who you are and what you've done.

The who-you-are part requires that you understand the kind of person you are and know the kind of job you want. Ask yourself, "What do I like to do? What am I good at? What salable skills do I have? What have I accomplished? The answers to these questions should be written on that blank sheet of paper, then transferred to your résumé after you have refined them.

If you have been a homemaker, look back at your past history. Did you help your husband in his business? Did you help manage his office or keep the books? Were you active in a political party, raising funds or helping your candidate get elected? Even if your candidate lost, you have relevant material for your résumé. Did you write campaign ads or participate in promotion or public relations for your party? Were you chairperson for the United Way campaign in your neighborhood? Did you raise funds for your church or synagogue? Did you do volunteer work? Have you had any special training that could be used by a corporation in a specific job? For example, if you have a knowledge of computers, you could train a company's employees in their use.

If you've been out of the job market for several years because you retired and decided to go back to work, the same principles apply. Use your past experience to frame your résumé. While you were "retired" you may have done voluntary work, helped out a friend in business, or engaged in hobbies. These accomplishments can be included in your résumé.

Homemakers shouldn't forget to include work done after college, before being married. This experience can also be used on your résumé. Many women during the course of their married lives perform daily jobs that are relevant in the corporate world. For example, a homemaker is a manager, a planner, a diplomat, an administrator, a writer, a practitioner of public relations, a politician, a problem solver, a nurse, a telemarketer, and a counselor and adviser, to mention some of her many and varied skills. In fact, many of the most important and desired skills, as Nella Barkley of the Crystal-Barkley Corporation notes, are used outside the workplace.

But these skills are valid and important, because they can be transferred to the corporate world. The ability of a person with good interpersonal skills, for example, is invaluable in the business world. So don't sell yourself short.

Let's look at some sample lines with specific headings that might be included on a homemaker's or widow's résumé. Management:

- Created, wrote, and produced advertisements credited with winning local election.
- Planned, executed church's annual fund-raising campaign. Result: $30,000. Largest amount raised in church's 50-year history.
- Organized, coordinated local United Way campaign. Increased donations 40 percent over previous year—all-time high.

These sample accomplishments give you an idea of what to include. Use short, punchy, action words. When you can mention figures and percentages, do so. For example: Increased sales 25 percent; reorganized department, which resulted in net gain of $10,000 to bottom line.

Common Mistakes—and How to Avoid Them

Résumés should be concise and to the point. Too many are overlong and wordy. They don't zero in on the job seeker's abilities or accomplishments.

Poor punctuation, faulty grammar, and misspellings are guaranteed to destroy your chances of getting an interview, let alone a job. Superior writing skills are valued by virtually every employer in today's competitive job market. Put them to work on your résumé.

A résumé that is poorly typed and printed also will ruin your chances for an interview. If you don't have a word processor or computer and printer, have your résumé produced at a printing shop. Look on the low cost as an investment in your future. Never send a résumé done on a dot-matrix printer unless it is excellent letter quality.

A résumé that is poorly laid out is another common mistake that can eliminate you from a job interview. The résumé should be esthetically pleasing to the reader. That means it should be written on white, off-white, ivory, or buff-colored, 8½ × 11 quality bond paper. Legal-size and off-size paper is not easily filed, so don't use it. Although some job hunters like to use offbeat colors, 50-plus professionals should stay on the conservative side. Avoid colors unless you are in a creative field, such as art directing or graphics designing, for example, where the résumé can reflect your style. Aside from being neatly typed and laid out, there should be enough white space on each side and at the top to give each page of the résumé a pleasing appearance. Don't cram every page with as much type as you can get on it. Common sense and good taste are the guidelines here.

The résumé needn't list all your accomplishments. It should highlight what you have done so that an employer can recognize the value of your experience and appreciate your potential to contribute to the company. What you want to do is to skim the cream from the top of your experience and put it on paper.

Compiling résumé information that isn't relevant to the job you are applying for is a waste of your time—and reading it is a waste of the would-be employer's time. It is important to key your résumé to the specific job you are applying for. Custom-tailor it.

Don't make the mistake of filling your résumé with a lot of technical jargon. However, you can use buzz words that apply to your particular field. Your résumé should read easily, and be instantly understandable. Too much technical jargon, especially if the interviewer is not an expert in the subject, can make you a noncompetitor.

Drafting Your Résumé

Writing a selling résumé is not so difficult. If you haven't written one recently, you can put a rough draft together in about an hour and a half if you follow the step-by-step instructions in this chapter. From that rough first draft you'll refine and polish it until it meets professional standards.

Several years ago we put a number of college students through weekend job-finding seminars. One of the drills was having them write a résumé in the afternoon, then refining it that evening. The students were amazed that after an hour and half they had put together rough résumés. We then spent time with each student critiquing and correcting what they had done. At the end of the evening, they were armed with résumés they had written. You can, too. The key is to get that all-important information about your interests, skills, and accomplishments on paper. Once that is done, you are ready to assemble the facts in a concise and readable format.

What You Should Know

Length. There is no one correct résumé length. It can be a page, a page and a half, or two pages, depending on your experience. In a recent survey by the Employment Management Association of 240 people who make employment decisions, 75 percent said a résumé longer than two pages is too much. Unless you are involved in a special job situation that requires a detailed history (or "curriculum vitae") of your work life, the maximum length should be two pages.

My feeling is that if you can apply for the job you want

with a tight, well-written, one-page résumé, it will be to your advantage. Career counselor Kate Wendleton, President of the Five O'Clock Club in New York City, sums up the length problem nicely. She says, "It has to be as short as it has to be, but long enough to tell the story." The best résumé is one that makes an interviewer read what you have written.

Originality. Don't be afraid to be creative and original when writing your résumé, as long as it is within the bounds of good taste and common sense. It's a personal advertisement for you, a marquee that touts your skills, a marketing tool designed to sell your talents to an employer.

Résumé Preparation Services. As an experienced professional, you should be able to write your own résumé. Although many companies offer résumé-writing services—for a fee— we consider this a waste of your money and valuable time. The reason? Only you have the information necessary to write your résumé. Consequently, it makes sense for you to spend the time developing this information and putting it on paper.

The best way to write a résumé today is with a computer and a printer. With a computer it's easy to correct typing mistakes and misspellings and quickly rearrange paragraphs. A computer or a word processor also makes it easy to write different versions of a résumé for specific job situations. In short, using a computer or word processor is a great time-saver.

Software Packages. If you haven't written a résumé in a number of years, consider one of the many résumé-writing software packages you can use with a computer. Although these software-produced résumés are usually directed to college students, they offer experienced professionals time-saving advantages in terms of design and layout. For example, they take the drudgery out of setting up a format and aligning margins and checking spelling. The programs give step-by-step instructions for preparing a résumé, and prompt you by asking questions about previous jobs and the specific skills you used to perform them. Programs provide lists of specific job categories for those who are uncertain about what they want to do, and ask questions as to what job hunters like to do to help the decision-making process. They also explain and illustrate examples of different types of résumés.

For example, *Career Navigator*™: The Computer-Powered Job Search System, developed by Drake Beam Morin, Inc., is a complete job-finding guide that includes four floppy disks and a detailed instruction manual. It is easy to use, even if you've never worked with a computer before. Under the section "Develop Your Job Search Tools," the user has seven choices. Let's select "How to Write Effective Résumés." This is what the computer monitor shows:

Action to take

    Edit
    Print
    Create
    Delete

You want to create your résumé, so you specify that section. A résumé form appears on the screen with headings: Objective, Summary, Skills Summary, Work History, Education, and Other. Fill in the required information from material you assembled earlier in the program. When you are finished, edit your material, delete or change, and then print it. You have a completed résumé. It may still be in rough form, but now you have something to work with and refine.

The Perfect Résumé Computer Kit created by Tom Jackson and Bill Buckingham also helps you build your résumé, from thinking about your career direction to printing the finished product. It comes with two disks—*The Career Consultant* and the *Résumé Builder*. The *Career Consultant* helps you formulate the résumé by making you clarify your career direction, identify significant skills, and shape your résumé. The *Résumé Builder* is your permanent file of résumé information, which helps you organize and design a variety of résumé formats to suit your needs. This includes setting margins and arranging sections.

For example, here, is a paragraph from the kit.

WRITE YOUR RÉSUMÉ

Now it's time to develop the paragraphs that make up the body of your résumé. From this you can create a Chronological, Functional, or Targeted résumé. Your work in this section becomes the core material used by the *Résumé Builder* disk in creating the final version of your résumé.

If you decide to use a computer program to prepare your résumé, read the software package label carefully to make sure it suits your particular needs.

Types of Résumés.

Let's define the different types of résumés and decide which kind is best for you. The next exercise is to write a résumé step-by-step.

The three basic types of résumés are: chronological, functional, and targeted. There's also another, more freewheeling style that might be called creative. This type is intended for people who are in creative fields, such as advertising or publishing. Let's look at each type of résumé.

Chronological. This type of résumé is literally a chronology of your work experience; it starts with your current position and works backwards, with a brief description that applies to each position you have held. Each description should be written with your job goal in mind. Designate the time period you held each job by year (e.g., 1989–1992).

The chronological résumé is more suitable for college graduates than 50-plus professionals, but it may serve your purposes for specific situations. If you plan to continue working in your career area of expertise, the chronological résumé is a good choice because it demonstrates how your career has progressed. Your work experience is listed by date, beginning with your current job and chronologically going back to the earliest job. If you use dates, don't go back more than 20 years. You can also write a chronological résumé without using dates. However, to offset possible age discrimination, using dates within the 20-year experience range is recommended. Career counselor Kate Wendleton suggests writing the number of years you worked on each job, not the dates. According to Ms. Wendleton, it's best to omit the dates because they don't help your case. Use the method you feel makes the best presentation.

Functional. The functional résumé lists your job function and accomplishments in short, punchy paragraphs, starting with the most important ones and then working down in descending order. For example, it highlights your accomplishments and marketable skills such as designing, financing, managing, and writing. It both supports and emphasizes what you have done. Dates are not always written in the functional résumé because of the way it is set up, which makes it a good choice for the 50-plus professional, including homemakers and widows. It is also a good résumé for career changers and people reentering the job market because it permits the job hunter to list a broad range of work experience skills. Again, dates can be included or left off. Companies you worked for are listed at the bottom of the résumé.

Targeted Résumé. As its name indicates, the targeted résumé is sent to the person in the organization responsible for the specific job you want. The Objective/Job Target zeros in on the position you want. It must be specific and state precisely the job you are seeking. Under the following categories—Skills, Accomplishments, and Work History—emphasize your qualifications and literally target your résumé to the job at hand. This résumé has to be carefully written in order to be successful. The targeted résumé is the easiest one to write once you have assembled the necessary information. Work history—the companies you've worked for—are listed at the bottom of the résumé.

Creative Résumé. This type of résumé is geared toward specific types of jobs in creative professions. The writer highlights specific work he or she has done, citing several examples, starting with the most important one and working backward. Although the typography used may be larger, varied, and more striking, careful judgment and good taste should prevail.

Before you write your résumé, it's necessary that you do some thoughtful soul-searching, especially if you've been out of the job market for a while. A résumé is not a detailed history. It is not a biography. You are putting on paper a highly selective work history that presents to a would-be employer the most important accomplishments in your work life.

How you present this information is vitally important. For example, if this material is written in a dull, uninteresting manner, the gloss of your accomplishments is dimmed. You have to write it as you would an advertisement. You want the employer to buy the product—you. You can't be modest or bashful when you write your résumé. You have to be pleasantly aggressive. Looking for a job is like being in show business. If you hide your light under the proverbial bushel, someone else will get the prize.

How to Structure Your Résumé.

Let's go through the main résumé categories that you will use. Start with a blank sheet of paper or use a word processor or computer. At the top of the page, type your name, address, home phone number and work phone number, assuming you can talk freely. If not, omit your work number. You can center your name at the top of the sheet with your address and phone number(s) directly below. Some job hunters prefer to center the name at the top, with the address on the left side of the paper and the telephone number(s) on the right side.

The next item on your résumé—an important one—is the Objective or Job Target, which tells the reader the job you want. This should be a clear and concise statement no longer more than three lines.

Next comes the Summary of Qualifications or Capabilities. Under this heading list single-line sentences preceded by a bullet or a brief two- or three-sentence paragraph. These headings can be used with both the chronological and functional résumés. The targeted résumé should state your job goal in one brief sentence.

The sample résumés in this chapter can be used to tailor your résumé to your particular needs. No matter what type of résumé format you use, the information you incorporate into it will essentially be the same.

Beneath the work history at the bottom of each résumé include one short line that reads: "References available on request." A college graduate seeking that first job might list several references with telephone numbers for the interviewer to call. But a 50-plus professional should be more circumspect. Regardless of whether or not you are working, you don't want another employer or interviewer calling your references to ask about you unless you have the job in hand. Tell the interviewer not to call your references until he or she okays it with you. People make mistakes and more than one job hunter has been hurt by indiscriminate telephone calls that caused problems with his or her boss, especially in situations where the applicant has decided not to switch jobs.

Another reason: You don't want your references to be subjected to a stream of phone calls. When you include "References available on request," you control who gets called when.

On each of the different types of résumés you can incorporate your own format to suit your needs as long as it is well designed and presents the information in a structured format geared to interest the potential employer. The résumés shown here should be used as guides. Don't be afraid to experiment and create a résumé that you are comfortable with and serves your needs.

In conclusion, your résumé should feature a job objective and a summary of your qualifications—or both. It should highlight your skills and your relevant work experience. It should contain a work history and include your educational background. And it should offer the interviewer references on request.

Once you've prepared your résumé, keep several copies available in the event you have to change or upgrade it to meet a new job situation. It is recommended that you update your résumé at least once a year. Save all your worksheets, too. You may have occasion to use them again.

Examine the sample résumés in this chapter and then compose your own. It is an important document and your passport to the working world and the job you want.

CHRONOLOGICAL RÉSUMÉ

R. Robert Roberts
8 Firewood Lane
Huntington, NY 11700
516/222-2222

EDITOR-IN-CHIEF/PUBLISHING EXECUTIVE. Experienced in all phases of magazine/book publishing, consumer and trade. Expert in administration, editing, writing, rewriting, production, graphics. Especially strong in creating new ideas that interest both readers and advertisers to generate more profits.

TECHNICIAN MAGAZINE
FASTRACK PUBLICATIONS   1984-Present

> *Editor-in-Chief.* In charge of monthly magazine for automotive service industry and Detroit and import car executives. Created new editorial direction, revitalized editorial contents, covers, graphics. Result: dramatic increase in reader interest. Magazine rose to No. 1 from No. 3 in its field.

> New editorial concept resulted in high editorial readership scores. Example: Super Research Inc. in 1987 study stated, "This is the first study we have ever conducted for a technical magazine, where every editorial item scores in excess of 100 index points.

MODERN CARS MAGAZINE   1971-1976

> *Managing Editor.* Supervised staff of seven. Planned, scheduled monthly contents. Assigned stories and art work. Made major contribution to magazine's circulation growth from 800,000 to 1,500,000.

> Conceived, planned special sections on variety of automotive subjects that resulted in 10% increase in advertising revenues.

Regularly wrote feature, how-to articles. Wrote monthly column devoted to latest developments in automotive technology.

Traveled to major U.S. cities, Europe, and Far East on story assignments.

PROFESSIONAL ASSOCIATIONS

American Society of Magazine Editors
International Motor Press Association
American Business Press
Who's Who in America·

PUBLISHED WORKS

Author—"A Job With a Future in Automotive Mechanics," Grosset & Dunlap, hard cover. In second printing. Most successful book in company's "A Job With a Future" series.

Author—articles published in variety of consumer magazines.

Story consultant for major publishers.

EDUCATION

M.B.A. New York University
B.A. Hunter College of the City of New York. Journalism and political science.

References available on request.

Note: The chronological résumé lists your most recent jobs and works backward to your earlier positions. It's easy to read, and highlights your accomplishments. It is a good résumé for a 50-plus professional who remains in his or her field because it demonstrates continuity and growth. This résumé writer went back only 20 years in his career. Dates can be left off if individual so desires.

FUNCTIONAL RÉSUMÉ

Joan Moran
5 Hacker Drive
San Francisco, CA 94116
414/666-7777

MANAGEMENT Conceived and implemented reorganization of major retail food chain in 10 Midwest states into three centralized divisions reporting to me. Result: reduced waste 15%, increased profits 12%, productivity 6%. Company moved from fifth place to second place in its field.

SALES Planned, budgeted, and executed novel sales plan for $100 million high-technology company. Took company from $14 to $38 million in sales in three years by reorganizing 15-person sales force, realigning territories, retraining, and motivating personnel.

MARKETING Responsible for marketing name-brand housewares in the United States and Canada. Developed promotional material that described products and their costs in one brochure that was used in both countries, eliminating second brochure formerly used in Canada. Result: $15,000 annual savings.

TECHNICAL Created technical training course for engineer-salespersons selling high-tech equipment. Course helped salespersons increase sales by simplifying presentations to nontechnical managers. Course was made mandatory in company's two other technical divisions.

EMPLOYMENT	1986-present	Division manager, Retail Foods Corp., Dallas, Texas
	1983-1985	Sales manager, Computers, Inc. San Francisco, Calif.
	1976-1982	Marketing manager, Home Housewares, St. Louis, Mo.
	1970-1975	Training manager, Hart Technical, Amityville, N.Y.
EDUCATION		B.S., Mechanical Engineering, Purdue University

References available on request

TARGETED RÉSUMÉ

Jonathan Mix
10 Lake Drive
Nashville, TN 37202
615/466-6666

JOB TARGET Chief executive, computer industry

CAPABILITIES
*Proven motivator of executives and employees
*Experienced in developing cost-saving budgets
*Accomplished in corporate and capital development
*Technical background in both software and hardware
*Experienced in planning, building, new plant facilities
*Established working relationships with industry executives in Asia and Europe

ACCOMPLISHMENTS
*Repositioned company, developed new product line that increased sales 10%
*Reduced and realigned executive staff to speed up decision making, improved efficiency
*Developed Far East task force that increased company's sales over Japanese competitor's by 4%
*Instituted robotic manufacturing in three of four plants to make company more competitive in global marketplace

WORK EXPERIENCE	*1983-present	Chief executive officer, Dyno Corp.
	*1979-1982	Vice-president, Dyno Corp.
	*1976-1981	Division manager, Humbert Corp.
	*1969-1980	Technical manager, Aero Corp.

EDUCATION

M.B.A., New York University
B.A., Stanford University

References available on request

CREATIVE RÉSUMÉ

RAY CORN ● GRAPHIC DESIGNER ● 5 GRAM ROAD ●
BROOKLYN, NY 11222
718/888-8888

JOB OBJECTIVE Graphic Design executive

SKILLS
Ability and experience in creative advertising designs, editorial layouts, spot illustrations, comprehensives, presentations, type design and specifications, photographic, mechanical, and production supervision.

EXPERIENCE
1989—Designs, Inc., Vice-President, Graphic Design
1982—Technical Catalogue Service, Art Director
1981—Ace Publications, Associate Creative Designer
1977—New York Daily Press, Senior Art Director
1970—New York Daily Press, Assistant Art Director

EDUCATION
New York University, A.A.S. degree
Pratt Institute
Cooper Union

References available on request

This creative résumé is simple, direct, and features eye-catching design. It shows growth and experience and gives no indication the sender is 58 years old.

CHAPTER 7

Writing Effective Cover Letters

Cover letters are an integral part of the job-hunting campaign. They are your direct mail campaign, and if well written they can make a difference. When you write a letter to an employer about a job, it should be flawless. That means it should be sincere, enthusiastic, easy to read, and technically perfect. It should be written on your stationery with your name, address, and telephone number imprinted at the top. The paper—white, off-white, ivory, or beige—should be of good quality.

The ability to communicate is a much sought-after asset in the business world, and you can gain an advantage over your unknown competition by the letters you write. For example, when you interview with an executive, you may walk out thinking that you did well, allowing yourself a sense of elation. You believe you have a good chance of getting the job. Certainly you're up with the top candidates, you tell yourself.

Think again. Take nothing for granted, especially when looking for a job. It is estimated that only 5 percent of all job applicants take the time to send follow-up letters. And no matter how well you think the interview went, the executive who interviewed you is a busy person. He or she may forget about you the minute you walk out the door. That's why the follow-up letter is so important.

Creating a Don't-Forget-Me Impression

Which job applicant will be remembered by the interviewer? Common sense indicates that the individual who most successfully markets his or her skills will get the job. That's human nature playing its part. Let's look at several good reasons for writing effective cover letters. In this chapter we'll feature 12 different letters you can easily tailor to your specific needs, and then discuss the merits of each one. The sample letters featured in this chapter can also be used by job hunters seeking part-time work. They only have to be changed to fit the individual's specific needs.

Remember: When you thank a person for his or her time, you flatter that individual and express an interest in the job as well. Thank-you letters are called "love notes," and believe it or not, they work. Don't be bashful about writing them to express your sincere and honest feelings.

A thank-you note gives you the opportunity to expound upon something you discussed during the interview. It also gives you the chance to bring up something you didn't discuss, or to demonstrate that you have a good knowledge of the company and its business.

Don't Be Afraid to Ask for the Job. Employers look for people with passion and enthusiasm for what they do. A thank-you note is an opportunity to tell the interviewer that the job seems particularly suited to your experience and qualifications, and that the possibility of working for the company is an exciting one for you. If you want the job, say so. How else will the interviewer know you are interested?

If you interview for a position in which you don't have much experience, you can use your letter to detail how your past experience and skills can be an asset to the company, and how you can bring a fresh perspective to the job.

Practice Good Manners. If, during the course of an interview, you are introduced to another person in the company, be sure to note that person's name and title and write a short note saying that you enjoyed meeting him or her and that you hope to have the pleasure of meeting again.

Writing letters to obtain a job is like courting a suitor. You want someone to say yes to your advances. It's like going to a dance and asking the best-looking man or woman to dance with you. They may say yes, or they may say no, but you'll never know the answer until you ask.

If you use these letters in your job-hunting campaign, you'll have a decided advantage because many people do not bother to write selling letters to get a job. It's difficult to run a letter-writing campaign when you have a job. When you are out of work, looking for a job and writing letters is a full-time occupation.

Don't forget the telephone, because it is an integral part of your letter-writing campaign. Once you've mailed your letters, following up via phone can give your job campaign a lift. Often a telephone follow-up can lead to an interview or even a new job lead. For example, one 50-plus professional recently sent a cover letter and résumé to the president of a company. The job hunter called a week later when the president happened to be out town, but his secretary said, "Oh, yes. The president got your letter and suggests you call Mr. Jones, the divisional manager. We sent him your résumé."

The result: A phone call to Mr. Jones with "Mr. President suggested I call you" produced an interview. Make that telephone work for you.

Writing letters is like sowing seeds. You never know when someone you've dealt with professionally is going to recommend you to another person. Most jobs are obtained through the process of networking. Professionally written letters can vastly broaden your network, including people you don't know, and increase your chances of getting a job. That's why it's important to put the extra effort into writing them.

Six Letter-Writing Rules

1. Target the company you want to work for.
2. Always address your letter to a specific person, by title. Make sure you spell his or her name correctly. If necessary, call the company and ask to speak to the manager's secretary. Verify the spelling of the manager's name and get his or her title.
3. Always send an original letter, never a photocopy. Many managers automatically throw photocopied letters into the wastebasket.
4. Tailor your letter to the specific position you are applying for, and keep it to one clear and concise page.
5. Date the thank-you letter the day of the interview, even though it is written the following day. Thus you can say: "I really enjoyed the opportunity to meet you today . . ." This indicates enthusiasm and interest in the job that will not be lost on the interviewer.
6. If you want the job, say so. If you don't ask for it, you may not get it.

Follow these rules and they will automatically set you apart from many job hunters.

Now let's take a look at the different letters you can use during the course of your job campaign.

The Cover Letter. A cover letter should always accompany your résumé. It should be no longer than five brief, easy-to-read paragraphs addressed to a specific individual. It should start with something personal, if possible. For example, you might begin this way: "Our mutual friend, Sam Jones, suggested I write you because of my experience in . . ." Or, "I read with great interest in last Sunday's paper your company's plan to start a new plastics division. Because of my experience in . . ."

In this short first paragraph you inject a personal note and give a brief description of your expertise and how it applies to the company's needs. This can be done in three or four lines.

In the second paragraph you highlight one or two outstanding achievements that are targeted to the company and the specific job you are applying for.

The third paragraph should emphasize some special work you've done in your field, or an award you received for your efforts.

The last paragraph states that you would like very much to meet this person to discuss job possibilities. The last sentence gives a specific day you will call.

This is a simple letter but it must be carefully thought out. Within that short three- to five-paragraph letter you communicate who you are and what you want, emphasizing the expertise and accomplishments that are listed in your résumé. The clincher is that last sentence promising to call on a specific day. You are giving yourself a legitimate reason for a follow-up telephone call.

The Résumé Letter. This letter is written in lieu of sending a résumé. It can be one page, or two pages, if you want to go into more detail. We prefer the one-pager because it makes it easier for the busy person who has to read it. The résumé letter has to be carefully crafted to be effective. What you are doing essentially is putting the highlights of your experience and work life in one letter. Carefully done, it can whet an employer's interest in you. It has an introductory paragraph, a middle section touting one's talents, and the "I'll call you next week for an appointment" sign-off. This letter can be very effective for the over-50 job hunter.

Appointment Confirmation Letter. Few job hunters take the time to write this letter, let alone think about it. But it puts an extra arrow in your job-search sling. It gives you the opportunity to make an additional impression on the interviewer. You'll be a known name on that first interview, and that could give you the edge when it comes to making the final selection.

Interview Thank-You Letter. This letter gives you the opportunity to thank the interviewer for the time he or she spent with you, to tell how positive you feel about the company and the prospect of working for it. It also gives you another chance to describe how your background and experience can contribute to the company. In this letter, you also inform the interviewer that if he or she has any questions or needs additional information, to please call you. Finally, it provides an opportunity to make a follow-up telephone call a week later about your job possibilities.

Second Interview Thank You. A second interview means you are in the running for the job. The competition is narrowing. In this letter you say once again how much you enjoyed the meeting, and that you are delighted to find that your previous experience seems to match the company's so well. Then you can state that you are more enthusiastic than ever about working for the company.

A second interview may lead to a third. If this occurs and an appointment is made at the second interview, state how you are looking forward to the next meeting with the specific people involved.

This is another good example of the "love letter." You are telling the company and its personnel that you like them and want to work for them.

Job Acceptance Letter. This is another letter that is too often overlooked by job seekers. It lets the interviewer know you are delighted to have been selected for the job. You say that you look forward to starting your new job on a specific date. It also indicates that you have been offered the job, should the company change its mind. Although this rarely occurs, it can happen. The last short paragraph thanks the interviewer or manager for the time he or she spent with you. The last line tells the person you appreciate the confidence he or she has in you, and that you will do everything you can to justify it. A different but deft touch for an experienced professional.

Referral Letter Thank You. When friends, and sometimes individuals you don't know, are introduced to you at interviews and refer you to another person who may be able to help you in your job hunt, don't fail to write a thank-you note. The person to whom you wrote the letter will remember your thoughtfulness. This is a form of networking that could pay dividends later on.

Didn't Get the Job Thank-you Note. This is a difficult letter to write and one that most job hunters neglect. Why should you take the time to write it? For several reasons. The employer is not likely to get many thank-you letters such as this one. It indicates that you are a considerate, well-mannered person, and it gives you an opportunity to request that this manager keep you in mind should he or she hear of a job in your field. It's possible to get leads for jobs from rejections.

Didn't Get the Job Letter Follow-Up. This letter isn't suitable for everyone, but sometimes it leads to a second interview. If you think it's worth it, try it. You have nothing to lose. Certainly the interviewer will remember you. You've gone through the interview process and have been turned down for the job. You feel the job is made for you. So you write to the company again, expressing your disappointment because you thought you were right for the job.

The next step is to follow up with a telephone call and request another interview. If this fails, you might say that you'd like to contact the company again in six months. Admittedly this is an unorthodox approach, but sometimes it works. The danger to avoid is making a pest of yourself, but nothing ventured, nothing gained.

Relocation Letter. Job hunters seeking work in other parts of the country often have an advantage. When a manager receives a letter from an out-of-town applicant, he or she is more likely to answer it than if it came from a job candidate in the local area. To be successful in these circumstances, you have to target the company or companies in which you want to work. It's a good idea to subscribe to local newspapers for several months to familiarize yourself with the locality in which you are seeking employment.

The next step is to write various companies to let them know you will be visiting their town on such-and-such a date and ask if they can arrange an interview. Target several companies and set up interviews with them for the days you plan to visit.

Executive Recruiter's Letter. Letters to executive recruiters, or head hunters as they are commonly called, need only be a form letter on your stationery. Executive recruiters only call when they have an assignment for a specific job, so the chances of hearing from them are not good. On the other hand, you never know when one will call so it is worthwhile sending them a cover letter and a copy of your résumé. Sometimes you will receive a postcard acknowledging that the executive recruiter received your résumé, whereas others won't respond unless they have a client assignment.

It's best to leave no stone unturned during your job-hunting campaign. You never know when you are going to uncover a treasure.

Answering Classified Advertisements. Classified advertisements can be answered with a form letter, but not a photocopy. Although many job hunters send photocopy letters in answer to such advertisements, we believe the letter should be written on your stationery. The reason: it will stand out like a beacon in a blizzard of photocopy submissions.

Don't expect too much from classified advertisements in newspapers, especially in large cities such as New York, Chicago, Los Angeles, and Washington, D.C. Many trade and business magazines also run classified ads, and many of them are available in your local library. Examples include *Engineering News Record, Publishers Weekly, Chemical Engineering*, and *Aviation Week & Space Technology*.

Classified ads, especially those in large newspapers in major cities, draw a large response. A Sunday ad, for example, may draw 400 or more letters. If you rely on such ads to get a job, you can quickly starve to death.

These ads are another aspect of the job-hunting campaign, however, and it's possible to get a job by answering them; just don't spend a lot of time on them. Set up a form letter in which you fill in the blanks. Even if you use a typewriter to answer classified advertisements, the form letter is easy to fill in and mail. Although the chances of getting a job through classified ads are much less than networking and targeting employers, many people have had success going this route. Don't overlook any possibility that could result in your getting a job.

When answering an advertisement, clip it and tape it to an 8½ × 11 sheet of paper together with the date you mailed your letter and résumé. This way you'll be able to keep track of your responses.

When you answer a newspaper ad, tailor your form letter to precisely what is asked for in the ad—with one exception. Don't include the salary, which many such ads request. The reason: you don't want to specify a salary that may be too high or too low, which would eliminate you from the competition. If the person who reads your résumé likes your qualifications, the chances are good he or she will call you.

Blind ads can be tricky, because they don't list the advertiser's name. You reply to an anonymous post office box or telephone number. Companies use blind ads for several reasons: they don't want people in their company to know about the potential job; they may be moving into a new field; or they may have a bad reputation.

The drawback to a blind ad, if you are working, is that it

could be your own company that is advertising. If this is true, the consequences of your submitting a résumé are obvious—you might end up applying for your own job!

Don't overlook poorly written ads. Oftentimes those who write classified ads do so at someone else's request. They may not be qualified to write them and they may know little about the job being advertised. If you spot an ad that carries a hint of the job you may be looking for, answer it. You never know what is at the other end and you may hit the job jackpot.

Sample Letters

The following sample letters can be adapted to your job-hunting campaign.

COVER LETTER

Richard Ogden
8 Sand Lane
Las Vegas, NV 89121
702/444-5555 home
702/445-5556 business
Date

Terry Tole, Manager
Sales Division
King Computer Sales Corporation
48968 New Castle Avenue
Encino, CA 91316

I noted with great interest your advertisement for a sales manager in yesterday's paper. Because this position seems particularly suited to my experience and qualifications, I am enclosing my résumé for your consideration.

Currently, I am the assistant sales manager of the Miles Computer Corporation where I reorganized the company's product line and sales approach. Result: product sales increased 8% per year for the past three years. In addition, I turned a losing operation into one that is now realizing a profit of more than $3 million annually.

I have 20 years of experience in computer sales and am a proven producer. I would like the opportunity to discuss this position with you and will call next week to make an appointment at your convenience.

Sincerely,

Richard Ogden

enc.

RÉSUMÉ LETTER

8 Ocean Avenue
Belmar, NJ 07719
201/999-9990
Date

Mr. John Smith, Editorial Director
Lovelace Publications
1445 Broadway
New York, NY 10017

Dear Mr. Smith:

I noted with great interest in today's *Daily Chronicle* the article stating you are planning a new automotive aftermarket magazine and are seeking an editor-in-chief. As you will note from my enclosed résumé, I am currently chief editor of *Consumer Cars* but would like to return to my first love, the automotive aftermarket. Because Lovelace Publications is the kind of company with which I would like to be associated, I would like to arrange an interview at your convenience.

My experience includes the following:

At *Consumer Cars* I created a new editorial direction that revitalized the magazine's contents, covers, and graphics. Result: a dramatic increase in reader interest that catapulted the magazine to No. 1 in newsstand sales in its field.

The new editorial concept resulted in record-high readership scores in our field. Example: A-1 Research in its recent study stated: "This is the first study we have ever done where every editorial item scores in excess of 100 points."

I also am completely familiar with the automotive aftermarket companies and executives, both domestic and foreign. I am also heavily involved in industry affairs.

Your new automotive aftermarket magazine seems particularly suited to my experience. I would appreciate the opportunity to meet you and discuss the possibility of working with you. I will call next Wednesday to set up an appointment. Thank you for your kind consideration.

Sincerely,

James Driver

enc.

APPOINTMENT CONFIRMATION LETTER

9 Chad Road
White Plains, NY 10607
914/666-6666
Date

Miss Nancy Hanks
ABC Company
10 Beach Street
Neponsit, NY 11694

Dear Miss Hanks:

This note confirms my appointment with you scheduled for 11:00 a.m. next Tuesday. I look forward with great pleasure to meeting you.

Sincerely,

Hannah Hopes

INTERVIEW THANK YOU

1234 Channing Street
Chicago, IL 60607
312/222-7777
Date

Mr. Charles Olsen, President
Olsen Corporation
10 Olsen Drive
St. Louis, MO 63130

Dear Mr. Olsen:

I really enjoyed the opportunity of meeting you today and very much appreciate the time you spent with me. The manufacturing manager's job we discussed seems particularly suited to my business background and qualifications. I left your office with great enthusiasm about the possibility of working with your company.

When I got home, I gave some thought to the production line problem we discussed. I have an idea that might help you solve this problem. I'd like to discuss this idea at your convenience.

Thank you again for your consideration. I look forward to meeting you again.

Sincerely,

Maria Chan

SECOND INTERVIEW THANK YOU

One Cove Road
Huntington, NY 11743
516/333-3333
Date

Mr. Blake Jones, Vice-President
Financial Corporation
3 Melody Lane
Boston, MA 02116

Dear Mr. Jones:

I enjoyed the opportunity to see you again today and meet Mr. Brown. I was truly impressed with the Financial Corporation and the work you are doing. I especially liked the tour of the company with you and Mr. Brown. It is a much more complex organization than I had originally envisioned.

I went away extremely impressed with your operation. The possibility of working at Financial Corporation is an exciting one for me. After reviewing your plans, I am more enthusiastic than ever about the contributions I can make to the company because of my experience in the financial field.

Thank you again for your time and courtesy. I look forward to talking with you next week.

Sincerely,

Marilyn Wilson

JOB ACCEPTANCE LETTER

14 Bowie Lane
Atlanta, GA 30365
404/323-2323
Date

Mr. Matthew Mason, President
Garment Manufacturing Company
Atlanta, GA 30365

Dear Mr. Mason:

I was delighted with your phone call yesterday inviting me to join the Garment Manufacturing Company as manager of the retail division at a beginning salary of $52,000 a year plus commission. The starting date of Monday, June 25, at 8:30 is fine and I look forward with great pleasure to working with you.

Thank you again for all the time you spent with me. I appreciate the confidence you have in me and want you to know that I will do everything I can to justify it.

Sincerely,

Jeb Suitor

REFERRAL LETTER

8 Broadway
New York, NY 10003
212/512-1234
Date

Mr. George Gange, Manager
Human Resources Company
383 Madison Avenue
New York, NY 10017

Dear Mr. Gange

I want to thank you for referring me to Tom Clancy at the Blanket Corporation and sending him my résumé. Because of your thoughtfulness, I had an hour-long interview with Mr. Clancy and there is the possibility of a job opening there in the near future.

I very much appreciate your efforts on my behalf and will let you know the outcome of my meeting with Mr. Clancy. Thanks again for your help and courtesy.

Sincerely,

Marsha Myers

DIDN'T GET THE JOB LETTER

151 Hull Street
Washington, D.C. 20460
202/999-8888
Date

Mr. Dan Young, Vice-President
CB Company
352 State Avenue
Washington, D.C. 20460

Dear Mr. Young:

I must confess that I am truly sorry that things did not work out for me at the CB Company. I was looking forward to the possibility of working with you. However, I realize that someone has to lose out when it comes to making a hiring decision. It was a pleasure to meet you and I thank you for all the time you spent with me.

Mr. Young, I would appreciate it if you would keep me in mind should you hear of any openings that become available in my field. Thank you again for your interest.

Sincerely,

Joan Ogden

DIDN'T GET JOB FOLLOW-UP

16 Town Road
Denver, CO 01701
303/600-0000
Date

Mr. Lawrence Coin, President
Roger Enterprises
32 Prairie Avenue
Denver, CO 01701

   I was extremely disappointed to receive your letter today
eliminating my candidacy for the job we discussed. Mr. Coin,
the purpose of this letter is to request that you reconsider this
decision.

   My reason for making this request is that of all the companies
I've interviewed with during my job search, Roper Enterprises
was far and away my first choice. I also have a special interest
in your company's products because of my experience in this
field.

   Although my request may seem unusual, I am writing because of my special interest in your company and the contributions I believe I can make to it. I will call you next Thursday to
see if we can meet again.

Sincerely,

Jon Stone

RELOCATION LETTER

Chester Caruthers, Ph.D.
345 Lexington Avenue
New York, NY 10017
212/888-9999 home
212/888-7777 business
Date

Mr. Malcolm Powell
Chief Executive Officer
Powell Enterprises Inc.
Wayside Boulevard
Walnut Creek, CA 94596

Dear Mr. Powell:

I am an experienced chemical engineer who specializes in research and development. My reason for writing is that my company is transferring its facilities to Dallas, Texas, in the near future and I am moving my family back to Walnut Creek, which is my hometown.

I will be coming to Walnut Creek in January, and I would very much like to set up an appointment at your convenience. Judging from the research I've done on your company, I believe my qualifications and past experience are particularly suited to your needs in the pharmaceutical field. Enclosed is a copy of my résumé.

I will call you next Friday to make an appointment during my January visit to Walnut Creek. Thank you very much for your consideration.

Sincerely,

Chester Caruthers, Ph.D.

enc.

CLASSIFIED ADVERTISEMENT LETTER

141 East 88th Street
New York, NY 10028
212/398-7654
Date

Mr. Ronald Shag, Vice-President
Shag Corporation
20 Broad Street
Morristown, NJ 07960

I noted with great interest your advertisement for a (name position) in last Sunday's paper. Enclosed for your consideration is a copy of my résumé.

For your information, my background includes X years in the (insert your field) in which I have:

(list your accomplishments)
_____
_____

I would like to arrange an interview at your convenience to discuss this position with you and look forward to your reply.

Sincerely,

Lorna Jones

enc.

LETTER TO EXECUTIVE RECRUITER

21 Yancy Street
Philadelphia, PA 19106
913/662-6262
Date

Mr. Jonathan James
Bull Executive Search
Independence Square
Philadelphia, PA 19106

Dear Mr. James:

I am seeking a new position in the (name of) field. Enclosed for your consideration is a copy of my résumé. As you can see, I have extensive experience in the (name) industry. I would appreciate it very much if you would keep my résumé in your active files.

Please do not hesitate to call me at work or home regarding present or future employment with one of your clients. Thank you for your kind consideration.

Sincerely,

Roberta Brian

enc.

CHAPTER 8

Proven Interview Techniques

The job hunter, a trim gray-haired man, strode quickly and confidently through the door into the poshly paneled office of the executive recruiter, smiled, stretched out his hand, looked directly at the man standing behind the desk, and said, "How do you do, my name is Tom Smith."

The man behind the desk, an executive recruiter, said, "I'm Chester Caruthers, please sit down." When they were seated, Caruthers said to Smith, "You have a high energy level." Smith was off to a good start.

First, he was properly dressed. Navy blue suit, white shirt, dark blue socks with a small pattern, a good-looking red tie, and highly polished black shoes. When he shook hands with the head hunter, he gave him a firm handshake and looked straight at him. He did everything right. It's imperative that the over-50 job hunter look sharp, be sharp, and give the impression of being an enthusiastic and vital person who radiates energy and confidence. Watching your weight and diet and exercising regularly are an essential part of your job-hunting campaign. If you present a washed-out image at interviews, you'll have a difficult time getting the job you want.

Create a Winning Image

Smith had all the right things going for him. The head-hunter noted immediately that the applicant was a confident, well-dressed, high-energy person by the way he walked into the room. You are onstage the minute you walk through the interviewer's door, and he or she will be watching you closely for the immediate impression you create, which will be positive or negative. You may be able to overcome a negative image as the interview progresses, but the odds are against it. Start with a positive impression and you increase your chances for success. You never get a second chance to make a first impression.

The Question of Age

"How old are you?"

That was the next question the headhunter asked. Smith smiled and said, "I'm 39 going on 51."

The headhunter casually remarked, "You look much younger than 51," then switched quickly to the interview and the job at hand.

Face it, the subject of age may come up during interviews even though this question is forbidden by law. But some interviewers, intentionally, or because of ignorance or insensitivity, may ask it. How do you handle it?

There is no easy solution. You are looking for a job. You don't want to irk the interviewer and possibly destroy your chances of getting a job. One way to is to gloss over it as Tom Smith did in the preceding anecdote. He made a quick decision to let it pass and go on with the interview. Your answer to the age question depends on your reaction to the situation.

The best response under most circumstances is to tell the interviewer that you don't think your age is a problem. You are applying for the job because of your experience, training, and highly qualified skills. Then specify how and why you should be considered for the position in question.

James Challenger, president of Challenger, Gray & Christmas, a Chicago-based outplacement company, says, "Tell them."

A Touch of Humor. Tom Jackson, chairman of Equinox Corp., a New York City human resource consulting company, suggests you might use humor. For example, "I'm old enough to do this job, really." Or, "I don't mind telling you my age, but first let me ask if there are any age restrictions to this job." In this case, says Jackson, you are gently reminding the interviewer that this is not a proper question to ask.

The best answer to the question is to give your age. Some people deduct five or ten years from their ages, but there's always the possibility of being discovered. If you are confronted with an extreme case of age discrimination (which is difficult to prove) you are better off continuing your job search.

The interview is your chance to claim the job by your performance. Unfortunately, the most qualified people don't always get the job; those who are most adept at interview techniques are the ones who do. It's up to you to convince the interviewer that you are the best person for the job. It's that simple.

Dealing with a Younger Person. As a 50-plus professional you've got to be ready for anything. Most important at an interview is to radiate an attitude of confidence. Job hunting today is far different from a short few years ago. Nowadays you have to think in terms of a multicultural workplace with employees from a variety of ethnic backgrounds. You may be interviewed by a black, a Hispanic, an Asian, or by a person half your age or younger. You have to be comfortable talking with such people, and convince them that you are the best person for the job because of the skills and the experience you bring to the workplace. This is a difficult assignment.

When dealing with interviewers, don't look surprised or make a comment such as "I was not expecting to be interviewed by a woman." You should appear accepting and at ease to the interviewer.

When interviewing with a younger person, be easygoing and relaxed in the way you comport yourself. If you are kept waiting, don't complain, indicate annoyance, or impatiently tap your feet or fidget. Always be gracious and flexible, to overcome any prejudices the young person may have about dealing with an older individual.

Under the Microscope. Another important point: You are being observed the minute you walk into the reception room. Treat the secretary behind the desk the same as you would the interviewer or the president of the company. If you are rude or abrupt with the secretary, or complain because you were kept waiting, the word will surely get back to the person you are there to see. More than one job opportunity has been lost by an insensitive job seeker who didn't know the importance of being polite to office personnel. Remember, courtesy doesn't cost anything, but it can pay big dividends.

If a secretary tells his or her boss what a nice person that was, so polite and pleasant, it goes into the plus column. It wouldn't be the first time a secretary's comments resulted in a job hunter's landing a job—or losing it.

When you walk into an interview—be prepared. Arrive a few minutes early; never be late. If, for some reason, you are delayed, call ahead to say you'll be late and explain why. Bring copies of your résumé and other materials you think may be of value, even though they may not be used. That doesn't mean walking into the office laden with materials. Only bring material you feel is important, and that fits comfortably in a briefcase in the event you need it. In addition, you must be impeccably attired for the interview. When you walk into the office it should be with energy and enthusiasm. Greet the interviewer with a smile and wait for him or her to offer you a seat.

Never take it upon yourself to be familiar and call the interviewer by his or her first name. Don't chew gum. Don't use slang. Don't smoke, even if the interviewer invites you. Why not smoke if you are given permission? Many companies today frown on smoking and prohibit it in all or parts of their offices. If you are in a basically nonsmoking office and light a cigarette, you could ruin your chances for the job, so don't risk it. Notice whether people are smoking as you go to meet the interviewer. Are there No Smoking signs prominently displayed? To drive this point home, a recent survey by Robert Half International found that one in four smokers lose out when competing for a job against equally qualified nonsmokers.

When you enter an interviewer's office, try to get a quick psychological profile of the person behind the desk. For example, is the office neat, with a place for everything and everything in its place? Is it disorganized, with papers piled up on the desk? What kind of pictures are on the wall or on the desk? Family, sports, boats, pets? How is the interviewer dressed? Conservative or casual?

Observing the details in the office such as photos and wall decorations can provide a clue to the kind of person you will be dealing with. The more you know about the company and the person interviewing you, the better your chances of having a substantive meeting. This is one of the reasons researching a company and its personnel prior to an interview can be so helpful. Is the interviewer a serious type or one with a sense of humor? Is the interviewer relaxed, intense, or laid back? If possible, you want to key your responses to his or her personality.

Breaking the Ice. One mature job hunter recently had an interview with a company that employed a majority of women in its work force. While waiting to see the interviewer, he noted that the human resource reception room was filled with women. He was the only male in the place. When he walked into the interview he was faced by a young woman. Sitting down, he leaned forward in his chair, looked directly into her eyes, and said in a serious manner, "May I ask you a question?"

"Certainly," she said.

"Do you ever hire males in this place?" he asked.

They both laughed and the subsequent interview was comfortable and relaxed. In this instance, it was a good way to break the ice, but there's an element of danger involved if the person behind the desk is unresponsive. This is the kind of judgment a job hunter has to make. If you are successful, you raise the interview to a higher level and put yourself in the running for the job. If you guess wrong, it can spell disaster.

Often an interviewer will start with small talk about such subjects as the weather, sports, or women's fashions. The interviewer is not making idle chitchat to kill time. He or she is attempting to get a feeling for the type of person you are. Are you comfortable, easy to talk to, relaxed? The purpose is to see if you are the kind of person who fits into the company's culture. Will you get along with other people in the company? Are you a team player? Such talk can lead into the interview and give you a decided advantage. Use such an opportunity to develop a relationship with the interviewer and contribute to the conversation. Always be concise when answering questions.

The Art of Small Talk. Recently a 50-plus-year-old journalist was looking for a job. The president of the company, who was going to interview him, had written a book. By chance, the job hunter had read the book and also knew an executive from his former company who was a close friend of the person he was going to see.

The job hunter walked into the executive's office and sincerely complimented him on the beautiful office decor. The small talk led to the fact that the job hunter had read the executive's book and had worked with a mutual friend. The book was discussed at length and the job hunter spent an hour and a half with the busy executive.

Did he get the job? Despite what he considered a terrific interview, he doesn't know whether he would have gotten the job, because he got the one he was seeking elsewhere. This anecdote points up the importance of what might seem like an inconsequential part of an interview. When you are polite, sincerely compliment someone, and demonstrate that you relate well with others, you enhance your chances as a potential employee. Small talk is an important part of business and it can serve you well in an interviewer's office.

Don't say you are looking for a new challenge. It's a cliché which, when you think about it, has no meaning. Every job hunter is looking for a "new challenge." Don't join the crowd.

Another point to remember: When you are invited to interview for a job, it means the company is interested in you. When this happens, be prepared. The interview is your ticket to getting a job. The more interviews you have, the better your chance of success. If you appear unsure, nervous, or shy, you won't make a good impression and may lose the opportunity to clinch the sale. A company has to make a decision when it comes to hiring someone. Let it be you.

Three Rules for Interviews

Says Davis Small, director of career planning at the University of Houston, "There is too much stock put in names and degrees when it is the interpersonal characteristics that get a person a job. It is the intangibles that make the difference in the job selection." Small stresses three rules for interviews: (1) research the company, (2) anticipate the questions to be asked, and (3) develop questions of your own.

What separates the cream-of-the crop professional from the run-of-the-mill job seeker are those who can interact in the interview, pick up on something the interviewer says, and use it to make intelligent comments. Interviewers do not want to hear a canned speech. They'll recognize it immediately, because they've heard it a thousand times. Use your experience and imagination to give relevant, honest answers to questions.

Interviewing is a two-way activity. The interviewer wants to determine what kind of person you are. Your purpose is to get as much information as you can about the company and the potential job. It's possible the job isn't one that you really want, and you have to determine this during the interview. Consequently, you should be prepared to answer questions that may be asked, but also to ask questions to determine if the company meets your needs and expectations.

The Right Answers. You are not going to be interviewed like a college graduate. You may be asked, "Why are you looking for a job after being retired for three years?" Or "Why do you want to work for our company?"

Your answer to the first question might be: "Frankly, I didn't really 'retire.' I did take some time off to travel. But I've kept busy doing some consulting work for my old company and freelancing. But I found I missed the day-to-day work and contact with people. I've done some research on your company and believe, because of my experience and specific skills, I can make an immediate contribution if you hire me for the job you advertised.

"For example, I understand you are having some trouble in your retail division. I've had a lot of experience in this field and I'm familiar with your problem area. I also have many executive friends I can call on, because I've maintained contact with them. I'd like the opportunity to discuss this situation with you."

To the second question, you might answer: "I've been reading about your company and the new manufacturing plant you've just completed. I'm a mechanical engineer with a great deal of experience in manufacturing, especially in robotics, which I understand is an important part of your process. I know several of the executives in the company that produces the robotics line and have visited their factory in Japan. I'm also familiar with the robotic startup problems you're having on the line. I've dealt with them before and am sure I can help you."

Use questions to your advantage by giving specific examples of how you can make an immediate contribution to the company should you be hired. You are selling competence and problem-solving ability. By preparing for potential questions before the interview, you should be able to give creative answers to virtually any question the interviewer asks.

Wanted! Professionals Who Can Fix Things. Companies want creative people who can solve problems. It's one thing to say you are a problem solver, but it's another to prove it. You can do this by pointing to specific problems you've solved in the past. Better still, if you can relate your experience and skills to a company's problems during an interview, you'll be one step ahead of the competition. Obviously, this can't be done in all cases, but these are the kinds of situations to look for when researching a company. Problem-solving situations can be invaluable to a job hunter because they will impress the person doing the hiring.

Learn to Listen. Listening is also an important part of the interview process. Pay close attention to what is being said so you can frame your answers to the questions. A professional interviewer has a reason for everything he or she says. Try to determine what information the interviewer is seeking. For example, he or she might say, "How did you like working for the XYZ company?"

This is an obvious question. The interviewer is trying to determine if you will bad-mouth your previous company. If you do, it's likely that you'll do the same to his or her company. Always speak well of past associates and companies.

Your answer: "It is a first-class company. I enjoyed working there."

Taking Charge. In the course of your job search it's very possible that you'll meet some interviewers who are unqualified or inept. In such cases you can't sit back waiting for something to happen. Sometimes you have to take charge of the interview, depending on the situation, and initiate questions about the job. What responsibilities does it have? What is expected of the person who fills it? What other people in the company are involved? Although such interviews can be difficult, never show impatience or indicate that you are annoyed about the unprofessional interview. Be polite, stay cool, do your best, and follow up with a thank-you note and a telephone call.

If you think the interviewer's ineptness might prevent you from getting the job, you can write to the human resource manager or the interviewer's boss saying you didn't think the interview went well and you'd like another chance to discuss your qualifications for the job. This can be a delicate situation, but you can say that the chemistry between you and the interviewer was poor. You really want the job and feel you are eminently qualified for it. Do this diplomatically, without casting blame, and you may get another chance with a different interviewer.

Problems Minorities May Face

Minorities are sometimes the victims of blatant unprofessional behavior. If you are a minority and find yourself in an interview situation that is obviously racist, Robert Brocksbank, chairman emeritus of the Dallas-Based Council on Career Development for Minorities, advises action. Get up, say, "You haven't heard the last of me," and leave. Then write the company president a letter complaining about the treatment received, and giving the interviewer's name and title.

Minorities should also seek out companies that actually practice affirmative action. Aside from talking with people in the company, look for minorities and women in executive positions. Then phone and arrange an interview or two and ask frank questions about the company's hiring and promotion policies for minorities and women. You don't want to join a company where you'll be running in place.

Robert Brocksbank says it better: "Work for a company where you'll be happy, one that encourages you to do your best, where you don't have to take off your skin before you go to work."

Go for It!

Recently a 50-plus professional woman interviewed for a job she really liked and wanted. She left the interview feeling that things had gone well and that she was right for the job. She was concerned that her age might be a problem because of her résumé and extensive past experience. When she got home that evening her husband asked, "How did it go?"

She replied she thought everything went well but feared someone else might be hired.

"Do you really want that job?" her husband asked.

"Yes, I do," she replied.

"Then pick up the phone tomorrow morning and tell them."

After some convincing, the next morning, with some trepidation, the woman called the human resource manager who had interviewed her and said, "I think I'm the best person for the job, and I really want to work for your company."

The result: The personnel manager called her in for another interview and she got the job.

This story is a classic example of making things happen. You can't afford to be bashful. If you want the job, ask for it. That doesn't mean every time you say you want the job you're going to be hired, but it does increase your chances of success. Procrastination doesn't pay in love, war, or business.

If you lack confidence—a common ailment for people of all ages—you'll have to overcome this drawback. To succeed in business and in life you must believe in your abilities and be willing to take the initiative when the situation calls for it. Even if you fail, as you will on occasion, you will increase your confidence and enhance your reputation because you were willing to try something new or different. Too many mature men and women are afraid to take a chance unless circumstances force them to do so.

How to Dial a Job

The telephone is a valuable tool for the job hunter because interview appointments are made on the phone. Don't be afraid to make cold calls if you hear of a job in a particular company. First send a résumé and cover letter, then follow up with a phone call to arrange an interview. Here is an example of a job hunter who used the phone to his advantage, thought creatively, and literally talked himself into an interview with a tough, no-nonsense executive who was not used to being questioned.

Several years ago a 50-plus job hunter called an executive to request an interview a week after he sent a cover letter and a résumé. He got through to the executive, who was noted for being difficult, and asked when it might be convenient to set up an appointment.

"I don't think it's worth my time to see you," he was brusquely told. "You have no experience in my field."

There was a moment of silence as the job hunter thought about what to say. Then he replied, "Mr. Executive, you could be making a big mistake."

There was a short pause on the other end of the phone. The executive, in a puzzled voice, asked, "What do you mean?"

The job hunter then briefly described his previous job in which he had gone into a new area of his industry, performed well, and won an award for his efforts. "Though I haven't had experience in your field," he said, "I have done well in the jobs I've had. If you hire me, I'll bring a fresh perspective to your company that your other employees may not have."

Another short pause, then, "Good point. See me tomorrow morning at eleven o'clock," the executive said, and hung up.

Each interview encounter is different. You have to be prepared to talk with many different types of people. Evaluate each one and then lead into the interview according to your concept of the individual you're facing. Chances are you'll be right.

Formulate specific thoughts about your immediate and long-term goals. This is important to your success. What do you want from the job? You have to answer that question and then articulate it for the interviewer so that he or she can evaluate whether or not the company and job are right for you.

Practice, Practice, Practice. In this age of instant photography and movies, it is worthwhile to practice interviews with friends. It may seem silly at first, but it works. Watching yourself on film will be a revelation, and you'll be shocked at the flaws you'll see. These can be corrected and overcome with practice. Friends can also be good critics and help you develop your interviewing style.

When seeking companies to interview, don't overlook small businesses in your area. They offer many opportunities to the 50-plus professionals. Many small companies have trouble finding trained people to meet their needs. They're looking for experienced professionals who can come aboard and perform immediately.

The secret to a successful interview is to be yourself. Remember, you are the seller, not the buyer. James E. Challenger, president of Challenger, Gray & Christmas, a Chicago-based international outplacement consulting company, claims that in well over 50 percent of all interviews, job seekers lost out by switching their roles from sellers to buyers. "In so doing," he says, "they quickly remove themselves from consideration for that job." You are there to tell an employer what you can do for the company, not what the company can do for you.

Finally, know when to stop talking and end the interview. Don't overstay your welcome. You should get a sense of when to end by watching the interviewer. If not, you might say, "I know you are busy, so I won't keep you any longer. Thank you for your time. I'm really interested in the position we discussed. If you have any questions or need additional information, please don't hesitate to call me."

Looking Good

Earlier we mentioned the importance of dress at the interview. You want to look as young as possible. Obese people usually have a more difficult time getting a job, so try to control your weight. The best way to dress is according to the company culture. A visit to the company before your interview is well worthwhile. Note how the employees of the company dress, especially the executives. This look-and-see method is better than asking employees for their opinions. They may have different ideas, depending on their individual perceptions and the departments in which they work. Dress as you would if you already had the job. Certain professions such as banking and law have conservative dress codes, and obviously these should be heeded when you are interviewed for a job in such an organization.

Another consideration is the part of the country in which you work. California and Texas dress norms are different from those in New York and Boston. It is better to err on the conservative side when it comes to clothes. For example, in professions such as publishing, advertising, and the arts, a sports jacket and slacks are acceptable, but for mature professionals a suit is recommended for all interviews.

Says Marsha Fox, Drake Beam Morin vice-president, "I think the older worker needs to look as young as possible. It's one thing to sell maturity, it's another thing to look as if you are lacking vitality. The older worker needs to buy a really nice suit for a job interview. There can be nothing tattered or weary about the self-image presented. There has to be energy exuded. No one wants to hire someone who seems tired or lethargic. Buying new shoes, or polishing your shoes, and a new suit that's really spiffy and fits, these things are important."

It's important to remember that fashions, like the rest of the world, have changed. In the 1990s it's not necessary to dress as if your clothes were designed from a corporate cookie-cutter pattern. Confidence in your appearance is a must. A neat, tailored suit or dress with appropriate accessories will portray an image of a professional, self-assured job hunter. Proper fit and quality tailoring are a must in the clothes you wear.

The Tailored Woman. For women, suits and separates can be coordinated with tasteful accessories to convey an up-to-date look. Women have broken away from the man-tailored suit to create a more individual image. In addition to traditional colors such as navy blue, black, gray, shades of maroon, green, and camel can be coordinated into your wardrobe. Dresses should be in muted colors. Suits and blazers should be in plain or neutral colors. Plunging necklines are taboo, as are slit skirts that reveal too much leg. Skirts can be pleated, straight, or dirndl, worn slightly below the knee. Shoes should be pumps with a low or medium heel, and polished.

Accessories can add color and flair to give you a stylish look and the chance to display your individuality. For example, a colorful scarf, stud earrings in gold or pearl, with a simple pearl necklace can create a simple and elegant image. Don't wear dangling earrings or an armful of bracelets; they can be distracting during the interview. You want the interviewer to concentrate on you, not on your dangling earrings or clanging bracelets. Stockings should be plain, with no patterns. Belt, shoes, and purse should also be coordinated with your outfit.

The Well-Dressed Male. Navy blue or gray suits in solid or pinstripe combined with a dress shirt in solid colors such as white, light blue, gray, or soft yellow are appropriate. Large and flashy cufflinks and rings should be avoided. Single-breasted suits with a vest can be worn with a collar-pin shirt if you want a more formal look. Double-breasted suits are also popular and acceptable attire for interviews.

Ties should be in muted colors, solids, pinstripes, or small patterns. Red, or a tie with a combination of red, is preferred.

Hose should be calf-length, preferably in dark colors to match the suit. Hose with a small pattern are acceptable. Avoid wearing firehouse-red hose to an interview. Belts should be black or blue leather.

Shoes should be black or dark brown, depending on the color of the suit. Wingtips or cap toes are preferred, although dress loafers with tassels are acceptable for most interviews, except in ultraconservative companies. Shoes should always be highly polished.

Grooming is an important part of the interview. Hair should be clean and neat. The trend today is toward shorter hair for both men and women. Men should be clean shaven. If a beard or mustache is worn (some companies still frown on both hirsute growths) they must be clean and neatly trimmed. Nails must also be clean and well manicured. Nail polish should be subtle—a clear or pale shade is best.

Your overall look should present the unique you. When you walk into an interviewer's office you have fewer than 10 seconds to make an impression. This first image you create is crucial to the interview. Looking good, being comfortable with yourself, knowing that you present a confident, self-assured appearance will do wonders for your self-esteem. So lavish great care and attention on both your wardrobe and your grooming. Send a signal that you are a person with a winning personality, one to be taken seriously, certainly one to be considered for the job at hand.

CHAPTER 9

Job-Hunting Strategies That Work

There is no magic formula or secret system to finding a job. New jobs are created every day. According to the Bureau of Labor Statistics almost one worker in five enters or returns to an occupation he or she did not work in 12 months earlier. Your chances of finding employment are good if you conduct your campaign in a systematic, businesslike way.

If you are 60 years old as you read this, and in good health, chances are you'll live another 20 to 25 years or more. If you are in your fifties, you have an even longer potential work life. Consequently, it's important that the job you get, whether full- or part-time, is one you like and enjoy, one that fits in with your needs and lifestyle. Also, the demographics in the 1990s and beyond favor you because of the experience and other intangible attributes you bring to a job market in need of professional and technical skills.

The purpose of your job-hunting campaign is to obtain an interview with the person in a company who has the power to hire you. The three basic keys that unlock the door to a job are: knowing what you want to do, having a plan, and executing your plan. It's that simple. The complex part is finding the job of your choice. That comes in the execution of your plan, accomplished by performing a number of steps

135

to achieve your goal, steps taken by millions of job hunters before you.

Your résumé is important, but it does not tell the employer that you can do the job. It is a calling card designed to influence the person who receives it. It is up to you to make a selling proposal, demonstrating by words and past deeds that you will be an asset to the company. You must convince the employer during interviews that it is good business to hire you.

A job hunter is like the conductor of a symphony orchestra. He or she orchestrates a campaign that includes a broad range of activities. The campaign requires planning, knowledge, practice, time, and effort to bring it all together. To conduct a successful job search, the over-50 professional must be adaptable, innovative, flexible, and willing and able to learn and to take risks.

It's the Details That Spell Success

A successful job search requires that you use every available source. Focus on the ones you feel will be most productive, but don't ignore the others. As you become involved in the job search you'll get a sense of what areas will produce the best results for your job-hunting campaign.

Remember, the more people you contact and the more effort you put into the job search, the better your chances for success. Job hunting is also a matter of attending to details. Leave no stone unturned; you never know when a job opportunity is going to pop up. Often such opportunities come from surprising and unexpected places.

What are the sources that produce the best results for job hunters? The National Center for Career Strategies recently reported that only 14 percent of 14,500 employed people got jobs through help-wanted advertisements in newspapers. The most effective method of getting a job is networking or personal contacts, which resulted in jobs for 70 percent of those seeking them.

The Jobs Are There—You Have to Find Them

This is especially true for the 50-plus professional. Chances are you will get your job through a personal contact. But the job hunt also mandates that you write letters, respond to classified newspaper advertisements, make telephone calls, delve into the hidden job market, look for job banks in your area, contact executive recruiters, talk to friends, relatives, business acquaintances, and strangers, use the Yellow Pages, and read newspapers and industry magazines for information you can use in your search.

Now let's examine various job-finding strategies you can use.

Networking/Contacts. Contacting persons who can help you get a job is your best chance for success. The purpose of networking is to expand your list of contacts by meeting more and more people through friends and referrals. The more people you know and contact, the better your chances of hearing about jobs and getting an interview. It's not surprising that the best and most obvious way to find a job is through networking. As an experienced professional you have developed many business friends and acquaintances in companies within the industry in which you worked. These are excellent sources to call for information about current jobs or potential future positions.

In both good and bad times, there is always movement in companies with new jobs being created, people leaving for new positions, retiring, or being terminated. In larger companies changes are constantly taking place, especially in today's volatile job market. Such changes open doors for 50-plus job seekers as new departments are being formed and new positions created. Frequently, companies cut into the muscle of their staffs in an attempt to trim costs and later find they must rehire people to perform needed work on a full- or part-time basis.

As a networker, you are a known commodity if you are

recommended for a job by someone in the company or an acquaintance who knows that interviewer or employer. An employer wants to feel confident that the person hired is capable of doing the job. A personal recommendation from someone who knows you is to your advantage. A good referral saves a company the time, trouble, and the expense of conducting a job search. In many large companies it is standard practice to give a cash award to employees who refer qualified people who are hired by the company.

Use every source you know, and don't be bashful about calling even casual acquaintances or people you don't know if you hear of a job lead. It could help you land a job.

Here's a typical case. A professional manager working on a new job with a new company for only two months was suddenly let go because the company had cash-flow problems. On the day he left, a co-worker suggested that the manager call a public relations director in a major company with a possible job opening. The manager was so distraught about being let go that he never followed up. A month later he met the person who had given him the woman's name and number on the street.

"Did you call Miss X?" asked his former coworker.

"No," said the job hunter.

"They're still looking. I'd give her a call," said the contact. "Don't forget to tell her I told you to call."

The next day the job hunter called Miss X, mentioning his co-worker and said, "Mr. Y suggested I call you. I understand you have a potential job opening in your company for a person with my experience."

"Oh, yes," said Miss X. "Call our vice-president, Mr. S. Tell him I told you to call. His number is . . ."

The job hunter called, got the first of several interviews, and three months later was hired. He barely knew the co-worker at his former company. The public relations woman and the vice-president at the major company that hired him were people he'd never met before. But because of his experience, skills, and the fact that he had several excellent interviews with the vice-president, he landed the job, beating out several competitors in the company that hired him.

Obviously it's preferable to have a friend or acquaintance recommend you for a job, but you don't have to know someone to get a good job lead. Make everyone you meet a contact.

Information Interviews. You may be familiar with this type of interview. Individuals uncertain about their choice of career can get information and trends about jobs in specific industries in this type of interview. It can also be used to obtain information about your specific field or industry. An information interview should be a planned process. This means when you walk into an information interview you have a throughly prepared list of questions to ask because you took the time to research the industry and the company. You are there to get information—not ask for a job. Busy executives who agree to spend time talking to you about their industry will not take kindly to being dunned for a job under the pretense of an information interview. Frequently job hunters do this, to their detriment.

If you use this technique, take the time to get information about the companies in the field, their needs, industry trends, the best areas to pursue in terms of job opportunities, and contacts the executive might give whom you can call for information interviews. Specifically ask for permission to mention the executive's name when he or she gives you a contact. You can also ask the executives you interview how they got into the industry, what their jobs encompass, and what companies may be hiring professionals with your skills in the near future. Also ask them for advice as to what avenues to pursue for someone seeking work in the industry.

Information interviews with executives of banks, insurance companies, and construction companies in the area can provide leads to new companies coming into the neighborhood, companies that are expanding or starting a new department or division. This is a good way to obtain information about what is going on in the business community in your area.

Such information can lead to new contacts, a potential interview, and possibly a job.

At the end of the information interview (don't overstay your welcome) thank the executive for his or her time and follow up with a thank-you note. If you do get a job in the industry, send a note to individuals you talked with, thanking them for their advice that was instrumental in helping you land a job. This will be the beginning of a new network of contacts that can be valuable later on.

Letter Writing. This is an integral part of the job-hunting process, albeit a time-consuming one. In your campaign, allot time each week for sending letters to new contacts, keeping track of letters mailed and answered. Letters should go to contacts acquired by your networking efforts. Letters should be sent to answer newspaper advertisements, to employment agencies, executive recruiters, and associations in your field. If you read of an executive being promoted or appointed president of a company, write a congratulatory note and say that you would like to join his or her team. Include a copy of your résumé. It's a long shot, but sometimes such letters can lead to an interview and new contacts.

Telephone Calls. The telephone is an invaluable job-hunting tool, so develop a confident, relaxed phone technique that presents a professional image to the person on the other end of the line. Use it to follow up a week after you've sent a cover letter and résumé to an executive requesting an interview. The best time to call a contact is between 8:30 and 9:00 A.M., during the lunch hour, or after 5:00 P.M. Chances are better that the executive may answer the phone during these hours, which gives you a direct contact and the chance to talk yourself into an interview.

During the day when a secretary answers, you'll have to react to what she says. For example, in some cases she may put you through to Mr. or Ms Executive without asking questions. More likely she will ask, "Who shall I say is calling?"

When you tell her, she'll probably ask, "What is this in reference to?"

Your response: "I told Mr. E I would call him today in reference to a letter I sent last week."

Sometimes this will get you through to Mr. E. If the secretary persists, which she may do because it is her job to screen calls, say politely, "I sent Mr. E my résumé last week and told him I would call him today." If you can say you mailed it because a friend of Mr. E suggested you do so, so much the better.

You may get a "One moment, please," while she checks with Mr. E. Many times you will get through, but sometimes you will not. The important point here is to always be polite. You are not trying to trick the secretary because he or she is the one who decides whether or not you talk to Mr. E, like it or not. If you conduct yourself in a pleasant, courteous manner, you won't alienate this person.

Our experience in making these calls is that most secretaries are polite and helpful. It is imperative when making such calls that your manners be impeccable. It is also important to realize that many executives attend office meetings or travel so that they aren't always available. Sometimes a secretary will say Mr. E isn't in, and ask you to call back next week. Or she may tell you Mr. E says there are no openings now. In this case thank the secretary for her help and ask if she knows of any potential future openings in her company or another company. Many good job leads have come from secretaries who were asked this question.

Don't be shy about making "cold" calls. They can be difficult, and the odds are against you, but they can also bring results. This doesn't mean going through the phone book making random calls. They should be planned so that you are calling a specific person who has the authority to hire. If you're wary of making cold calls, prepare a script of what you plan to say. You don't have to read it word for word, but use it as a guide. The person on the other end of the line is unpredictable. He or she may quickly end the conversation. Conversely, something may be said that will give you an opportunity to state your case and lead to an interview. A cold call is somewhat akin to making a speech to an unfamiliar audience. You have to get the audience's attention and then deliver your message. The telephone gives you another opportunity to make your case and get an interview. Used with style and imagination, it can be a creative tool.

Telephone interviews are being used by a growing number of small companies to screen job candidates. Consequently, it is important to develop a winning phone personality. You must be businesslike and friendly, speak in a relaxed voice, using good English, listen carefully to what the interviewer says, and follow up with a thank-you note. Here are four rules to follow: (1) call a specific individual; (2) call with a purpose; (3) know what you are going to say; (4) have a closing or clincher to end the conversation.

A Cold-Call Script You Can Use

Here is a sample script you can use to suit your needs for a cold call.

"Hello, my name is Jack Kramer. I'd like to talk with Mr. Ogden, please."

"May I ask what this is in reference to?"

"It was suggested that I call Mr. Ogden about the marketing manager's position with your company."

"One moment please."

"Hello, Ogden here."

"Good morning, Mr. Ogden. This is Jack Kramer. I'm calling about the marketing position that is open with your company."

"Well, we do have a position open. What experience do you have?"

"Mr. Ogden, I have more than fifteen years' experience with the Major Marketing Company. I created, planned, and implemented a number of award-winning campaigns at Major Marketing. My most recent campaign resulted in a 4 percent increase in market share and a 9 percent increase in sales. From what I've learned about your company, the position you have open seems particularly suited to my experience and qualifications. I would very much like to meet you to discuss this position. Can we set up a meeting later this week, at your convenience?"

"No, this week is out of the question. Why don't you send me a copy of your résumé."

"Mr. Ogden, I took the liberty of putting one in the mail to you yesterday, as soon as I heard about the marketing manager's position at your company. Why don't I call you the week after next, after you have had time to look over my résumé?"

"Fine, Mr. Kramer, call me Wednesday, the week after next."

There you have it. The job hunter made his cold call after learning about the job and getting the name of the person responsible for hiring. From this information he was able to give a brief but informative rundown of his experience and how it would fit in with Mr. Ogden's company. The clincher was to get an interview or have Mr. Ogden read his résumé. Under the circumstances, Kramer has put himself in the running for the job when he calls and gets his interview.

The Hidden Job Market. Much has been written about uncovering this mysterious-sounding job market. No one knows precisely how big it is, but it is estimated that approximately 80 to 85 percent of current jobs are unadvertised— hence the hidden job market. Whatever the percentage, it is a huge job source waiting to be tapped. The question is: How do you find the hidden job market?

First, you have to know what you want to do, then target the companies in the industry that can use the experience and skills you can provide. How do you find such companies in your area?

Start with the Yellow Pages, making a list of all the employers in your industry you can contact. Compile a list of both small and large companies. Read business magazines and newspapers' business sections for industry news and information.

What kind of information are you seeking? You want to know how well your target companies are doing, problems they are having, if any, executive changes, what's taking place in the field, trends, short- and long-term plans of the companies, information that gives you insight about these companies and their needs, the kind of intelligence that can be invaluable during interviews. Then compile a list of ways you can contribute to your target companies through your experience.

The next step is to arrange appointments with executives in your target companies. Sometimes you may have to go through a company's human resource staff to get to your target executive, although you have a better chance of hitting pay dirt by talking with the executive. Human resources can sometimes be a bottleneck, sad to say, and sometimes hiring decisions can get lost in a large company's bureaucracy. When you have the information you need about your target company, zero in on the area that interests you and contact the executive who has power to make hiring decisions. If the executive sends you through the human resource office, you'll enjoy an advantage because you were recommended by someone with clout. Remember in such cases that you have to impress the individuals who will interview you.

Another way to check out the hidden job market is to look at the job listings in major companies. Many companies routinely post job listings of new positions every week. Such job listings give the starting and mid-range salaries of positions and a brief but informative description of the duties involved. They usually include a contact, too. If you have friends in such a company, ask them to check out job listings that apply to you. In many companies, it is possible to walk in and take the elevator to the floor of your choice. In such cases you can ask a secretary where the job listings are posted.

Some companies won't allow you in unless you have an

appointment to see someone. This is done for security reasons by major companies in large cities. In such a situation, try to visit a friend or make an appointment with a human resource professional to get an opportunity to see the listings. Or you might ask to use the restroom. Job listings are usually displayed in a place where company employees can conveniently see them.

Once you've researched your target companies, you are ready to use your acquired information to convince the interviewer about the contributions you can make to the company. This is the way savvy job hunters can sometimes create a niche for themselves. By researching a company and its needs, the job hunter goes to the interview armed with information that can be used to pinpoint problems and needs with suggestions as to how they can be solved. This can result in an offer or the creation of a new position because of the job hunter's suggestions and experience. Such effort and expertise are not lost on intelligent interviewers or executives.

The kind of interview information job hunters need can be found through friends and acquaintances, in some instances. But industry and business publications such as *Business Week, Forbes, Fortune* magazine, and *The Wall Street Journal* can provide valuable information about such companies. *Standard Rate and Data*, which has volumes listing both consumer and trade publications, can provide additional information about these companies. What makes business publications so valuable is that they report regularly on the business world in the United States and abroad. They publish articles and profiles on companies and individuals, reporting trends, changes, successes, and failures. Keep up with the goings-on in the business world. The knowledge acquired will be invaluable during business discussions with your interviewers.

Trade magazines are another excellent source of information. *Aviation Week & Space Technology, Chemical Engineering, Data Communications, Engineering News Record, Mechanical Engineering*, and *The CPA Journal* are examples of industry magazines. Many of them also carry classified advertising for jobs. Most libraries subscribe to some of these magazines. If not, they're available from the companies that publish them. They are all listed in *Standard Rate & Data.*

Newspaper Advertisements. Classified advertisements in newspapers and magazines are potential job sources, although many times you will not receive an answer to your query. Nevertheless, this is another slice of the job-potential pie that should not be overlooked. *The Wall Street Journal* runs a classified advertising section every weekday, listing jobs in various parts of the United States. *The National Employment Weekly* publishes a classified help-wanted section every week together with job-finding articles.

Employment Agencies. These provide both full-time and temporary positions for those seeking them. A full-time employment agency charges a fee for getting an individual a job. However, the fee is usually paid by the client company—the employer—seeking a new hire. Fifty-plus professionals should not have to pay a fee. Be wary of any agency that insists you sign a contract. Usually, individuals looking for a job are asked to fill out a simple form, giving name and address and most recent jobs. Read it carefully, especially the fine print, and don't sign anything unless you understand it. A full-time employment agency may deal with a number of different jobs or specialize in specific disciplines such as accounting, management information systems, or engineering professionals, to name just a few categories.

After registering with an agency you have to follow up with your contact so that you are not forgotten. Agencies in big cities deal with large numbers of people, so take nothing for granted. Register with several agencies that handle employment in your field and follow up periodically so that you are not overlooked. In this area the squeaking wheel does get more grease.

Temporary Employment Services. These services hire people for a day, a week, a month, or longer, depending on the assignment. Temporary employment services are increasingly hiring retirees who want to work part-time or several days a week. A temporary employment service is also a good way for homemakers or widows to reenter the job market. Pay is usually on an hourly basis, depending on skills, experience, and the assignments. Some temporary services have executive assignments for companies that require such expertise. The temporary employee is hired and paid by the temporary service. Temporary employment is an excellent way to check out companies, and often leads to full-time employment.

Executive Recruiters. Head hunters, as they are commonly called, fill approximately 5 percent of the top managerial positions in the job market. When a company has a management position to fill, it calls in an executive recruiter. Fees vary, depending on the assignment, but they usually average about 15 percent of the executive's salary. Because the executive recruiter works only for the client company, the job hunter never pays a fee. The executive recruiter screens all candidates, examining the individual's background if that person is seriously being considered for the job. It's worth sending a brief cover letter and résumé to a number of executive recruiters, asking them to keep your résumé on file should they receive an assignment for a person with your qualifications. You may be called for an interview if there is a current search for a person with your talents.

If you are looking for a management-level position, don't rule out executive recruiting companies. Register with a number of them and if you change jobs, send them an updated copy of your résumé. If they have an assignment in your area, you may hear from them.

Alumni. College contacts are an excellent information source for men and women. By contacting the alumni association at your college you can get the names of graduates in the area in which you live. They can provide company names, contacts, and information that can give your job campaign a boost. Under such circumstances, it's a good idea to invite your old school contact to lunch. In addition to getting information, you have the school ties that you can talk about during lunch. This brings a more personal—and relaxed— touch to your job search that can broaden your networking contacts.

Associations. There are thousands of associations in the United States that you'll find compiled in the *Encyclopedia of Associations*, available in most libraries. The reference lists the association, the name of the director, address, and telephone number. Associations can provide information about the specific industry you are interested in, including names of companies and executives, their telephone numbers, and dates of association meetings in your area.

Job Banks. A recent report entitled "Job Banks for Retirees" by Helen Axel for The Conference Board discusses a current trend by companies to harness the skills of older or retired workers, a growing but underutilized labor pool. The Conference Board is a not-for-profit research organization supported by business concerns.

The report claims that because of job shortages and the large number of retirees in the United States, "businesses are beginning to face labor shortages, serious skills deficiencies among younger workers, and the disappearance of valuable skills as a result of mass retirements."

Says Helen Axel, "The job bank in its purest form is a labor pool with people with transferable skills who can move from one temporary position to another in a company as opposed to a contractor-specific assignment."

In recent years, an increasing number of companies have established job banks, using their retirees to build a dependable labor pool to fill temporary positions during heavy work periods. Some companies use retirees with special skills and those willing to learn such skills. The Travelers, for example, has recruited retirees to fill temporary positions in data and word processing. Companies also hire retirees who have not worked for them. The best information on the subject is contained in the New York City–based Conference Board's "Job Banks for Retirees." This report, No. 929, is available from The Conference Board, 845 Third Avenue, New York, NY 10022; $80.

"Job banks will grow in the 1990s," claims Ms. Axel. "I think they will grow faster in more informal ways rather than in a structured way. They are primarily located in certain types of industries that need word processing and computer skills where lots of bodies are needed."

Thus the trend is to job banks, which have been in existence for approximately 15 years. The best-known job bank is the Travelers Companies in Hartford, Connecticut. "Although company surveys and labor force statistics indicate a growing interest in older workers," according to the Conference Board Report, "relatively few firms to date have adopted formal policies or programs that promote or facilitate continued employment of their mature workers and retirees. However, as nonstandard work arrangements gain in popularity, and labor force demographics change, opportunities for retiree employment will undoubtedly increase. One arrangement that has had promising results in satisfying both retiree and employer needs is the internal temporary pool or job bank."

The report states that "Job banks appear to be prevalent in labor- and paper-intensive firms (such as banks and insurance companies), and in some manufacturing settings where particular skills are sought for technical and production jobs. Apart from those specialized job banks, the majority of jobs filled by internal pools require clerical, data entry, and word processing skills.

"The job bank is quite informal," says Axel. "The people are known, they're retired and come back. An anomaly is the Travelers Companies, which also hires from the outside. The job bank is particularly good for someone who left the company and has a good feeling for it, and vice versa. It is good for the employer and employee. And the setup is convenient because there is no expensive paperwork and the employer does not have to go through agencies to obtain employees."

The outlook, says the report is that "the aging population and work force, as well as the growing diversity of the labor market, will focus continued employer attention on innovative approaches to retaining and regaining retiree skills."

Small Business. This is an excellent area for the 50-plus professional to explore. Small business operators often have trouble getting trained employees. A recent survey reported that hiring competent help was No. 4 on the small business most-wanted list. Small businesses offering full- and part-time positions comprise an important segment of employers. If you want to work part-time, small business is an excellent field to cultivate for work. If you have had experience in a large company, your skills will be sought after and you have a good chance of finding a full-time or temporary position with a small company that needs your talents.

You can locate small business establishments in your field by looking at the Yellow Pages, in your library, or talking with executives in your utility companies. They often have records of businesses they serve. Local newspapers are another source. They may publish articles about the 50 or 100 top companies in your locality.

Another way to find small business establishments is to walk through the business area of your town or city. Go into the buildings and check the registry. Or ask the guard or elevator operator if there are any businesses in your field in the building. In smaller buildings without guards or elevators, knock on doors and ask to speak to the office manager. If he or she is not immediately available, talk to receptionists and secretaries about potential companies in the area in your specialty. You'll be surprised at the information you can pick up by talking with people in different offices.

The Salary Question

It's worth mentioning salary at this point because it is a delicate subject for the 50-plus professional who wants to work full-time. When the subject of salary comes up, you are walking a fine line. You don't want to quote a figure too high or too low because either extreme may ruin your chances of getting the job. The most important information you need is the market rate (the salary range) for the specific job you are interviewing for. Know your high and low range before you go to the interview.

How do you find the market rate? Reading the classified advertisements in the newspapers in your area is one way. Another method is to talk to friends who work in companies in your area. Or visit an employment agency in your town or city to find the going rate. This information is important, so take the time to learn the local market rate for your discipline.

In most interviews it is best when the employer brings up the subject of salary. If the figure given is too low, you can say, "That figure is below the market rate for this job." Don't be afraid to be politely candid with the employer. This is when you have to sell your experience and talents and, most important, your contributions to the job.

If you are asked what salary you want, be prepared to say what you want—and why. Each case is unique and you have to decide what salary to suggest or accept when the moment comes. On the other hand, you may have to take less money than you orignally planned, depending on the situation. The most important thing is not to undersell yourself or your talents.

Five Rules That Ensure Success

As you pursue your job search, here are five key points, which are vital to your success.

1. Be Creative. In today's competitive job market, creativity is an important asset for the 50-plus professional. Knowing this, what can you do to stand out from your competition? Here's an example used by a 50-plus editor who was looking for a job. He was interviewed by the vice-president and editorial director of a major publishing company for the editorship of a magazine that was having editorial problems. The interview seemed to go well and the editor was excited because the job was at the No. 1 company on his preferred list.

After the interview the editor went home and wrote the customary thank-you note—but included an extra one-page mini-critique of the magazine the editorial vice-president had given him to examine. He hadn't been asked to do a critique but thought this extra effort would separate him from the unknown competition.

Says the editor: "I went through the magazine, commenting on the articles, layout, and what I thought would have been a better cover story in the magazine. I realized this was risky and I didn't say, 'This is a terrible magazine.' That wouldn't have been very smart. I did say, 'This is an excellent magazine . . . but.' Then I made specific suggestions and comments, purposely keeping my one-page 'mini critique' short and to the point."

"I got the job," says the editor. "Later, the vice-president who interviewed me said my comments were 'right on target.' In fact, he told me I had been 'too kind' in my criticism."

As the editor pointed out, there is an element of risk in criticizing or making a suggestion in a letter, because you can eliminate yourself from the job. But if you use common sense tied in with your knowledge and experience, you can tip the scales in your favor and land the job.

This technique can be used by salespersons, financial professionals, copy writers, and advertising executives who know their industry and its needs. It also requires some imagination and thought to make it work. It's a job-winning formula when properly executed.

2. Adjust to Circumstances. There comes a time in a job search when nothing seems to go right. It is something that happens to every job hunter, so don't be discouraged if it happens to you. It is important when job hunting to do something every day. That means making telephone calls, making contacts, writing letters, and following up.

If you're not getting results, you may have to change tactics. Like a professional athletic team, if things are not going well, you have to readjust your strategy. This is all part of the job quest, which requires both know-how and imagination.

3. Don't Be Afraid to Take Risks. This doesn't mean doing something foolish. You take a calculated risk just as the editor in the preceding anecdote did. You think about what you intend to do, plan it, and weigh the consequences on the win-and-lose balance sheet.

What are some of the "risks" we're talking about? One example: Recently a 59-year-old woman with a Ph.D. applied to a company for a job that she was more than qualified to perform. The salary was less than she had wanted, but the company was near her home and it was a job that appealed to her. She sensed that her interviewer, in her mid-thirties, and in charge of the department in which she would work, was uncomfortable with the thought of hiring her.

As the interview came to an end she said, "Look, I realize you may be reluctant to hire me. But I want the job and I can do it well. I'll work hard for you and my experience will help to make your job easier. I hope you will take this into consideration when you make your decision."

The Ph.D. got the job. Chances are she wouldn't have, had she not voiced her interest in the job in a nonthreatening way. Was it worth the risk? In this case, yes.

4. Expect Success. You've probably heard this advice so many times that it sounds like a platitude, but a healthy can-do attitude is essential for a successful job hunt or anything else that you want to do well in life.

5. Be Persistent. This is one of the most important assets in your job-hunting arsenal. Ray Kroc, the late founder of McDonald's, hung signs at the company headquarters that read:

- "Nothing in the world can take the place of persistence.
- "Talent will not; nothing is more common than unsuccessful men/women with great talent.
- "Genius will not; unrewarded genius is almost a proverb.
- "Education will not; the world is full of educated derelicts.
- "Persistence, determination alone are omnipotent."

Remember these words. They constitute a formula for success.

CHAPTER 10

Temporary Employment Services

Temporary employment services are one of the fastest growing industries in the United States. They offer a variety of options to the 50-plus professional, to the widow or homemaker who wants to return to work, to a retiree anxious to get back into the job market, to a person planning to switch careers, and to a person who wants part-time work or flexible hours. Even the U.S. government uses the skills of temporary employees. A temporary employment services company can also help you obtain work in another part of the country if you are moving to a new location.

The temporary employment services industry has changed dramatically in recent years. Today, for example, many temporary services not only screen employees before hiring them, they also check their references. Many provide training, at no cost, on current PC word processing and spreadsheet software. They also provide informational seminars about the corporate culture employees will be working in, and tell them how to dress and how to comport themselves on the job. The importance of a positive attitude on the job is stressed. Temporary service companies also serve as consultants for clients who use their services.

In some cases, for example, a temporary service company

155

will place a full-time representative on site for a client who requires a large number of employees during peak work periods. The representative will discuss the needs of the company, the work required, and how its temporary employees can do the job for the client in the fastest, most cost-efficient way.

Standards Are High

Temporary employment services are careful about the type of individuals they hire. The reason: They guarantee the quality of their services. If notified promptly, according to the Alexandria, Virginia, based National Association of Temporary Services (NATS), temporary employment services will not charge their customers for unsatisfactory work done by an employee and will replace the employee if necessary. Today's temporary employment services develop working relationships with both their employees and their client companies because of repeat business and the fact that they rely on each other to achieve their goals.

As employers, according to NATS, temporary service companies "assume the obligations normally related to all employers and maintain this responsibility throughout the employment period."

The temporary employment services have a language of their own. The word "dispatch," for example, is generally used to refer to the act of assigning industrial temporary employees to report for work on customers' premises. "Job shop" is a colloquial term generally used to refer to businesses that supply longer-term temporary employees on a contract basis in technical or specialized areas such as engineering or drafting. See the Glossary for a complete temporary-help lexicon of terms.

New Hiring Trend. There is also a growing nationwide trend toward using the skills of 50-plus professionals—including gold-collar workers, those 60 years and older who have retired and returned to the workplace. Chicago's ABLE (Ability Based on Long Experience) is one organization that helps older people find jobs.

Shirley Brussell, the 69-year-old executive director of operations, says ABLE's goal is to provide employment opportunities for adults 55 years or older, to counsel them, train and retrain them, and send them back to school if necessary. ABLE was started in June 1977 and since that time has served more than 60,000 older workers and more than 5,000 employers in the Chicago metropolitan area.

"In the beginning," says Brussell, "there were a lot of fragmented efforts, none of which was coordinated with one body. We at ABLE felt the need to start a clearinghouse to bind disparate agencies into one coordinated effort."

Today more than 40 agencies are involved in senior employment in the ABLE network in the Chicago metropolitan area, plus a job hot-line telephone available to both older workers seeking employment and employers in need of personnel. The ABLE Chicago hotline number is 312-782-7700. This clearinghouse operation has multiple job listings that are based on job category and area, and links the 40 agencies in the network. ABLE provides executive, managerial, technical, secretarial, and blue-collar temporary help to employers seeking such skills in the Chicago area.

ABLE is unusual in that it is a nonprofit social agency, which was founded through the efforts of the Chicago Community Trust, a prestigious private foundation. It is supported by charitable trust funds, by grants, and by funds from individuals and the business community, including more than 50 corporate foundations, and the government.

In addition, ABLE operates a private temporary employment agency for persons 50 and older called APT (apt to fit your needs), which helps to finance the ABLE operation.

According to Brussell, there are more than 70 on ABLE's staff, plus several hundred volunteers. "We have far more jobs than we can fill," she says. "We can't always get a good match. But what we are proving is that young people and 50-plus older temps can work side-by-side and be simpatico."

Executives Wanted

In New York City, John Thompson, chairman of Interim Management (IMCOR), was chairman of KMG Hurdman when it merged with Peat Marwick. After a short period of time, he took early retirement. During his 30 years in public accounting, he noted that many companies spent a lot of money on overtime work. They had a need for good management talent, but didn't want to commit to permanent employees. In some cases they had no way to fill their need for time-sensitive work, short of hiring full-time employees.

What was needed, thought Thompson, was a service that supplied a whole range of expertise on an on-call basis. Result: Thompson started IMCOR, a temporary employment service that provides interim executive help for companies that require such services.

Thompson started his company in April 1988, and business is booming. He says there has been a need for this type of service for a long time. What made it work, he says, is that the downsizing and mergers and acquisitions that took place in the business world made available a large supply of very talented people, some of whom no longer want a full-time position. Thompson's solution was to bring together companies who needed executive help on a short-term basis with executives who could fill in on an interim basis.

Thompson says he places individuals in positions of chief executive officer, chief operating officer, chief financial officer, marketing and human resource managers, executives for negotiating license agreements, and a broad range of specialists from middle to top management.

Such executives, according to Thompson, may be on assignment from three months up to a year, depending on client requirements. Salaries for such temporary/interim executives generally range from $75,000 to $150,000 on a per annum basis, with some higher.

Assignments Vary. Executives who sign up with Thompson submit a résumé. They are screened and asked to fill out an extensive six-page questionnaire that focuses on functional and industry skills. Each person is then evaluated to see where he or she qualifies in IMCOR's talent pool. This information is then put into a computer. When a company asks for a specific type of expertise, a computer search is made to come up with appropriate candidates. There are extensive interviews between the candidate and the client before the selection is made, says Thompson. All fees are paid by the client company. According to Thompson, 25 percent of his out-of-work clients end up with permanent (full-time jobs) assignments.

One of Thompson's clients, Linda Plevrites, an accountant, worked at Time Inc. for 24 years. She started in 1964 "at the lowest rung of the ladder" and ended up as controller of the magazine division. She accomplished her career goals and "hit the wall" at 46 years of age when she asked herself, "What am I doing? I don't want to spend all my time doing this."

She quit her job, her husband sold his business, and they decided to enjoy themselves. Plevrites then took time off to go to the gym three times a week, take piano lessons, and do what she calls "fun things."

Nine months later she heard about IMCOR, a temporary employment service that placed executives. She contacted IMCOR, filled out the applications, went through the interviewing process, and was called in by an advertising agency to "act as an accounting manager, a controllership kind of function." Plevrites says, "You work at your whim, long and hard. It's similar to Time Inc. I stepped into something that fits like a glove. It's a lot of fun, with different problems and a different environment. People have been easy to work with."

Plevrites says she likes the sense of freedom. At this writing she and her husband are planning a six-month trip to Europe. "I don't think I'll ever take another job," she says. She and her husband may go into business together later on, but for the moment she enjoys her lifestyle, knowing that she can work where and when she wants.

Wanted! Mature Workers

In Tucson, Arizona, Bob Rheinhart runs Retiree Skills Inc., a temporary employment service that specializes in over-50 professionals. Twelve years in business, Retiree Skills is a franchise, according to Rheinhart. "When we first started," he says, "we had a heck of a time selling companies on temporary older workers. But every year it gets easier because of the need."

The benefits of using older workers, says Rheinhart, are their experience, dependability, skills, and low turnover, which are a big plus. "They can arrange their hours and work full-time or part-time," he says.

Rheinhart has 750 to 800 temporary employees registered at all times, and with the shortage of skilled labor, he sees the temporary employment field for 50-plus workers growing.

Sharon Canter, director of strategic information for Manpower Temporary Services, an international company headquartered in Milwaukee, Wisconsin, says: "Manpower is employing more and more senior workers who do not want to retire from the work force on a full-time basis. Through Manpower, seniors can maintain a flexible work schedule and earn supplemental income. According to Manpower, 50-plus employees now comprise almost 25 percent of the company's one million temporary workers, and their numbers are continuing to grow.

"We offer seniors a way to repot themselves into new careers through temporary office, light industrial, and marketing assignments. Our skills assessments, which uncover hidden talents, interests, and personal characteristics, enable us to assign senior workers to jobs that they enjoy."

Learning New Skills. Canter continues, "Although senior workers bring years of experience and knowledge to their job assignments, sometimes they want training in new skills. We offer them a way to update their skills for today's automated office. Skillware, Manpower's computer training program, is offered free of charge to our temporary workers. Written in everyday language, the training is hands-on and self-paced. The training is also reflective of the work they'll do on job assignments."

Manpower not only trains temporary employees in the use of computer hardware and software, it also provides training to the permanent staff of companies.

"We've found that senior workers are dependable, hard-working, and productive," says Canter. "When equipped with our Skillware computer training, they are also in high demand. Many customers call and request the same senior workers on a consistent basis."

Kelly Services Inc. is another international service company. Headquartered in Troy, Michigan, it provides temporary jobs to a diverse group of customers through its Kelly temporary services division. The company operates more than 900 branch offices worldwide, with 700 in the United States and Canada.

Kelly annually employs more than 580,000 people for short-term assignments at clients' facilities. It serves more than 180,000 customers and supplies temporary employees in more than 100 job classifications.

In 1987 Kelly was having difficulty obtaining temporary employees, particularly on the East Coast, according to Carolyn Fryar, senior vice-president. Says Fryar, "We could not recruit enough people to fill all assignments. We had to find different ways to find people with the skills we needed. We began recruiting over-50 people; we found they were retiring earlier than before, although being retired didn't mean they didn't want to work anymore. We thought this could be a possible solution to our problem and we created Encore in 1987 to target the 50 and older group."

The result, according to Fryar, is that approximately 10 percent of Kelly Services' approximately 560,000 work force are now 50 and over and they are actively being recruited. "The purpose of Encore," she says, "is to share the advantages of temporary employment with those seniors who want to work. Some of these advantages include flexible scheduling, a variety of work experiences, the chance to meet new people, and the opportunity to maintain current skills or learn new ones."

New Role for Mature Professionals. Houston-based Talent Tree Personnel Services, with more than 100 temporary employment and permanent placement branches throughout the country, has seen, in both its major and secondary markets, a steady rise in the demand for workers in the 50-plus age group. William L. Caudell, senior vice-president, says, "The trend of corporations to employ people on an 'as-needed' basis, has coincided with the shrinking number of younger people entering the work force and the growing number of retirees. The opportunities for the older workers are obviously increasing."

Caudell points out that unemployment statistics and the business mix of individual markets nevertheless dictate the types and numbers of people that temporary service companies require. He says, "The key to using temporary help employees is cost-effective productivity that often translates into skills . . . if the candidate does not have skills and experience relating to a client's equipment, software or work environment, his or her range of opportunities is obviously limited. Fortunately, these limiting factors can be overcome with proper training. Today the foolish discrimination against age or race is becoming much less of a problem."

Promote Your Skills. But as with any group, knowing how to market yourself is critical, says Caudell. "Although no segment of the society truly fits a stereotype, there is a general belief that the older worker comes equipped with a 'superior' work ethic. The older worker should use that to his or her advantage. Sell the strongest attribute, whether it is being on the job every day, being punctual, being willing to help out so that the job is completed on time, or being able to fall back on life's experiences, as they relate to a company's needs.

"Unfortunately, older workers often seem to be their own worst enemy when they are looking for a job. Regardless of how much someone wants to assist you in gaining employment, if you do not believe you can perform a job because of experience, skills, age, or ability, few people will give you a try."

Caudell says that if the older worker wants a full-time position, working first as a temporary is a means of building skills and confidence. And once work performance is proven, full-time jobs often become available. Working as a temporary provides an excellent means to meet the older worker's economic and lifestyle needs.

The New Image

Samuel Sacco, executive vice-president of the National Association of Temporary Services (NATS), says the perception of temporary help has changed dramatically in the last few years and is now perceived by business as problem solvers in the personnel area. Temporary services consult with businesses on the best and most efficient ways to use temporary employees. Incidentally, the industry now refers to temporary "services" rather than "agencies." "Temporary help services assign their own employees to customers who need extra temporary help on short notice," says Sacco.

Sacco gives three reasons for the rapid growth of temporary help services: "The business community is much more understanding and sophisticated in using temporary help services. The diversity of the temporary workers' skills has increased demand, with more alternative ways to use them. Temporary help services have branched into virtually every area you can name. Every day more than 100 positions ranging from janitor to computer programmer are filled by temporary workers.

"Second, temporary services offer flexibility that permits businesses to control the fixed costs of labor, the same as other overhead costs. If a job requires less than full-time help, it is more economical to employ temporary staffers who can do the job and who are readily accepted by business to solve personnel problems.

"The third reason is that technology has changed so rapidly that many businesses have a hard time keeping up. Equipment is an intricate part of the business operation, and has some controlling factor in the way the business is run. Businesses can't afford to have equipment sit idle or hire people who are not qualified to operate it. It takes six weeks to train a person in data processing. This is where the trained temporary employee services person steps into the picture."

New Opportunities. "As the labor shortage continues to get worse, we are going to see more and more companies using temporary employees," says Sacco. He also points out that the temporary services industry is doing a better job of identifying competent help, screening and testing applicants, and matching temporary workers to jobs. So important has the use of qualified temporary employees become to business, that seasonal temporaries are now a preplanned line item on many company budgets, according to Sacco.

The demand for temporary employees has soared from an average of 416,000 jobs a day in 1980 to more than a million in 1989. The $14 billion-a-year industry has been growing at an approximate rate of 15 to 17 percent annually for the past 10 years, according to NATS.

Temporary jobs are categorized into four groups, says Sacco. Here is the percentage of employment among temporary help industry segments as compiled by NATS:

- 63.5 percent of all temporary help jobs consist of office/clerical positions of every kind and skill level

- 15.4 percent of temporary work involves light and heavy industrial skills, ranging from assembly line work to product demonstrations to janitorial services
- 11.2 percent of the temporary help work force encompasses technical and professional positions such as engineers, accountants, draftsmen, computer programmers, writers, and editors
- 9.9 percent of all temporary help jobs are found in the medical segment, which includes registered and licensed practical nurses, nurses aides, orderlies and lab technicians for hospital staffing and home health care

Salaries for temporary employees range from about $4.00 to $21.00 or more an hour, depending on the assignment. However, Sacco points out that some temporaries such as chemical and electrical engineers or contractors in high demand can earn six-figure salaries, again, depending on the assignment.

Earnings and Social Security. A temporary job is an excellent way for retired professionals to supplement their Social Security income. However, there are limitations on what you can earn if you are receiving social security. For example, starting in 1991, the earnings limitation for people 65 to 69 is $9,720. Under age 65 the earnings limitation is $7,080. If you are under 65, you lose $1.00 in benefits for each $2.00 earned that is above the exempt amount; if you are 65 to 69, the reduction is $1.00 for every $3.00 above the earning limitation. Once you reach 70 years of age, there are no limits on how much you can earn. But you must file an application to obtain Social Security, and rules do change. If you have questions, call the Social Security Administration's national telephone number: 800-234-5772.

When you sign up with a temporary services company, you become an employee of that company. The temporary services company pays your salary and social security taxes, workers' compensation, and unemployment insurance. The temporary service company assumes responsibility for general liability and personal property damage.

Companies use temporary help because they don't want to be employers, says Sacco. He points out that NATS is a trade association with a commitment to the industry. Member companies number 1,000 and account for 85 percent of the sales volume in a universe comprised of approximately 4,000 national, regional, and independent temporary employment services companies that operate more than 10,800 offices throughout the United States. It is also important to note that NATS members pledge to abide by all Codes of Good Practices adopted by the association.

Targeting Quality Companies

The way to judge a quality temporary service company, according to NATS, whether it is a member or not, is determined by several factors. It begins when you telephone for information or an appointment. Is the person who answers friendly, professional, with good telephone manners? When you arrive for an appointment is the staff alert, organized, businesslike? Do you get the full attention of the people who interview you? Is the counselor friendly and concerned? Does he or she match your job skills to the assignment? If the answers to these questions are yes, chances are good you're dealing with a reputable company.

Questions to Ask. You will find temporary service companies listed in the Yellow Pages. Register with at least three of them. When you visit their offices, observe how they operate to see if they meet the requirements described earlier. This is the time to ask about fringe benefits. Although such fringes may vary according to the temporary service company, here are some questions you might ask:

Does the company offer paid vacations? If so, do hours accumulate from year to year or will you have to start from scratch each year? Some companies pay one week for every 1,000 hours worked.

Is there a medical and hospital plan? What are the benefits?

Does the company have seniority bonuses for their long-term employees?

Do you get paid for referring other workers?

NATS also suggests asking about how busy you will be. Many temporary service companies establish long-term relationships with their temporary employees because of the professional work they do. It is not unusual for a temporary employee to work on assignments for as long as six months when the job requires it.

Temporary Path to a Permanent Job

"Temporary work . . . is an excellent pathway to becoming rehired," says James E. Challenger, president of Challenger, Gray & Christmas, a Chicago-based outplacement consulting firm. "It also reflects the increasing tendency by many to contract work out to specialists on an 'as needed' basis to save on the expense of full-time salaries and expensive benefits packages.

"As firms become smaller and more cost-effective," he says, "they may hire out a variety of services, even including manufacturing and production workers, while maintaining a compact central core of managers. It is reflected in the growing popularity of the 'just-in-time inventory' approach to manufacturing that has been used successfully by overseas producers and is now being used here.

"Although temporary work lacks the stability of full-time employment, many managers prefer it because of the variety of the work involved and the flexibility in terms of working hours," says Challenger.

"Some are becoming permanent members of the temporary and part-time work force. At the same time, others are accepting temporary assignments and still maintaining their overall objectives of finding a full-time job.

"For the individual who still has his or her sights set on full-time, continuous employment, temporary work can provide a good stage because of the typically broad range of companies that a firm specializing in temporary workers deals with. More often than not, the person who makes a favorable impression and demonstrates significant contributions to the client firm's bottom line will receive a full-time job offer."

According to Challenger, some employers regard temporary workers with disfavor. They are often thought of as people who could not get a job and therefore become temporaries or consultants.

"For that reason, it is entirely possible that the manager who has chosen to do temporary work and then decides to seek full-time employment may be handicapped by having an unfavorable image just because he or she has accepted temporary work in the past."

The best approach is to accept the temporary or part-time assignments with the aim of converting those opportunities into full-time employment as soon as the appropriate job situation appears. Challenger's conclusions are based on his company's recent surveys of 600 managers, 25 percent of whom were discharged from companies with sales volumes ranging from $30 million to more than $1 billion.

Other drawbacks to temporary employment may include times when no assignments are available, working at a dull job, or working in an environment that you dislike. In such cases, ask for a new assignment.

Despite these perceived drawbacks, NATS says the three primary reasons people choose temporary employment are: (1) the appeal of variety in job assignments; (2) work environments; and (3) the ability to gain new and valuable work experience. Temporary employment also gives 50-plus professionals returning to the job market the flexibility to arrange their personal and professional work lives according to their dictates, the chance to learn new skills, earn extra income, or scout the job market to investigate a career change or find a full-time position.

See the Glossary for a lexicon of temporary-help terms.

CHAPTER 11

Advice for Minorities

"Work for a company where you'll be happy, one that encourages you to do your best, where you don't have to take your skin off before you go to work" is Robert Brocksbank's advice to young minority-group college graduates about to enter the business world. Brocksbank's strong words apply to any member or any minority group seeking employment at any age.

Brocksbank, a champion of minority employment, a consultant with Mobil Oil Company, and chairman emeritus of the Dallas-based Council on Career Development for Minorities, points out that many minorities are in fields where the transfer of skills is not recognized. For example, making the transition from the military to academe or from teaching to the business world can often be difficult. Brocksbank says that many such minorities came from good jobs, have impressive credentials, and many are Ph.D.'s, but they have difficulty finding employment.

"The real division in our society is not black and white," says Brocksbank. "It's those with hope and without hope. Those without hope don't try—and don't make it."

Although the job hunt is difficult, it is not impossible. The minority 50-plus professional has more hurdles to conquer

170

than his or her white counterpart. In additon to racism and prejudice that may be lurking behind an interviewer's smile, the workplace is more competitive and cutthroat today because of cutbacks, mergers and acquisitions, and increased competition at home and in the global marketplace. The result is that companies are slimming down and gearing up for the bottom-line battle for profits and increased market share in the 1990s. This makes it more difficult for anyone looking for a job, and places another barrier in the path of minority professionals seeking employment.

Beating the Odds

The minority job hunter, even more than his or her white counterpart, has to use every skill and resource available. In writing this chapter, we've talked with a number of talented and successful minority professionals from various walks of life who have fought the lions in the job arena and walked away, though not without scars, setbacks, and some defeats. But overall they overcame and succeeded in America's corporate jungle. Here is the advice they offer to today's over-50 minority professionals.

Says Lois Davis, in her mid-50s, "If someone had told me a few years ago that I would be a Philadelphia lawyer, I would have laughed." Davis, who didn't enter law school until she was 43, now works for the U.S. Attorney's office in the civil division. She represents the government in a variety of cases such as discrimination, medical malpractice suits, bankruptcy, drug seizures, or unpaid small business loans, to mention a few examples.

A friendly, accomplished, and energetic woman, Davis grew up in rural Charles County, about 20 miles south of Washington, D.C. When she was eleven, her father, concerned about her educational opportunities, moved the family to Washington, D.C., where Davis attended junior and senior high school. Her high school years were significant, says Davis, because Washington, D.C., schools were still segregated in

1954 when she graduated from high school. Her teachers motivated and encouraged her, she says, especially her chemistry teacher.

"There were two separate school systems, black and white," says Davis. But it happened that many of her teachers had Ph.D.'s. Some had attended schools like Harvard, but couldn't get jobs in the private sector. As a result, Davis got a first-class education.

When she enrolled in Howard University, she decided to major in chemistry, which she felt was her only option, other than math, because of her mathematical abilities. "All women at that time who took math ended up teaching," she says, "and I didn't want to end up teaching math."

In 1962 Davis married her husband, Wayne, whom she met when he was a senior at the University of Connecticut. After they were married, her husband joined the FBI and began to move around the country. Davis lived and taught math ("the irony," she says) in Washington, D.C., New York, Detroit, and Newark. She had the first of her two daughters in New Jersey and stopped working until 1976.

Getting Involved. "It was an exciting time of life," says Davis. She began to become involved in community affairs, which she credits with helping her become a lawyer. But Davis wanted new worlds to conquer. So when a friend suggested that she go to law school, Davis liked the idea, because "It brings together all the social science and scientific training I had. I love to talk and negotiate, all the things I did working for the community."

She studied for the Law Student Aptitude Test (LSAT) and scored in the 92nd percentile. A Phi Beta Kappa at Howard University, Davis says, "I could have gotten into any law school in the country with my credentials."

In 1980 she attended the first year of law school at Indiana University/Purdue University at Indianapolis where the Davis family lived. When she first arrived, she said to herself, "I'm too old for this," and walked into a room to meet with seven other late-bloomer lawyers-to-be ranging in age from their thirties to one woman in her sixties. "We became good friends," says Davis. "We studied together and supported each other."

Davis graduated in December 1983 from Wayne State University Law School in Detroit, Michigan, where her husband had been transferred. During one summer vacation, she worked at the U.S. Attorney's office in Detroit. Upon graduation she landed a job in Detroit with Butzel, Long, Gust, & Klein, where she worked for a year and a half before her husband was transferred to Philadelphia.

In Philadelphia, Davis joined a firm with 200 lawyers, where she worked for two years. Then she heard the U.S. Attorney's office needed a trial lawyer. "I wanted to be a trial lawyer," she says, "I really like the work." She applied for the job and got it. Davis learned that life changes quickly and that after five years as a Philadelphia lawyer, she is committed to her job for now. "Later, I'll make an evaluation," she says. "In the meantime, don't try to plan it all out" is the advice from this Philadelphia lawyer.

No Easy Solutions

Willard Anderson, director of training for ITT Corporation, says: "The over-50 group, in my opinion, tends to suffer in large measure from what I call 'oppressive psychosis.' We grew up in an era where it was necessary to be suspicious of almost any and everything. We look at the past ten years and what has happened to affirmative action along the way. You mesh that with what the average 50-year-old today has grown up with, and, psychologically speaking, the thought is, 'I'm not going to be able to find meaningful employment, the odds are stacked against me,' which tends to create a problem initially. And that is, 'It's not fair.'

"To some extent, I think that is true. Look at the business side. Mergers and acquisitions have taken their toll and in terms of numbers, there are not a lot of jobs out there. I would say that the psychological end is the toughest part. Now it's not easy for anyone to get employment today. I don't know of any profession where people are just walking through the doors and signing up. It's tough on everyone. But the minority has to be strong and tenacious and understand that, generally speaking, it will take anywhere from three to six months to land a job.

"So today, the toughest thing is getting over the hurdle psychologically and saying to yourself, 'There is a position somewhere out there for me and I'm going to find it.' "

Connecting. "Now how do you find it? Networking is one way. You speak to the people you know who are working and occasionally you'll find someone who knows of a job possibility. But that's not easy. Oftentimes we don't want people to know we are out of work and we don't use our networking contacts. Be willing to admit you are looking for a job and work toward that end.

"The other thing I don't think minorities always pay enough attention to is the willingness to move. This is another aspect of job hunting. I talk to quite a number of people in this job who call, seeking advice. I ask them, 'Are you mobile?' And the answer, generally speaking, is 'No, I don't want to leave New York.' Or 'No, I live in New Jersey, and I like New Jersey.' Or 'I love Connecticut.' I think that's a mistake, because if you decide to just pick off a piece of the market, and that's the only one you plan to approach for employment, that creates a larger problem for you. You go where the job is.

"It's easy for me to say because I've been gainfully employed all my life and I've never really had to do a lot interviewing. I had a military career prior to joining ITT."

Anderson emphasizes the importance of self-worth. The former chief master sergeant in 1976 was selected outstanding airman in the U.S. Air Force. And in 1977 he was selected by then Alabama governor George Wallace as the outstanding enlisted representative in the state.

"I was considered an individual on the move, very professional, and the kind of person you really want to have on the job. But when I was interviewed for my first position with an ITT company, I was made an offer with a dollar value that made me laugh. The interviewer asked me what was funny. I told him I thought the compensation was too low. That I couldn't really come to work for that amount, because I brought willingness and ability to the job and I knew where they were going to place me. As a result, I felt I should be compensated for the kind of performance I knew they were going to get from me."

Believe in Yourself. The company upped the ante and Anderson got the job. "I started a very low level job and today I'm the director of training and development for the corporation worldwide," he says. "I feel it is important that you have a good, solid feel for what you are worth on the market. That is not to say that all interviewers or people who are in charge of hiring are going to try to get you as cheaply as possible. I know this is a fair corporation and there have been a lot of changes over the years. But there are still companies out there, especially if you are a minority, that will try to get you cheaper. It happens. Oftentimes it is found out and it causes problems.

"When it comes to interviews, you have to understand the interviewing process. You have to know what the company is looking for, have your objectives set, and be confident. If you find that the person is prejudiced, then you remain the person you know you are. And if it doesn't work occasionally, it just doesn't work. That happens a lot. If we decide we'd like to file a charge as a result, and we have our facts correct, I say do that. One must do what one feels one must do."

Anderson says it's important to have a good idea of what you want to do. What kind of work would you like to do, especially if you are a retiree who's been out of the market for a while and wants to get back in? He advises using various employment agencies, including the government, and organizations like the Urban League, and allowing them to help you seek the kind of employment you want. In that process you should find out what it really takes to be employed at that level or in that kind of job. Once you have that information, you have another decision to make. Do I want to do what it takes to get that job? For instance, if you've been a teacher and out of the profession for a while, it may be necessary to return to college to take a course or two to become certified in a state where you may have moved. If you're willing to do these things there's a good chance you'll be able to find employment. Not at the level you may seek at first, but employment to the extent that you'll be satisfied, if not happy.

As to prejudice, Anderson says: "It's one of those things that has been with us since the beginning of this country and it's still there. There was a big swing at one point. Companies did a lot of outreach and almost all of the companies had a meaningful number of minorities. The pendulum has begun to swing the other way now. I would imagine a part of that has to do with the mergers and cutbacks and the lack of the number of jobs. The question is: 'Can they get hired?' Have there in fact been some changes?"

Fresh Winds of Change. Anderson goes on, "There's been a tremendous amount of changes. Specifically, this corporation. I'm very proud of ITT in terms of some of the things I know it has done. Some companies, I would imagine, like others, tend to exist based on the environment that they are in and in many instances they're not yet the way we'd like them to be. But it seems that demographics are going to do something about that in the near future if I can believe what I'm reading. So the problem to some extent will be solved in the next decade or two."

Prejudice Is Still with Us

Dr. Bailey Jackson, associate dean for academic affairs at the University of Massachusetts, and consultant to major corporations and universities on multicultural organizational development, recalls when he began his career and was interviewing for a job on Wall Street, the interviewer suggested he might be more interested in boxing than computer science. This despite the fact that Dr. Jackson graduated at the top of his computer class.

"It's not as blatant today," says Dr. Jackson. "People are smart enough not to ask such questions, but then they won't consider your application seriously." He also notes that blacks and Latinos have become smarter in identifying racism when it rears its ugly head. It is subtle—Dr. Jackson calls it "sophisticated"—and harder to see.

When it comes to "corporate fit," Dr. Jackson says it is rarely people who are black or Latino, but white. "Qualified" is another word used to discriminate, says Dr. Jackson, because the black or Latino does not have "white qualifications" that some companies mandate.

Dick Clarke, premier minority recruiter in the country and president of Dick Clarke Associates in New York City, says most professionals are aware of the kinds of prejudices that one expects. "It's never overt," he says. "You must assume going in you are going to encounter it somewhere along the way."

"Be focused, be prepared, and be articulate," advises John L. Estrada, program development director, human resources, at the Amoco Corporation in Chicago. "Don't look at the job hunt in a negative way," he says. "Know you will encounter difficult issues and deal with them."

Estrada says minorities who have left big corporations or government employment don't like change. "They want to go back to what they left, and they can't," he says. Minorities in this situation have to evaluate themselves, and concentrate on their strengths and abilities. "Look at other job markets," says Estrada, "smaller companies and organizations that view minorities' abilities with greater value. Such companies typically will not look so much at the minority aspect, because they are more interested in the bottom line. There is value added to a smaller organization. The bottom line today is that you are not always needed by big corporations and you have to come to terms with that."

Reenter with Know-How. People who reenter the job market have to make a transition. They have to go into the job market with a smile, be sincere, and fit in. One major problem Estrada sees is that in many cases minorities have not properly investigated what they want to do. They have to tell a would-be employer what they can do and how they can fit in. "This is where you have to be focused, prepared, and articulate," claims Estrada.

A good resource of potential employers is area magazines like Crain's *Chicago Business* that annually list the 100 largest corporations in the area, both public and private, their financial health, and the number of employees. Utilities are another good source of information about growing companies.

Another source is associations such as the Black Business Alliance, National Black MBA Association, U.S. Hispanic Chamber of Commerce, Hispanic Organization of Professionals and Executives, National Society of Hispanic MBAs, National Association for the Advancement of Colored People, and the Association of American Indian Affairs, to mention a few. You can find the names, addresses, and telephone numbers of associations in your field by looking them up in the *Encyclopedia of Associations* at the library.

Executive recruiter Richard Clarke calls attention to the "Last in, first out" syndrome. He says Lifo as it applies to minorities has been a consistent pattern of corporate behavior. "What does surprise me," he says, "is that the people coming out of the military are having similar problems, although, on reflection, my experience has been that general officers—these are generals—who come out of the regular army that are not minority, tend to find employment very quickly—mostly with companies that are in some aspect of the industrial-military complex. You get terrifically efficient, accomplished black generals—who come out and have a very difficult time finding employment. Some of them are logistics experts, army, air force, marine, as well as naval officers. When you hear that such people have difficulty finding jobs you're disappointed because these are, in my mind, very special people and they deserve a higher degree of respect from people in the hiring process."

Clarke also notes that 43 percent of respondents to a 1987 survey of 5,000 minority group managers commissioned by his company said there was less opportunity to advance than there had been in 1982. Half claimed they had been treated differently or unfairly because of their color.

Winning on Talent

There are some bright exceptions, of course. A CEO who headed one of the largest construction programs in the country is Charles Williams, a black major general who had recently retired from the army. He was in charge of constructing bases around the world and was in charge of the New York City School Construction Authority, a $4.3 billion enterprise. Clarke points out that there have been some successes, and General Williams is one of them.

General Williams is the first and only black in the United States to head a technical organization of the type and complexity of the New York City School Construction Authority. As a major general and director of management in the U.S. Army, Williams advised the Chief of Staff and the Secretary of the Army. "They relied on me to provide advice on all management aspects of the army," says General Williams. He trained as an engineer via the Corps of Engineers, got his MBA from Atlanta University, and attended the Kennedy School at Harvard for Senior Managers in Government Programs.

Sell Your Know-How. "You can't market yourself as a black (or minority)," says General Williams. He points out that he didn't seek the School Construction Authority job. "I was contacted by a search firm," he says. General Williams mentions three advantages minority officers leaving the service can sell when looking for jobs in the private sector. They are:

- You are highly disciplined and a person who has had a tremendous amount of responsibility.
- You are the right age—in General Williams' case, 49—with 15 or more years of pure executive-level experience.
- You have important assets: almost 30 years of hands-on construction (or whatever military credentials) and management experience and a high learning curve in your field.

General Williams believes in strong preparation and seeking jobs that will give you hands-on experience. Strive to make your work experience portfolio as strong as possible. He believes in his case the best man got the job and race was not a driver.

Most minorities have gained their skills in major corporations—Fortune 500 companies, says Clarke. The simple reason is that there was more access there because of the civil rights laws, therefore there was increased motivation on the part of major corporations to seek out and employ qualified minorities. These minorities have gained valuable experience over the years, says Clark, but because of mergers, acquisitions, and downsizing, they've been the victims of "unequal equal opportunity." They've been the last in and the first out.

Don't Overlook Small Companies. Clarke says, "The particular experience they've had with major organizations is very valuable to smaller organizations that have not had the benefit of having a well-trained Fortune 500 person to bring these skills to bear in a smaller area. Albeit, they are not going to get the salary, the bonus and other perquisites. But I know people who have gone to small organizations and what they've gotten is a reasonably good salary, and in many cases negotiated a piece of the action—bonuses, and certainly cerebral satisfaction.

"I think it may be a mistake to pursue another Fortune 500 company with the idea that you are taking into that arena experience that companies need. It is most likely that there is someone already occupying that chair, or that the chair will remain empty because of the company's desire to improve profitability or whatever reason the company had for such cutbacks."

Dr. Thomas M. Law, president of St. Paul's College in Lawrenceville, Virginia, notes that minorities, after age 50, in terms of retirement, face the problem of no matter how good they are, or have been, they've worked in professions in many cases that did not pay well. Consequently they are not able to maintain their lifestyle by taking retirement or part-time employment. They have not had the opportunities to amass a decent financial base so that they can comfortably back away. They often lack the option of a good retirement fund or the normal expectancy that they can be absorbed into another profession. Dr. Law says industry puts up a barrier to minorities by not looking at the quality and expertise minority professionals bring to the workplace. He also notes that many people in education and administration, managers with administrative skills that are transferable, are frequently not considered for employment.

"We actively recruit retired executives from Fortune 500 companies because we know they have expertise," says Dr. Law. "If you look at the trials and tribulations black colleges go through, the wealth of information and expertise they offer, you realize they manage to make bricks without straw.

"I do realize that minorities must have something very unique so that companies can see they will have an impact on the balance sheet," says Dr. Law. "If you are fortunate enough to have the skills in demand or something unique to market, then the company will see that you can help the balance sheet."

Dr. Law sees the relationship between major corporations and minorities getting better in the years to come. He is optimistic about more options for younger minorities in the workplace so that they won't have to go through many of the travails that over-50 people did. "Plan on a more even playing field," he says. "It is not going to be even, but it will become more so as people become better prepared."

Attitudes Are Changing

Cathy Fyock of Innovative Management Concepts, a management consulting firm in Louisville, Kentucky, sees a change in attitudes with employers becoming more receptive to older workers. Fyock, who counsels corporations on hiring employees, cites the case of a high-tech company that had a practice of giving employees early retirement. The company soon discovered it was not only losing a valuable source of state-of-the-art technical skills, but the retirees were going to work for the competition.

"There is a changing mind-set," says Fyock, "albeit it is taking place slowly." It is a change in terms of companies beginning to understand the importance of the older consumer, especially in service companies that have direct contact with customers. It's important to have older workers serving older customers in banks, in retail establishments, and many of the service industries."

Opportunities in Service Industries. Need is also tied in with the older consumer, claims Fyock. Typically, service industries have been harder hit by the labor shortage and are more receptive to the nontraditional segment. Minority status and age are not as important as the ability to do the job, especially with the baby bust, labor shortages, and lower employment rates. Overcoming some of these misconceptions and stereotypical thinking opens doors to competent people in the work force. Savvy companies do what is necessary to retain and train workers.

Fyock also points out that there are multiple kinds of opportunities in the fast-food business. "You can start at the bottom without prior experience and work up to fairly high-paying jobs in a couple of years, including benefits," she says.

Experienced professionals can solve problems and deal with customers. Fyock describes the case of a 57-year-old woman who started as an hourly employee in a fast-food emporium and in two years worked up to assistant manager, and then training manager. "The opportunities are there," says Fyock.

Choosing the Right Company

Recruiter Dick Clarke says, "There's an equation I always use. You go to work for a company that makes something the public is buying—or a service that's being rendered—by a company catering to what we call a 'diverse population,' which is a euphemism for blacks, Hispanics, and women. If the company makes ball bearings, forget it, because the product doesn't have any particular identification in the marketplace. But if you are making food, beverage, or clothing, or other products that people have the ability to identify by brand—those are the kinds of companies you want to target. Especially look at the small and emerging companies—and I emphasize the small and emerging—because those are the companies seeking managerial ability. They are less likely to be concerned about the race or sex of the person. They're often starved for management and that's where you want to take your skills.

"When looking for a job," says Clarke, "wear the proverbial corporate uniform. Go forth and assume that the person interviewing you is examining the content of your character rather than the color of your skin. If you are looking at a smaller company, there may be a bit of what I call visual surprise. But once you get down to talk about the nitty-gritty—nobody gives a damn. If you are a quality control person coming out of IBM or Polaroid or Xerox or a company like that, and you go to work for WC Widget Software Manufacturing, the company executive is saying, 'Gee, this guy is bringing me 20 years of IBM. I don't care if he's purple.' "

A Surprise Advantage. Clarke notes that an interviewer may be somewhat surprised to see a minority walk through the door. Don't be put off by that, he says. Focus on making your point. Take advantage of the interviewer's surprise. Say, "I know you may be surprised to see me. But if you'll just focus on my résumé and talk about the contents of it and my experience, you may be pleasantly surprised." Then, says Clarke, talk about how you can help the company. Focus on the positive and make your points.

Floyd Dickens, an electrical engineer and CEO of 21st Century Management Services, a Cincinnati-based management consulting firm, says minorities need to use their natural intelligence to determine whether interviewers are racist or sexist. Indulge in idle chitchat for a few minutes to size up the interviewer and develop the approach you plan to take. "If an interviewer seems prejudicial," says Dickens, "I'd be very aggressive and interview them. On the other hand, if the interviewer is sensitive, open, and direct, I would be less aggressive and put more emphasis on information."

Show-and-Tell Interviews. Dickens says white interviewers often expect minorities to be nonaggressive. "What happens," he says, "is that minorities, especially blacks, get caught between a rock and a hard place." He cautions against being nonaggressive and polite and claims it is much better to err on the strong side.

"It's important to convey an attitude of 'Look what you'll lose if don't hire me. Look at the difference I can make,' as opposed to saying, 'Oh, please hire me because I need a job.' And interview the interviewer to find out what the company can do for you. You have a right to work in an organization you'd like to call your own."

Another way to influence the interviewer, says Dickens, is to say, "Let me show you what I've done." He suggests bringing a portfolio of your work, like an artist, that vividly demonstrates your achievements. These materials can include magazine articles you've written, newspaper clippings, reports you've produced, and a set of written one-pagers that highlight your interpersonal skills, problem-solving and leadership abilities. Bind this material into a leather notebook and you'll have an impressive presentation of what you've done and what you can do. "Think of it in terms of an acting appearance," says Dickens.

Discard Excess Emotional Baggage. "When you are out of a job at age 50," says recruiter Clarke, "you've probably got a couple of kids finishing high school, or in college or grad school, and your house is almost paid for. You've got a lot of emotional weight to carry. Don't carry the emotional weight of race into the interview process. Pursue the job in a positive way, because you can get really depressed in the job-hunting process if you assume the person you are talking to is going to discriminate against you.

"With the demographics being what they are today, companies that are going to stay competitive are going to have to deal with a diverse employment market. Intelligent companies are going to hire good people from diverse backgrounds. Employers will in this and the next decade have to hire an older pool of employees to meet their need for experienced workers.

"Although it may not be apparent to 50-plus-year-olds going into the job market, they are indeed going to be the market of the future. They are going to have something to sell in a seller's market for a change. They should maintain the attitude of 'Hey, I've got something to offer your company.' Not with an arrogant approach, but one that says, 'Look at the future, look at the demographics. I'm going to be here at least for the next 20 years because there is no mandatory retirement at 65. I'm not the kind of person who will be changing jobs every couple of years. So I'm bringing you solid experience and the probability of being a loyal, long-term employee.' "

A Diverse Future

How to manage a work force that is diverse is the wave of the future, according to Dr. R. Roosevelt Thomas, Jr., the executive director of the American Institute for Managing Diversity at Morehouse College, where he is also secretary of the college. The corporate world is not set up for a diverse work force, especially for those returning to it, says Dr. Roosevelt, because they are different, they don't quite fit into the corporate culture. People have to be prepared to deal with this reality.

There must be a greater sensitivity to these types of differences, says Dr. Thomas. It's important to understand the culture of the organization: can the organization meet the requirements of managing a diverse work force or are they too demanding? The system is not set up to deal with the uncommon aspect of work-force diversity and there will be some gnashing of teeth as the corporate gears of change try to mesh.

In a given organization, says Dr. Thomas, managing diversity permits a knowledgeable and understanding manager to harness the full potential of employees because there will be a minimum of blatant racism and sexism. The corporation's motto might be "We is us," which means employees are accepted for what they are and what they do rather than their color or ethnic background.

As these changes in attitude and need take place in this decade, the job market for minorities will continue to improve. That doesn't mean it is going to be easy, but it does mean that if you have the required skills and the self-confidence to pursue your career goal, there is a job waiting for you to find it.

See Appendixes VI, VII, and VIII for organizations that can help.

CHAPTER 12

Companies That Hire 50-Plus Professionals

New job opportunities will present themselves in the 1990s, especially for those able to meet the challenge of change. Education and knowledge will open doors into specialized occupations and new jobs that have not yet been created. The author's research into the status of the 50-plus job seeker in relation to company hiring confirms that skilled mature professionals are in the midst of these changes and trends, and will be needed to fill vacancies, particularly in technological and service industries. Our research shows that most progressive major companies have a positive attitude; they hire and appreciate mature employees.

A Hidden Resource

Before looking at the particular needs revealed by our survey of companies that hire 50-plus workers, it is important to examine the workplace of the 1990s and the changes that are taking place in it. Among the human resources of an American company, the mature employee remains a gem embedded under an outcrop of unspoken discrimination. Unlike the Japanese, who revere the elderly and have no demarcation for the end of a person's work life, American business man-

187

agers often shunt aside employees who have reached the age of 50 or more. The charge is usually hard to prove, but is evident in the careers of too many over-50 professionals whose jobs are dead-ended or terminated. The Equal Opportunity Commission reported 24,710 claims of age discrimination in 1987. Discriminatory practices are evident to Christopher Mackaronis, head of the Advocacy Programs of the American Association of Retired Persons (AARP), whose employment equity office is deluged with protest calls every week.

Doubtless, there are many more 50-plus professionals sidetracked, pushed out, or retired early, whose stories never become known. This, despite the fact that people have longer, healthier work lives than ever before, and some industries have a serious need for such workers. For displaced employees, the solution could be a new job or a new career with companies in need of their talents.

A Fast-Changing World. The technological revolution has enhanced the quality of people's lives and has served to extend them as well. Although it was once feared that widespread use of computers would put people out of work, the opposite, in fact, has happened. Since 1982, 16 million new jobs have been created, and the number of people employed has reached a record 62 percent of the working-age population (Department of Labor, 1989). In some areas of the country more new jobs have been created than there are people to fill them.

Labor shortages are due largely to demographic factors. Together with an increase in technology demanding more skilled workers, there has been an increase in demand for products and service from a burgeoning consumer population—the baby boomers born in the 1940s and 1950s. At the same time, there is a smaller work force entering from the population born in the 1960s and 1970s, and a diminishing number of older workers remaining as their cohorts take early retirement.

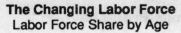

The Changing Labor Force
Labor Force Share by Age

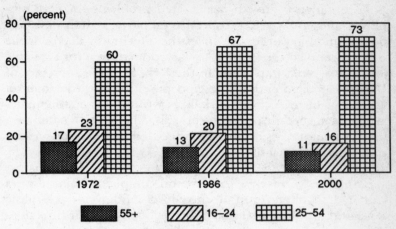

Source: Bureau of Labor Statistics

The chart above shows the decline in younger (16–24) and older workers (55-plus) as part of the nation's work force.

Company mergers have increased the number of large corporations and reduced the number of mid-sized companies. Dr. Marvin J. Cetron, president of Forecasting International Inc., writing in the *Journal of Career Planning and Development*, cites business deregulation as the cause of companies' merging and enlarging. Although companies have become fewer and bigger, many mid-sized businesses have disappeared, and a proliferation of small companies offering special services or products has survived. In this economic environment, the large technological and service industries need knowledgeable employees, but opportunities also exist for the small entrepreneur, temporary worker, consultant, or independent to find a niche. Some of the best openings are in the fields of technology, finance, health care, and hospitality.

Change Brings Problems

Technological growth has created problems for both employer and employee. Prospective employers often have difficulty finding workers to meet their technical needs, while new entrants to the job market lack preparation for available jobs. This "skills gap" cited in the Report of the Secretary of Labor (1989), notes that young people entering the job market are deficient in such basic skills as writing and mathematics as well as in specialized technical skills. The mismatch between jobs and employees available has focused national concern on problems of education.

Employers' Concerns. A common complaint of employers is that the current crop of entry-level employees lacks basic skills and attitudes that make for productivity: self-direction, initiative, and effective work habits. Some companies have formed a liaison with schools for improving educational preparation, whereas others are increasing their in-house training.

Technological developments have reduced the need for manual labor and increased the number of jobs that require skill and experience, making 50-plus professionals appropriate candidates for current employment needs. As changes in the workplace continue, the necessity for retraining of workers will increase. This is true of older workers as well.

The Carnegie Corporation Project on Aging has advocated education and retraining throughout a worker's lifetime. The Age Discrimination in Employment Act requires equal opportunity in training for employees of all ages. According to a study by B. Rosen and T.H. Jerdee ("Investing in the Older Worker," *Personnel Administrator*, 70 [Apr. 1989], pp. 70–74), self-paced and practical on-the-job training has worked best for companies that have implemented training programs for older as well as younger workers. Increased productivity, higher morale, and cost benefits are company advantages accruing to those who have adopted training programs. In their search for competent employees, some companies have turned to their own retirees, whereas others are seeking out older workers who are experienced in their fields. More and more companies are hiring 50-plus professionals to solve their labor problems.

Dr. Ken Dychtwald, author of "Age Wave: The Challenges and Opportunities of an Aging America" in *Training and Development Journal*, envisions the aging population as affecting company systems and changing workers' lives. No longer will retirement be routine at age 65. With increasingly better health and vitality among the new young, life spans extending into the eighties and nineties will be divided into several careers, with intermittent periods of schooling and sabbatical leaves. In the manner of universities, Wells Fargo since 1977 has provided "personal growth" sabbaticals to its employees of 10 years or more. The trend is for employers themselves to provide education in their specialties. International Business Machines asks its managers to take 40 hours of training per year; Bell Labs offers workshops and courses, not necessarily job-connected, to its employees. Baptist Medical Centers, a $300 million corporation, retrains and uses its older employees as mentors.

Importance of Education

The drop in manufacturing and increase in service industries calls for a higher level of skills—for computer systems analysts, scientists, and health professionals—and for a frequent change in skills as companies strive to compete with new technologies. Professional and managerial jobs are projected to rise by 6.7 million; in contrast, operative and laborer jobs will rise by much less, 450,000, according to the Department of Labor (1989). A greater percentage of jobs will require higher learning. For the employee to be successful in the labor market, this means learning technical skills, adjusting social skills, and revising both as new situations arise. Higher levels of math, language, and reasoning skills will be needed.

Enjoy Your Work Life. Job satisfaction has become more important to employees, whatever their age. Dr. David L. Birch, president of Cognetics Inc., has observed that for recent college graduates, control over their own lives and careers is paramount. This is also true for older workers: the chance to be of service, to feel useful, is most important. In the analysis of the basic needs of working people by the cognitive psychologist Abraham Maslow, a hierarchy of needs emerges.

They begin with the most basic: a person's physiological need for security and freedom from anxiety, to a need to belong, to have the friendship of others, to gain their respect and esteem, and finally to achieve what Maslow called "self-actualization," the realization of one's maximum potential. In terms of employment conditions, the salary provides the basic physiological necessities and more, whereas the workplace provides a sense of order, of belonging, of social acceptance, self-respect, and the chance to use one's abilities. These elements in a prospective job, then, should match fairly closely the job seeker's expectations of reward for work. For example:

1. The salary should satisfy the worker's needs and lifestyle; working conditions should be safe and pleasant.
2. The climate of the company, its organizational tone and method of operating, should be one in which the employee can function comfortably.
3. The employee's associates, immediate superior, and peers and subordinates, should be people with whom he or she can cooperate in a friendly yet businesslike way.
4. The tasks on the job should provide a sense of self-respect, the opportunity for self-expression, and a feeling of accomplishment.

Realistically, most workers achieve these levels of satisfaction to some degree. Usually, the first two are met and given no further thought; the need to socialize successfully, except where there is strong conflict within a department, is often achieved. But the last, self-actualization, is the most difficult and constantly sought-after goal. As people develop and gain knowledge and experience in their careers, however, the goal of professional achievement becomes increasingly important. To many retirees returning to the employment market, a sense of challenge and satisfaction can be the most important job element they seek. Corporate organizations also strive for their goals of profitability and success. A close fit of company and employee renders mutual satisfaction.

What Corporate America Wants

What is corporate America's attitude toward the 50-plus professional employee? Do companies value the experience, know-how, and skills such employees bring to today's marketplace? Will companies hire 50-plus professionals on a part- or full-time basis to meet their staffing needs now and in the future? If so, what kinds of skills and talents and experience are they seeking?

To answer these and other questions about mature workers, we conducted a survey and compiled a list of companies that hire 50-plus workers. The survey, conducted in conjunction with the writing of this book, indicated a strong interest of companies in the older worker as a source of experienced, reliable service.

For this study, the older worker was defined as 50-plus years of age. A brief questionnaire was mailed to 300 randomly selected members of the Employment Management Association, the largest organization of human resource managers in the United States. These personnel officers were asked to assess past performance of older employees, the future needs of their companies, and their current hiring practices with reference to the 50-plus worker.

Sixty-one of the 300 members contacted responded. The responses to each of the multiple-choice questions were tabulated, and the written comments to open questions were recorded. The respondents were categorized according to their business product or service, and information from their answers synthesized. Although their comments concerning mature employees were positive, it must be noted that the returned sample is self-selected. Companies that may discriminate against the older worker may not have returned the questionnaires.

A Broad Spectrum. The responses came from a national variety of industries, reflecting their interest in the older work force and membership in the Employment Management Association (EMA). The greatest number of responses came from the fields of science and technology, with financial services and others following in striking similarity to the list of fastest growing fields in the Occupational Outlook analysis of the U.S. Department of Labor (see the accompanying chart), with one exception. Missing from the list of the present study, but strong in the "Occupational Outlook Handbook," are the Health Diagnosing and Treatment professions, currently in short supply and predicted to continue so. The lack of responses from this group probably reflects its absence from membership in the EMA. Agriculture and forestry, fields in which older workers are strongly represented, are also absent from this survey.

The responding organizations were divided by type as follows:

Among the respondents, the support for hiring the older worker was very strong. Ninety-seven percent answered yes to the questions "Have the 50-plus workers you've hired done a good job for your company?" and "Do you foresee your company's hiring 50-plus workers in the future?" Not one respondent marked the space "Do not generally hire older workers." Many indicated, in a "comment" space provided, that they did not discriminate on the basis of age, that they sought to hire the best qualified people for filling job vacancies. In general, companies indicated they had no set hiring policy, except to obtain the best candidate for the job. Some

Type of Organization	Percentage of Total Response
Scientific, technology, computer	25%
Finance and insurance	19%
Chemical and pharmaceutical	15%
Manufacturing	14%
Industrial products, energy	12%
Hospitality and food service	7%
Public institutions, education	3%
Others, miscellaneous	5%

Source: EMA

companies noted they had outreach programs directed toward the older worker.

"Does your company hire people who are 50 years old, or older?" the first question asked, had as responses, "Never," 0; "Sometimes," 58%; "Frequently," 42%.

"If you do hire mature workers, at what level are they employed?" was answered with "Entry level," 47%; "Experienced in your field," 93%.

The larger than 100 percent total resulted because some companies marked both choices, indicating they hired older workers at both entry and experienced levels. Comments included by the respondents supported the 93 percent companies' desire for workers with experience and indicated that hires were on a senior and high-technology level.

Do You Have the Required Skills?

Directed at ascertaining the types of jobs available to the mature hiree, the question "What kind of jobs do the mature workers most often fill?" gets these answers: "Clerical, secretarial," 56%; "Technical," 66%; "Managerial," 63%; and "Professional," 73%; indicated a preponderance of hiring at the technical, managerial, and professional levels, depending on the type of company and its needs. The variety of skills called for related to the special product or service of the company.

What Companies Seek. When asked about skills sought, companies responded with the particular needs of their businesses. Among those most frequently sought were the following:

Communication skills
Problem-solving skills
Sales, customer service
Banking experience
Technical skills
Scientific knowledge
Accuracy, accounting
Sales experience
Experience in the industry (whatever it happened to be)
Computer-related skills: engineering, design, manufacturing, peripherals
Finance, math skills
Hospitality experience
Marketing

Science and technology, banking, and manufacturing industries led in responding and requiring particular skills suited to their industries. Although they were not asked about the personal qualities of employees, apparently it was important to human resource managers, because their comments included the personal qualities they sought in an employee. Here are the qualities they cited as important:

Positive attitude
Steady personality
Ability to learn
High energy

Intelligence
Good work ethic, commitment

A space was left at the end of the questionnaire for comments from the respondent. Many took the time to lace their information with personal anecdotes; others provided printed material that described their company's operations and employment opportunities.

What Companies Say. A Pennsylvania bank reported that it actively recruited in the senior market, winning a Champion of Older Workers Award from the state of Pennsylvania. It had hired more people over 55 than any other medium-sized employer in the state.

Another bank: We "consider all applicants equally without regard to age. We have filled positions in all areas of our company with individuals over the age of 50."

A Japanese automobile company: "We view 'over 50' employees as extremely valuable to our organization. We have not targeted this group for specific jobs, but we hire older Americans for any jobs."

An electrical technology company: "We utilize 50-plus workers and retirees as consultants, i.e., in technology, sales, advertising."

Communications equipment manufacturer: "We consistently have looked at skill sets, never the age factor."

Hospitality organization: "As the work force ages, we see ourselves hiring more older workers, both in our field operations and in our staff positions."

A computer company: "We frequently offer positions to experienced, senior people. Two-thirds of our sales work force in the western U.S. are over the age of 40. Many of these are over 50. . . . We see a true value in experienced people calling on major clientele."

The hospitality industry, whose usual work force of teenage and young adults has shrunk, has had to rethink its employment strategies, as have many other industries today. As the industry continues to grow, it is turning increasingly to an older population that could help meet its staffing needs. The American Hotel and Motel Association invites older individuals to apply for work. Days Inns recruits among senior citizens, having found them to be ideal employees. At Hampton Inns, mature employees are highly valued for their excellent skills in dealing with people.

Tapping the Older Worker. The food service industry, which has traditionally relied on young recruits, is also tapping the senior population for help. Taco Bell's offers of part- and full-time entry-level jobs include consideration and information about Social Security benefits. With a special "McMasters" program, McDonald's recruits older workers and provides them with training and flexible work schedules. By directing its recruiting drive toward older workers, Naugles, a West Coast restaurant chain, more than tripled its employee retention rate. Other companies that have programs for older workers are Arby's, Kentucky Fried Chicken, and Wendy's. Among the restaurants interested in the older worker are Marriott and General Mills.

In finance, banking, and insurance, businesses in which physical dexterity is inconsequential, the mature employee's work life is extended. At Travelers Companies, retirees are hired on a part-time or temporary basis. The company keeps a working list—called a "job bank"—of former employees who are utilized according to company needs and employee availability. When the Great American First Savings Bank of San Diego began hiring older people as tellers, its turnover rate was drastically reduced. The banking industry also values experience in its employees. Sun Bank, N.A. recruits through local senior citizens' agencies, and The Provident Bank in Philadelphia actively recruits in the senior market.

Cashing In on Needed Skills

Senior workers who have accumulated a wealth of business and industrial skills are invaluable in their special fields. After they have retired, they are often asked to come back, and some companies, to close the skills gap in their ranks, offer gradual retirement and part-time return deals to their employees. Varian Associates, a high-tech manufacturer, has a retirement transition program that permits employees to reduce their work hours before taking full retirement. One worker, a highly specialized equipment tester at the company, opted for full retirement and then decided he didn't like it. In his late sixties he returned to the company, where he now works several days a week. Varian's program benefits the company and its skilled employees, permitting them the opportunity to work and to enjoy leisure time.

Grumman, the Long Island defense contractor, has a phased retirement program, as well as a policy of rehiring those who wish to return. Its retention of experienced employees permits the company to gear up quickly for production, when it is awarded a new contract. At Polaroid Corporation, workers may take up to six months of unpaid leave to try retirement before making a final decision. These programs, though few in number, serve to retain the skilled senior employee.

Summary

Social and economic changes are favorable for the over-50 job market. Population growth followed by decline has created a demand for workers. Technological developments call for workers with special knowledge and skills. Additionally, jobs for unskilled and entry-level employees are in demand, but these offer low pay.

Leading the field in employment opportunities are technology, science, and health care. The need for financial services, marketing, and sales help on all levels is increasing.

Hospitality and restaurant industries are also in dire need of employees. Service and manufacturing industries need professional, technical, and administrative help, including clerical workers.

Many advantages accrue to the companies that engage older workers: a more efficient and productive work force, higher employee morale and loyalty, and a stable and reliable work force.

Most companies seek employees with experience in their fields, and many top companies have programs designed to attract and retain older workers: part-time and flexible hours, shared jobs, phased retirement, retiree job banks, job redesign and training, and sabbatical leaves.

Companies That Hire Over-50 Workers

Adolph Coors Co.
311 10th St.
Golden, CO 80401

Boehringer Ingelheim
Pharmaceutical Inc.
90 East Ridge
P.O. Box 369
Ridgefield, CT 06877

Chase Lincoln First Bank
One Lincoln First Square
Rochester, NY 14643

Chivas Products Ltd.
13177 Nantucket
Sterling Height, MI 48078

Cubic Corp.
9333 Balboa Ave.
San Diego, 92123

A. Duda & Sons Inc.
P.O. Box 257
Ovieda, FL 32765

General Instrument Corp.
2355 W. Chandler Blvd.
Chandler, AZ 85224

Giant Food Inc.
P.O. Box 1804
D549
Washington, DC 20013

Mack Trucks Inc.
Box M
Allentown, PA 18105

Pacific Concept Systems Inc.
dba Emil Villa's Restaurants
1200 Lakeshore Ave.
Oakland, CA 96606-1627

Host International Inc.
1 Marriott Dr.
Washington, DC 20058

Stanford University
Old Pavilion
Stanford, CA 94305

Store 24, Inc.
184 Riverview Ave.
Waltham, MA 02254

The following companies were cited in The Conference Board's "Job Banks for Retirees" report as ones that utilize the skills of 50-plus workers.

The Aerospace Corp.
2350 E. El Segundo Blvd.
MS/MI 448
El Segundo, CA 90245

Ameritrust Co.
900 Euclid Ave.
Cleveland, OH 44101

Cigna Corp.
One Logan Sq.
Philadelphia, PA 19103

Combustion Engineering Inc.
900 Long Ridge Rd., Box 9308
Stamford, CT 06904

Corning Inc.
Houghton Pk.
Corning, NY 14831

Dayton-Hudson Inc.
777 Nicollet Mall
Minneapolis, MN 55402

Digital Equipment Corp.
111 Powdermill Rd.
Maynard, MA 01754

General Mills Inc.
One General Mills Blvd.
Minneapolis, MN 55426

Grumman Corp.
1111 Stewart Ave.
Bethpage, NY 11714

Harris Trust & Savings Bank
P.O. Box 755
Chicago, IL 60690

Honeywell Inc.
Honeywell Plaza
Minneapolis, MN 55408

IBM
Old Orchard Rd.
Armonk, NY 10504

J.C. Penney Co. Inc.
14841 N. Dallas Pkway.
Dallas, TX 75240

Motorola Inc.
1303 E. Algonquin Rd.
Schaumburg, IL 60196

Polaroid Corp.
549 Technology Square
Cambridge, MA 02139

Pillsbury Co.
200 S. 6th St.
Minneapolis, MN 55402

Sovran Bank
One Commerce Pl.
Nashville, TN. 37219

3M
St. Paul, MN 55144-1000

Union Carbide Corp.
39 Old Ridgebury Rd.
Danbury, CT 06817

Varian Associates
611 Hansen Way
Palo Alto, CA 94303

Wells Fargo Bank, NA
464 California St.
San Francisco, CA 94163

The Travelers Corp.
One Tower Sq.
Hartford, CT 06183

CHAPTER 13

For Entrepreneurs Only

This is the age of the entrepreneur, a time when one of the most popular American dreams is to own and operate a business. The reason: You are your own boss—you don't have to take orders from anyone. In short, you have the freedom to do what you want, come and go as you please, and make all the important decisions. And the money you earn is yours. It sounds too good to be true.

It is too good to be true. It's not easy to start and run a business, and it is important for would-be entrepreneurs to separate hopes from reality. Despite all the ballyhoo about starting a business and being financially independent, the entrepreneurial road can be a treacherous one for persons of any age who don't know how to avoid its many potholes. Though there are advantages, operating a business requires knowledge, dedication, time, effort, skill, and good planning and management. Many people who do plunge into the entrepreneurial pool do not have the managerial know-how nor the perseverance necessary to succeed. If you are considering this road, look before you take the risky leap to what could be financial ruin. This is especially true for the 50-plus professional.

Yet small business is one of the foundations of the U.S.

economy. Small business generated the majority of new jobs in the United States between 1980 and 1986. In 1989, the United States had a total of 5 million business companies. Of this number, all were small businesses except for 12,000. In addition, the United States also had 15.9 million nonfarm, self-employed proprietors in 1989. Proprietorship, or small business income, increased from $287.5 billion in 1986 to $316 billion in 1987, a 9.9 percent increase.

According to Department of Commerce data, in 1982 there were 2.6 million women-owned businesses and 843,000 minority-owned businesses. By 1987, the number of women-owned sole proprietorships had risen to 4.1 million, a 57 percent increase since 1982. Of the 10.6 million jobs created in the United States between 1980 and 1986, 6.6 million were in small business, a job contribution share of 63.5 percent.

The fastest growing segment of entrepreneurs is women. According to the Small Business Administration, women comprise more than 50 percent of the U.S. population and currently own about 30 percent of the nation's businesses. Many women and minorities go into business for themselves when they realize they have little or no chance of moving into senior corporate management.

The number of black-owned companies in the United States increased from 308,000 in 1982 to 424,000 in 1987, a 38 percent rise, according to a survey by the Commerce Department's Census Bureau. About 3 percent of the nation's businesses were black-owned in 1987.

The major cause of most small business failures is poor management, according to SBA statistics; therefore proper preparation and knowledge are important. If you are determined to start and operate a small business, the best advice is to choose a field you know. Then, if you're still determined to pursue the entrepreneurial road, here are some cold facts you need to consider.

Statistics to Ponder

Let's look at these facts and some startling statistics on the subject from Donald Sexton, professor of management and human resources at Ohio State University and the William H. Davis chair holder, at the American Free Enterprise System. According to Sexton:

- Sixty percent of all U.S. businesses bring in a gross revenue of $25,000 a year or less.
- Ninety percent of all U.S. businesses have gross sales of $100,000 a year or less and employ fewer than five people.
- The vast majority of businesses that start with $25,000 their first year don't grow. Five to six years later, their sales are still $25,000 a year.
- Usually, if the owner has a plan and a vision at the start, he or she will see growth.
- Fewer than 10 percent become big businesses.
- About 94 to 96 percent of U.S. businesses have less than a million dollars in sales.
- Fewer than 650,000 U.S. businesses are actually growing and creating new jobs. And the top 10 percent of those businesses are generating about 93 percent of all new jobs.
- The future of most businesses, depending on where they're positioned, is determined at the time they start.

No Guarantees. These facts and figures dramatically demonstrate that starting a business does not automatically put you on the road to riches. In fact, according to Dun & Bradstreet, in the first five years or less, 51.8 percent of all new businesses fail. Getting started in business requires an enormous amount of know-how and hard work by the entrepreneur. The more a person knows about the market and the business he or she plans to enter, the better the chances of success.

It's one thing to talk about being an entrepreneur, it's something else to take the plunge and face reality. Bud Clarke did when he started his communications and design company, now called Clarke-Thompson. The company designs promotional material for magazines and also designs and produces magazines. It also does corporate image work and prepares posters and in-store (point-of-purchase) promotions in bookstores.

Even though he had prepared well for his launch and had experience and contacts in his chosen business when he started, Clarke says, "There was tremendous apprehension, even though I had a number of jobs lined up."

Past Experience Invaluable

Clarke, an art director and graphic designer at a major publishing company in New York City, had been responsible for the graphics of three magazines. After 12 successful years with the company, and a well-earned reputation for creativity, he felt his career was "not going the way I wanted it.

"The time spent at the publishing company was invaluable, especially the contacts I made," says Clarke. "I worked with three publishers who are now with different magazines—and all three are now Clarke-Thompson accounts." Clarke's initial apprehension made him so aggressive about getting clients that within six months of starting the business he had to take on a full-time assistant, Pat Thompson, who became his partner.

Clarke's advice to would-be entrepreneurs: "Keep your staff and company as lean as possible, and use freelancers to help over the rough spots. Hire competent people. This is especially important for a small company." He and Thompson worked hard to develop a relaxed office atmosphere in which staffers are congenial and work well together. "Every Tuesday," says Clarke, "our staff meets to review new ideas and discuss every account, where we are and where we're going. Then we have 'show and tell,' where everyone brings in samples of outstanding work done by other firms. We keep our people as informed as possible. It's good business."

You Must Be Involved. Careful, hands-on management is essential, says Clarke. He tells how he had to dismiss a book-keeper who didn't keep accurate records and gave inaccurate financial reports, which resulted in the company's spending too much money. Clarke says he and Thompson had to learn when and how to do the selling, and not to oversell. They had to estimate the work flow and the size of the business operation to minimize having to hire extra help. A partner makes it a lot easier to share the burdens and the difficult problems, he says.

But it was a tough struggle financially, for Clarke, who has been in business nine years and did not show a profit until the fifth year. During the first five years, Clarke-Thompson kept reinvesting in the business, especially in computers. "You are going to work harder than you ever worked before," says Clarke, "It's ongoing. You can never let up, but the rewards are absolutely worth it in terms of self-satisfaction."

How to Get Started

The first step in becoming an entrepreneur is to determine the type and nature of the business. The entrepreneur who has the best chance of succeeding should have some business experience and go into a business with which he or she is familiar.

And then you have to ask questions. Is there a need for the type of business you're proposing? Are you suited to running such a business? Does it involve a product? If so, how will you produce it? Where and how will you distribute this product? Are there competitors making a similar product? Do you have financing to produce the product?

Do you have people/staff to help you? And most important, do you have the managerial skills and market savvy to make your product a success? Do you have access to professionals like a financial adviser, legal counsel, and marketing expert to whom you can go for counsel before you make decisions that may adversely affect your business?

As a would-be entrepreneur, you have to ask yourself hard and specific questions. For example, "What do I know about the business I'm going into? Have I had similar experience?" Similar experience makes it easier to launch a successful enterprise. Will I have enough cash flow to sustain me in a start-up operation? Can I get financing if I need it? Most important, am I willing to put in the long hours and hard work necessary to succeed?

The Start of a Business Journey

If your answer to these questions is yes, the next step is to develop a detailed written plan, including the goals you want to achieve. You must also have the right kind of business ownership—sole proprietorship, owned by one individual—is the most common. Then you need the necessary licenses and permits that may be required from city, county, and state agencies. A lawyer versed in business law will help you with the legal requirements. The key to success is to be prepared. But as in love, war, and business there are no guarantees for success.

An Expert's Advice. Joseph R. Mancuso, president of the Center for Entrepreneurial Management in New York City, looks on an entrepreneurial venture as the beginning of a journey. And he offers three rules that must adhered to if would-be entrepreneurs expect to be successful.

- Rule 1. "Write a business plan," says Mancuso. "Put it on paper. It's like taking a trip. You get on the highway and follow road signs. It's better to look at a map, plot your trip, and save yourself a lot of trouble." After you've written your business plan, says Mancuso, show it to friends and business acquaintances. The purpose: to have them critique it, to make it better, to look for short-cuts, to update and improve it. Work on the plan until you are satisfied with it and then follow your own directions.

- Rule 2. Don't go it alone. You may be the smartest person in the world, says Mancuso, but you need someone who is experienced, who knows the ropes, like an accountant, a banker, or a lawyer who knows the entrepreneurial pitfalls to avoid.
- Rule 3. Keep your customer in mind throughout the process. Mancuso says entrepreneurs are too often wrapped up in office procedures, their bank accounts, and literature, and they forget about the customer.

Keep an Eye on Cash Flow

Another pitfall is running out of money too fast. This is a common problem, says Mancuso, and it provides the acid test. Those who run out of money but manage to keep their businesses going are successful; those who don't, fail. Being an entrepreneur is not a casual activity, says Mancuso. If you treat it that way, you are not going to succeed.

Bill Bygrave, academic coordinator for entrepreneurship at Babson College, offers another warning to the typical over-50 entrepreneur, who has worked 20 or 30 years with a major corporation, and who enjoys a nice income with stock options, fringe benefits, health insurance, pension plan, and four-weeks' vacation. "That person," says Bygrave, "suddenly goes haywire, gets fed up, wants to make a fortune, and reads all the right magazines for the wrong reasons. We tend to overemphasize the ones who make it, and not tell enough about those that failed and why."

Look Before You Leap. "Weigh carefully giving up a job with good wages and benefits," advises Bygrave. "New entrepreneurs always face slim years and positive cash flow usually doesn't occur for three or four years. Unprepared entrepreneurs risk their savings, their homes, and even their marriages when they tread into the dangerous and difficult shoals of business."

Are entrepreneurs a different breed? Do they have different characteristics that set them apart from other people? Boston University's Dr. David McClelland advises aspiring entrepreneurs to do a self-assessment. "Do you have the right personality?" he asks. "If not, don't."

Dr. McClelland says he found back in 1953 that people high in achievement motivation, people essentially interested in doing things better than they have been done before, people motivated to do things more efficiently and to find new ways of doing things well, make the best entrepreneurs. An entrepreneur is a different type of personality than a manager, and many managers make lousy entrepreneurs, he says.

If you have in the past been successful in selling, tried new and faster ways to get things done, are an observer of what goes on around you, and want to do something well as long as you are in control, you have the makings of an entrepreneur, according to Dr. McCelland.

Where to Get Help

If you've made up your mind to go for it, a number of organizations are available to help. Start with the Small Business Administration. It has more than 100 offices and a staff of approximiately 3,700 employees throughout the United States. The SBA helps businesses become more efficient and profitable through a number of advisory, training, and educational services. In addition, it has an extensive network of volunteers, colleges and universities, and other private and public organizations.

The SBA is divided into three operational levels: the central office in Washington, D.C.; regional offices in 10 major cities—Boston, New York, Philadelphia, Atlanta, Chicago, Dallas, Kansas City, Denver, San Francisco, and Seattle. Each region encompasses several states. District offices are located throughout the United States, and these offices are the contact points for small businesses needing information and assistance.

Most small, independent businesses are eligible for SBA assistance. To be eligible for SBA loans and other assistance, a business must meet a size standard set by the agency. Information is available from any SBA office around the country.

A good way to start your quest for information is to call the Small Business Answer Desk (800-827-5722) in Washington, D.C. It is set up to answer callers' questions about how to start and manage a business, where to get financing, and provide other information required to operate and expand a business.

Helping women become successful entrepreneurs is a major goal of SBA. Women comprise more than half of the U.S. population and currently own more than 25 percent of its businesses. It makes a special effort to assist women, minorities, the handicapped, and veterans to start and stay in business because of the unusual difficulties they face. In 1983, SBA began organizing a series of business training seminars and workshops for women business owners and for women who want to start a small business.

The Key Ingredient for Success. In a recent nationwide attitude survey on successful women entrepreneurs conducted by Avon Products Inc., a cosmetics company headquartered in New York City, the most important quality given for entrepreneurial success was perseverance (50 percent). Twenty-nine percent of the female entrepreneurs said they derive far more satisfaction from offering a quality product or service than from sales growth or personal income. And 26 percent said they enjoyed satisfaction that comes from having more control over their lives.

The women in the Avon Report do not consider lack of business skills as the major obstacle to business, but they do believe that acquiring competence in various business activities, such as management and marketing, are crucial to entrepreneurial success. When asked to name the most satisfying aspects of business ownership, only 2 percent said "personal income." Thirty-eight percent defined success in terms of happiness or self-fulfillment, whereas only 12 percent measured it in sales growth and profit.

Help for Minorities. SBA also offers special programs to assist members of minority groups who want to start a small business or expand an existing one. In this effort, SBA has combined its programs with those of private industry, banks, communities, and other federal agencies. The agency also makes loans available to physically handicapped small business owners and private nonprofit organizations that employ handicapped persons.

SBA's Business Development Program is extensive and diversified. It includes free individual counseling, courses, conferences, workshops, problem clinics, and a wide range of publications. Many of these publications are free, and charges are nominal for those that are not.

Counseling is provided by the SBA Development Staff: the Service Corps of Retired Executives (SCORE), and its corollary organization of active businesspersons, the Active Corps of Executives (ACE), and numerous professional associations. SCORE and ACE help small business executives solve their operating problems through one-on-one counseling.

A nationwide organization, SCORE offers management counseling and training through 13,000 retired volunteers with extensive business experience and special skills; the average SCORE counselor has 35 years of business experience. SCORE operates out of SBA offices and in more than 700 other locations. Their counsel is free and confidential. A small fee is charged for specialized services. If the SCORE counselor feels you are not ready to go into business, he or she will tell you. The counselor will also work with a new applicant as long as necessary.

Where to Get Counseling. Small Business Institutes (SBIs) organized through SBA are found on approximately 500 university and college campuses. At each SBI, senior and graduate students at schools of business administration and their faculty advisers provide on-site management counseling. Students are guided by the faculty advisers and SBA management assistance experts and receive academic credit for their work.

Small Business Development Centers (SBDCs) provide managerial and technical help through the private sector, through university facilities, and through local state and federal agencies. These organizations access technical help, research studies, and other types of specialized assistance of value to small businesses. The centers are generally located in academic institutions and provide individual counseling and practical training for small business owners.

The federal government offers a broad range of services to would-be entrepreneurs. Knowing the type of business you want to start and its goals, however, will result in faster service when you seek help or information from the SBA.

An excellent source of business information for women is the American Women's Economic Development Corps (AWED) in New York City. During the past few years, AWED has helped more than 72,000 women who have attended training courses, received individual counseling, and participated in network meetings, conferences, and lectures. The courses include practical information about advertising, marketing, record keeping, sales, insurance, law, and finance.

How Do You Stack Up As an Entrepreneur?

Do you have what it takes to make it successfully on your own? Not sure? Take this quiz to see how you measure up to 2,500 entrepreneurs surveyed by the New York–based Center for Entrepreneurial Management.

The quiz is designed to rate you against the personality profile of the typical entrepreneur, so don't be discouraged if you do not score well, cautions CEM President Joseph R. Mancuso.

1. How were your parents employed?
    a. Both worked and were self-employed for most of their working lives
    b. Both worked and were self-employed for some part of their working lives
    c. One parent was self-employed for most of his or her working life
    d. One parent was self-employed at some point in his or her working life
    e. Neither parent was ever self-employed

2. Have you ever been fired from a job?
    a. Yes, more than once
    b. Yes, once
    c. No

3. Are you an immigrant, or were your parents or grandparents immigrants?
    a. I was born outside the U.S.
    b. One or both of my parents were born outside the U.S.
    c. At least one of my grandparents was born outside the U.S.
    d. Does not apply

4. Your work career has been:
    a. Primarily in small business (under 100 employees)
    b. Primarily in medium-sized business (100 to 500 employees)
    c. Primarily in big business (more than 500 employees)

5. Have you operated any businesses before turning 20?
    a. Many
    b. A few
    c. None

6. What is your present age?
   a. 20 or younger
   b. 21–30
   c. 31–40
   d. 41–50
   e. 51 or older

7. You are the _____ child in the family.
   a. Oldest
   b. Middle
   c. Youngest
   d. Other

8. You are:
   a. Married
   b. Divorced
   c. Single

9. Your highest level of formal education is:
   a. Some high school
   b. High school diploma
   c. Bachelor's degree
   d. Master's degree
   e. Doctor's degree

10. What is your primary motivation in starting a business?
    a. To make money
    b. I don't like working for someone else
    c. To be famous
    d. As an outlet for excess energy

11. Your relationship with the parent who provided most of
    your family's income was:
    a. Strained
    b. Comfortable
    c. Competitive
    d. Nonexistent

12. If you could choose between working hard and working smart, you would:
    a. Work hard
    b. Work smart
    c. Both

13. On whom do you rely for critical management advice?
    a. Internal management teams
    b. External management professionals
    c. External financial professionals
    d. No one except myself

14. If you were at the racetrack, which of these would you bet on?
    a. The daily double—a chance to make a killing
    b. A 10-to-1 shot
    c. A 3-to-1 shot
    d. The 2-to-1 favorite

15. The only ingredient that is both necessary and sufficient for starting a business is:
    a. Money
    b. Customers
    c. An idea or product
    d. Motivation and hard work

16. If you were an advanced tennis player and had a chance to play a top pro like Jimmy Connors, you would:
    a. Turn it down because he could easily beat you
    b. Accept the challenge, but not bet any money on it
    c. Bet a week's pay that you would win
    d. Get odds, bet a fortune, and try for an upset

17. You tend to "fall in love" too quickly with:
    a. New product ideas
    b. New employees
    c. New manufacturing ideas

    d. New financial plans
    e. All of the above

18. Which of the following personality types is best suited to be your right-hand person?
    a. Bright and energetic
    b. Bright and lazy
    c. Dumb and energetic

19. You accomplish tasks better because:
    a. You are always on time
    b. You are super-organized
    c. You keep good records

20. You hate to discuss:
    a. Problems involving employees
    b. Signing expense accounts
    c. New management practices
    d. The future of the business

21. Given a choice, you would prefer:
    a. Rolling dice with a 1-in-3 chance of winning
    b. Working on a problem with a 1-in-3 chance of solving it in the allocated time

22. If you could choose between the following competitive professions, it would be:
    a. Professional golf
    b. Sales
    c. Personnel counseling
    d. Teaching

23. If you had to choose between working with a partner who is a close friend, and working with a stranger who is an expert in your field, you would choose:
    a. The close friend
    b. The expert

24. You enjoy being with people:
    a. When you have something meaningful to do
    b. When you can do something new and different
    c. Even when you have nothing planned

25. In business situations that demand action, clarifying who is in charge will help produce results.
    a. Agree
    b. Agree, with reservations
    c. Disagree

26. In playing a competitive game, you are concerned with:
    a. How well you play
    b. Winning or losing
    c. Both of the above
    d. Neither of the above

Scoring

Find the score for each of your answers below, and add up all the points to see how you rate as a potential entrepreneur.

```
 1. a = 10   b = 5    c = 5    d = 2   e = 0
 2. a = 10   b = 7    c = 0
 3. a =  5   b = 4    c = 3    d = 0
 4. a = 10   b = 5    c = 0
 5. a = 10   b = 7    c = 0
 6. a = 0    b = 8    c = 10   d = 5   e = 2
 7. a = 15   b = 2    c = 0    d = 0
 8. a = 10   b = 2    c = 2
 9. a = 2    b = 3    c = 10   d = 8   e = 4
10. a = 0    b = 15   c = 0    d = 0
11. a = 10   b = 5    c = 10   d = 5
12. a = 0    b = 5    c = 10
13. a = 0    b = 10   c = 0    d = 5
14. a = 0    b = 2    c = 10   d = 3
15. a = 0    b = 10   c = 0    d = 0
16. a = 0    b = 10   c = 3    d = 0
```

17. a = 5   b = 5   c = 5   d = 5   e = 15
18. a = 2   b = 10   c = 0
19. a = 5   b = 15   c = 5
20. a = 8   b = 10   c = 0   d = 0
21. a = 0   b = 15
22. a = 3   b = 10   c = 0   d = 0
23. a = 0   b = 10
24. a = 3   b = 3   c = 10
25. a = 10   b = 2   c = 0
26. a = 8   b = 10   c = 15   d = 0

Your Entrepreneurial Profile

Total Score	Analysis
235–285	Successful Entrepreneur. You can start multiple businesses successfully.
200–234	Entrepreneur. You can start one business successfully.
185–199	Latent Entrepreneur. You have always wanted to start a business.
170–184	Potential Entrepreneur. You have the ability but have not yet begun thinking about starting a business.
155–169	Borderline Entrepreneur. You have no qualifications but could still be in the running with a lot of training.
Below 154	Hired Hand.

The average score for the entrepreneurs in the CEM study is 239. Most of those surveyed come from homes where one parent was self-employed for most of his or her working life. Nearly 60% were the oldest child in their family, and more than 75% were married. About 56% said they wanted to start a business because they did not like working for anyone else.

A P P E N D I X E S :

Organizations That Can Help

The organizations listed in the following appendixes include career development sources, the 40 Plus Clubs, a list of employment agencies that cater to women and minorities, federal and state government employment centers, the National Urban League, and other organizations that offer advice for minorities. There are tremendous resources here for the over-50 job hunter. Don't overlook them. One of these agencies could lead you to the job you want.

Appendix I
Catalyst
"Catalyst does not do career counseling but works directly with corporate policy makers in behalf of women's leadership development," according to Vivian Todini, director of public relations. It is a national research and advisory organization.

Catalyst makes available a career-publication brochure. Write Catalyst for a copy of this brochure at 250 Park Avenue South, New York, NY 10003-1459.

Appendix II
Forty Plus
Founded in 1939, Forty Plus of New York Inc. was the first organization of its kind in the United States. The unique concept of running a self-help organization for unemployed executives who are 40 years old or more subsequently led to the founding of other Forty Plus operations throughout the country. Currently there are 16 Forty-Plus organizations, all separate entities, operating independently, but engaged in an informal network, according to New York's Forty Plus public relations chairperson.

According to the chairperson, "Forty Plus was founded to assist laid-off executives in their job search in the aftermath of a corporate takeover. In today's environment of increased mergers and buyouts, the need is greater than ever. In effect, Forty Plus is the original outplacement agency.

"The organization is structured similar to a regular corporation. The members staff all positions, volunteering two days of service weekly to help the other members find jobs. We have flourished for 50 years."

Forty Plus is a nonprofit, self-help, member-managed organization counseling unemployed executives in their job search. There are no paid employees. Members accept the responsibility to operate the organization as a condition for membership. This includes a volunteer Board of Directors.

Forty Plus has two types of members—Active (unemployed and Associates [alumni]). Active members are, without exception, temporarily unemployed, highly qualified and experienced executives. The number of Active members fluctuates as members find jobs and new members join. Forty Plus members who get jobs are invited to become associates. They receive newsletters and other communications to keep them informed about Forty Plus activities. They can continue to be screened for new jobs and may return to active membership at any time without paying a membership fee. Associates are obliged to pay an annual fee of $50. After six years of dues payments the Associate becomes a life member with no further dues. The organization has approximately 1,300 loyal alumni.

Forty Plus membership requires a one-time fee, which varies somewhat according to location. New York's Forty Plus charges $850—$100 is paid with the application and $750 upon becoming a member. A deferred plan is available for an additional $50. Any fee of $50 or more may be charged to Visa or Mastercard. In addition, members pay $6 per week as long as they are active. In a recent calendar year 99 members found new positions, often equal or superior to their previous positions. The average age was 52-plus. Salaries averaged $45,000 to $50,000, and ranged to $150,000. Length of stay for an active member averaged three to seven months. The success of members in finding jobs, according to Forty Plus of New York, is directly related to their commitment to the program.

The organization provides an extensive package consisting of peer support, job search strategy, member networking, career guidance, PC training, interviewing techniques, and how to reenter the job market. Forty Plus is a base of operations to conduct a job search—an office with telephone answering service, computers, training opportunities, and peer support.

Forty Plus receives regular listings and direct requests from employers seeking experienced personnel. A committee works continuously to obtain job orders from businesses, nonprofit agencies, and recruiters. A computerized talent bank matches members' qualifications to a job order and résumés are sent immediately. There are no placement fees to an employer or member.

Small groups meet regularly to discuss each other's job search strategies and activities. In addition, employed Associate members regularly assist Active members in securing jobs.

The membership committee reviews a candidate's qualifications, and upon its recommendation the candidate is voted into the organization by the membership. There is no discrimination on the basis of sex, race, or religion.

The requirements for membership are:

- Have recently held an executive or professional position with documented responsibilities and salary.
- Submit six references from former employers and business associates that are carefully checked.
- Be a U.S. citizen or permanent resident.
- Be at least 40 years of age, unemployed and actively seeking employment.
- Agree to devote time for the cooperative operation of the organization.

Some Forty Plus groups serve members from other states who can commute to the Metro area office: New York serves New York, New Jersey, and Connecticut; Philadelphia serves Pennsylvania, southern New Jersey, and Delaware; Chicago serves Illinois, Indiana, Iowa, and Wisconsin; Washington, DC, serves the District, Maryland, and Virginia. Forty Plus of Puget Sound, Seattle, has been chartered and expects to be operating around the latter part of 1991. The temporary contact is Jane McCormmach (206-682-2780).

Here is a list of the 16 Forty Plus organizations throughout the country, including address and telephone numbers.

FORTY PLUS ORGANIZATIONS ACROSS THE COUNTRY

CALIFORNIA

Forty Plus of No. California
7440 Lockheed Street
Oakland, CA 94603
415-430-2400

Forty Plus of So. California
3450 Wilshire Boulevard
Los Angeles, CA 90010
213-388-2301

Orange County Division
23151 Verduga Drive   #114
Laguna Hills, CA 92653
714-581-7990

COLORADO

Forty Plus of Colorado
639 East 18th Avenue
Denver, CO 80203
303-830-3040

Northern Division
3840 South Mason Street
Fort Collins, CO 80525
303-223-2470   Ext. 261

Southern Division
2555 Airport Road
Colorado Springs, CO 80910
303-473-6220   Ext. 271

DISTRICT OF COLUMBIA

Forty Plus of Greater
  Washington
1718 P Street NW
Washington, DC 20036
202-387-1562

HAWAII

Forty Plus of Hawaii
126 Queen Street   #227
Honolulu, HI 96813
808-531-0896

ILLINOIS

Forty Plus of Chicago
53 West Jackson Boulevard
Chicago, IL 60604
312-922-0285

NEW YORK

Forty Plus of Buffalo
701 Seneca Street
Buffalo, NY 14210
716-856-0491

Forty Plus of New York
15 Park Row
New York, NY 10038
212-233-6086

OHIO

Forty Plus of Central Ohio
1700 Arlingate Drive
Columbus, OH 43328
614-275-0040

PENNSYLVANIA

Forty Plus of Philadelphia
1218 Chestnut Street
Philadelphia, PA 19107
215-923-2074

TEXAS

Forty Plus of Dallas
13601 Preston Road   #402
Dallas, TX 75240
214-991-9917

Forty Plus of Houston
3935 Westheimer   #205
Houston, TX 77027
713-850-7830

UTAH

Forty Plus of Utah
1234 Main Street
Salt Lake City, UT 84117
801-533-2191

Appendix III
A Working List of Employment Agencies/Search Firms for Minorities and Women

CALIFORNIA

The Zivic Group, Inc.
1131 N. Brand Blvd.
Glendale, CA 91202
818-242-1835
Search Firm.
Minorities and women at managerial levels.

Jobs for Progress, Inc.
SER South Bay
3800 El Segundo Blvd., Suite 204
Hawthorne, CA 90250
213-970-0826
Search Firm/Employment Agency.
Minorities and women in administrative, blue collar, dp, finance/accounting, managerial, sales and technical positions.

Career Connection
10411 Woodbine
Los Angeles, CA 90034
213-202-8787
Search Firm.
Women in sales positions.

PDQ Personnel Services, Inc.
5900 Wilshire Blvd., Suite 700
Los Angeles, CA 90036
213-938-3933
Employment Agency.
Minorities and women in administrative, clerical, finance/ accounting, managerial, and sales positions.

PDQ Personnel Services, Inc.
888 S. Figueroa, #760
Los Angeles, CA 90017
213-627-4447
Employment Agency.
Minorities and women in administrative, clerical, finance/ accounting, managerial, and sales positions.

Urban Development Associates
P.O. Box 45421
Los Angeles, CA 90045
213-641-9885
Search Firm.
Minorities and women in administrative, dp, finance/ accounting, managerial, sales and technical positions.

PDQ Personnel Services, Inc.
10550 Sepulveda, #106
Mission Hills, CA 91345
818-361-4441
Employment Agency.
Minorities and women in administrative, clerical, finance/ accounting, managerial, and sales positions.

The Zivic Group, Inc.
555 Montgomery St.,
  Suite 1614
San Francisco, CA 94111
415-421-2325
Search Firm.
*Minorities and women at
managerial levels.*

CONNECTICUT

Derocher Associates, Ltd.
2320 Main St.
Bridgeport, CT 06606
203-579-0878
Search Firm.
*Minorities and women in
administrative, dp, finance/
accounting, human resources,
managerial, sales, and
technical positions.*

Wendell L. Johnson
Associates, Inc.
12 Grandview Dr.
Danbury, CT 06811
203-743-4112
Search Firm.
*Minorities in dp, finance/
accounting, managerial, sales
and technical positions.*

Phyllis Walker Associates, Inc.
580 Burnside Ave., 2nd Fl.
E. Hartford, CT 06108
203-528-2556
Search Firm/Employment
Agency.
*Minorities in administrative, dp,
finance/accounting, managerial,
and technical positions.*

DISTRICT OF COLUMBIA

The Interface Group Ltd.
1230 31st N.W.
Washington, DC 20007
202-342-7200
Search Firm.
*Minorities and women in
administrative, dp, finance/
accounting, managerial, sales,
and technical positions.*

Stuart-Donathan Associates
1000 Connecticut Ave. N.W.
Washington, DC 20036
202-223-4911
Search Firm/Employment
Agency.
*Minorities and women in dp,
finance/accounting, managerial,
and technical positions.*

GEORGIA

Whitlow & Associates
3390 Peachtree Rd., N.E.,
Suite 236
Atlanta, GA 30326
404-262-2566
Search Firm/Employment
Agency.
*Minorities and women in
administrative, dp, finance/
banking/accounting,
managerial, sales and technical
positions.*

Robert L. Livingston
Consultants
P.O. Box 568
Lilburn, GA 30247
404-925-8687

Search Firm.
*Minorities and women in dp,
finance/accounting, managerial,
manufacturing, sales, and
technical positions.*

ILLINOIS

Americas, Inc.
612 N. Michigan Ave., Suite 617
Chicago, IL 60611
312-664-7770
Search Firm.
*Minorities and women in
administrative, dp, finance/
accounting, managerial, sales,
and technical positions.*

David Gomez & Associates, Inc.
20 N. Clark, Suite 2525
Chicago, IL 60602
312-346-5525
Search Firm.
*Minorities and women in
finance/accounting positions.*

James H. Lowry & Associates
218 N. Jefferson St., 3rd Fl.
Chicago, IL 60606
312-930-0930
Search Firm.
*Minorities in finance/
accounting, managerial/
executive, sales and technical
positions.*

INDIANA

Alpha Rae Personnel
127 W. Berry St., Suite 1109
Fort Wayne, IN 46802
219-426-8227

Search Firm/Employment
Agency.
*Minorities and women in
administrative, dp, finance/
accounting, managerial, sales
and technical positions.*

MARYLAND

Davies Associates, Inc.
4800 Hampden Lane
Bethesda, MD 20814
301-657-3510
Search Firm/Employment
Agency.
*Minorities and women in dp
and technical positions.*

Clark, Clark & Clark Associates
7338 Baltimore Blvd., Suite 109
College Park, MD 20740
301-864-1117
Search Firm.
*Minorities and women in dp,
finance/accounting, managerial,
sales and technical positions.*

Wallach Associates, Inc.
6101 Executive Blvd.
Rockville, MD 20852
301-231-9000
Employment Agency.
*Minorities and women in
technical positions.*

Derocher Associates, Ltd.
P.O. Box 3714
Silver Spring, MD 20901
301-384-6625
Search Firm.
*Minorities and women in
administrative, dp, finance/
accounting, human resources,
managerial, sales, and
technical positions.*

MASSACHUSETTS

Selected Executives, Inc.
959 Park Square Bldg.
Boston, MA 02116
617-426-3100
Search Firm/Employment
Agency.
*Minorities and women in
administrative, dp, finance/
accounting, managerial, sales,
technical and other professional
positions.*

Xavier Associates, Inc.
1350 Belmont St.,
Williamsburg Sq.
Brockton, MA 02401-4404
617-584-9414
Search Firm/Employment
Agency.
*Minorities in dp, finance/
accounting, managerial, sales
and technical positions.*

MICHIGAN

B.P.A. Enterprises, Inc.
19967 James Couzens
Detroit, MI 48235-1840
313-345-5700
Search Firm/Employment
Agency.
*Minorities and women in
administrative, dp, finance/
accounting, managerial, sales
and technical positions.*

Ludot Personnel Services, Inc.
3000 Town Center, #2025
Southfield, MI 48075
313-353-9720

Search Firm/Employment
Agency.
*Minorities and women in
administrative, dp, finance/
accounting, managerial, sales
and technical positions.*

MISSOURI

Ebony Employment, Inc.
15 W. 10th St., Suite 600
Kansas City, MO 64105
816-221-2090
Search Firm/Employment
Agency.
*Minorities and women in
administrative, dp, finance/
accounting, managerial, sales,
technical and other professional
positions.*

NEW JERSEY

Minorities Opportunities
Unlimited, Div. of
REM Associates Roman II
134 Evergreen Place
East Orange, NJ 07018
201-676-8906
Employment Agency.
*Minorities and women in
administrative, blue collar, dp,
finance/accounting, managerial,
sales, technical, human
resources and all other
professional positions.*

The Hennessy Group Ltd.
385 Prospect Ave.
Hackensack, NJ 07601
201-487-6776

Search Firm.
*Minorities and women in dp,
managerial, and technical
positions.*

Howard Clark Associates
507 White House Pike
Haddon Heights, NJ 08035
609-547-7200
Search Firm/Employment
Agency.
*Minorities and women in
administrative, dp, finance/
accounting, managerial,
purchasing, sales and technical
positions.*

Subscription Personnel Services
1180 Raymond Blvd., Suite 1435
Newark, NJ 07102
201-623-6700
Employment Agency.
*Minorities and women in
administrative, dp, finance/
accounting, legal, managerial,
sales, and technical positions.*

NEW YORK

Bruce Robinson Associates
200 West 57th St., Suite 417
New York, NY 10017
212-541-4140
Search Firm.
*Minorities and women in
administrative, finance/
accounting, managerial, sales
and technical positions.*

Careers for Women
80 Fifth Ave.
New York, NY 10011
212-807-7633

Search Firm.
Women in sales positions.

Corporate Woman, Div. of
Gardner Associates
300 Madison Ave.
New York, NY 10017
212-687-6615
Search Firm.
*Minorities and women in
managerial and sales positions.*

Nippon Employment Agency
25 West 43rd St.
New York, NY 10036
212-704-9960
Search Firm/Employment
Agency.
*Minorities and women in
administrative, blue collar, dp,
finance/accounting, managerial,
sales, technical and other
fields.*

Sydney Reynolds Associates
342 Madison Ave.
New York, NY 10017
212-697-8682
Search Firm.
*Minorities and women in
managerial positions.*

H.C. Smith Ltd.
Two Stanley Keyes Ct.
Rye, NY 10580
914-967-8734
Search Firm.
*Minorities and women in
administrative, dp, finance/
accounting, managerial, sales,
technical and other positions.*

OHIO

R.A.N. Associates, Inc.
140 Public Sq., Suite 804
Cleveland, OH 44114
216-696-6699
Search Firm/Employment
Agency.
*Minorities and women in
administrative, dp, finance/
accounting, managerial, sales
and technical positions.*

H.C. Smith Ltd.
3051 Van Aiken Blvd.
Shaker Heights, OH 44120
216-752-9966
Search Firm.
*Minorities and women in
administrative, dp, finance/
accounting, managerial, sales,
technical and other fields.*

PENNSYLVANIA

John Patrick Associates
650 Blue Bell W., Suite 122
Blue Bell, PA 19422
215-643-3460
Search Firm/Employment
Agency.
*Minorities and women in
managerial and sales positions.*

Howard Clark Associates
P.O. Box 58846
Philadelphia, PA 19102
215-574-9690
Search Firm/Employment
Agency.
*Minorities and women in
administrative, dp, finance/
accounting, managerial,*

*purchasing, sales and technical
positions.*

LaMonte Owens, Inc.
805 E. Willow Grove Ave.
Philadelphia, PA 19118
215-248-0500
Search Firm.
*Minorities and women in
administrative, dp, finance/
accounting, managerial, sales
and technical positions.*

SOUTH CAROLINA

Southern Recruiters &
Consultants
215 Park Ave. S.E.
Aiken, SC 29802
803-648-7834
Search Firm/Employment
Agency.
*Minorities and women in
administrative, dp, finance/
accounting, managerial, and
technical positions.*

TENNESSEE

Recruiters National
3803 Hydes Ferry Rd., Suite B
Nashville, TN 37218
615-254-5283
Search Firm/Employment
Agency.
*Minorities and women in
administrative, finance/
accounting, managerial,
secretarial, and technical
positions.*

TEXAS

Ferrer Management &
  Personnel Consultants
2503 Limestone Dr.
Arlington, TX 76014
817-465-5271/467-3625
Search Firm.
*Minorities and women in dp,
finance/accounting, managerial,
sales and technical positions.*

Di-Rec Services
10501 N. Central Expwy.
Suite 306
Dallas, TX 75231
214-987-9834
Search Firm/Employment
Agency.
*Minorities and women in
administrative, dp, finance/
accounting, managerial and
technical positions.*

Minority Search, Inc.
777 S.R.L. Thornton Frwy.
Suite 105
Dallas, TX 75203
214-948-6116
Search Firm/Employment
Agency.
*Minorities and women in
administrative, dp, finance/
accounting, managerial, sales
and technical positions.*

Abel Gonzalez & Associates
P.O. Box 790845
San Antonio, TX 78216
512-494-0909
Search Firm.
*Minorities and women in
administrative, advertising/PR,
finance/accounting, managerial,
sales and technical positions.*

VIRGINIA

Reston Employment Service
1760 Reston Ave.
Reston, VA 22090
703-648-1895
Search Firm/Employment
Agency.
*Minorities and women in
administrative, finance/
accounting and technical
positions.*

Crickenberger Associates
P.O. Box 8082
Roanoke, VA 24014
703-345-8885
Search Firm.
*Minorities and women in
administrative, finance/
accounting, human resources,
and managerial positions.*

WASHINGTON

B&M Unlimited & Associates
1331 Third Ave., Suite 420
Seattle, WA 98101
206-223-1687
Search Firm.
*Minorities and women in dp
positions.*

John Gayton & Associates
810 Third Ave., Suite 442
Seattle, WA 98104
206-621-7913
Search Firm.
*Minorities in administrative, dp,
finance/accounting, managerial,
sales and technical positions.*

Appendix IV
Office of Personal Management Federal Job Information/Testing Center

Job openings are many and diverse in the federal Job-Testing Centers that are listed here. Jobs range from janitors to executives, including part-time employees. There is hardly a trade, profession, or skill that is not employed in some area of the federal government. The only criteria for hiring is the ability to do the job, educational background, and experience. For some jobs the marks earned on the civil service examinations will determine if you will be hired.

The government is the fairest equal opportunity employer in the country. There is no consideration given to a person's age, race, religion, sex, or national origin. To be considered for employment, each person who applies for a government job must fill out Form 171, which is available at the centers throughout the country. You may have to take a test for some jobs, depending on the position for which you apply.

The general schedule of government salaries is listed below. There are approximately 1.4 million federal employees between GS-1 step 1 and GS-16 step 5. Beyond this cap are senior executive service employees who are similar to division directors in the corporate world. Senior-level management personnel are career employees who have worked their way to what would be senior management positions in the corporate world. These are basically cabinet-level jobs.

1990 Federal White-Collar Pay Scale

	Step 1	2	3	4	5	6	7	8	9	10
GS-1	$10,581	10,935	11,286	11,637	11,990	12,197	12,544	12,893	12,910	13,232
GS-2	11,897	12,180	12,574	12,910	13,053	13,437	13,821	14,205	14,589	14,973
GS-3	12,982	13,415	13,848	14,281	14,714	15,147	15,580	16,013	16,446	16,879
GS-4	14,573	15,059	15,545	16,031	16,517	17,003	17,489	17,975	18,461	18,947
GS-5	16,305	16,849	17,393	17,937	18,481	19,025	19,569	20,113	20,657	21,201
GS-6	18,174	18,780	19,386	19,992	20,598	21,204	21,810	22,416	23,022	23,628
GS-7	20,195	20,868	21,541	22,214	22,887	23,560	24,233	24,906	25,579	26,252
GS-8	22,367	23,113	23,859	24,605	25,351	26,097	26,843	27,589	28,335	29,081
GS-9	24,705	25,529	26,353	27,177	28,001	28,825	29,649	30,473	31,297	32,121
GS-10	27,206	28,113	29,020	29,927	30,834	31,741	32,648	33,555	34,462	35,369
GS-11	29,891	30,887	31,883	32,879	33,875	34,871	35,867	36,863	37,859	38,855
GS-12	35,825	37,019	38,213	39,407	40,601	41,795	42,989	44,183	45,377	46,571
GS-13	42,601	44,021	45,441	46,861	48,281	49,701	51,121	52,541	53,961	55,381
GS-14	50,342	52,020	53,698	55,376	57,054	58,732	60,410	62,088	63,766	65,444
GS-15	59,216	61,190	63,164	65,138	67,112	69,086	71,060	73,034	75,008	76,982
GS-16	69,451	71,766	74,081	76,396	78,190	79,438*	81,708*	83,978*	85,470*	
GS-17	79,762*	82,420*	85,078*	85,470*	85,500*					
GS-18	86,682*									

* The rate of basic pay payable to employees at these rates is limited to the rate for level V of the Executive Schedule, which would be $78,200.

OFFICE OF PERSONNEL MANAGEMENT
FEDERAL JOB INFORMATION/TESTING OFFICES

ALABAMA

Huntsville:
Southerland Building
806 Governors Dr., S.W., 35801
205-544-5802

ALASKA

Anchorage:
Federal Building
701 C St., Box 22, 99513
907-271-5821

ARIZONA

Phoenix:
U.S. Postal Service Building
522 N. Central Ave., 85004
602-261-4736

ARKANSAS

Little Rock:
Federal Bldg., Third Floor
700 W. Capitol Ave., 72201
501-378-5842

CALIFORNIA

Los Angeles:
Linder Building, 3rd Floor
845 S. Figueroa, 90017
213-894-3360

Sacramento:
1029 J St., Rm. 100, 95814
916-551-1464

CALIFORNIA (*cont.*)

San Diego:
880 Front St., 92188
619-293-6165

San Francisco:
211 Main St., Second Floor,
Room 235, 94105
415-974-9725

COLORADO

Denver:
P.O. Box 25167, 80225
303-236-4160
Physically located at 12345 W.
Alameda Pkwy., Lakewood, CO

For job information (24 hrs. a
day) in the following states:
Montana: 303-236-4162
North Dakota: 303-236-4163
South Dakota: 303-236-4164
Utah: 303-236-4165
Wyoming: 307-236-4166

For forms and local
supplements dial 303-236-4159

CONNECTICUT

Hartford:
Federal Building, Rm. 613
450 Main St., 06103
203-722-3096

DELAWARE

(See Philadelphia, PA listing)

DISTRICT OF COLUMBIA

Metro Area:
900 E. St., N.W.,
Rm. 1416, 20415
202-653-8468

FLORIDA

Orlando:
Federal Building and
  U.S. Courthouse
80 N. Hughey Ave.,
Rm. 229, 32801
305-648-6148

GEORGIA

Atlanta: Richard B. Russell
  Federal Bldg., Rm. 960
5 Spring St., S.W. 30303
404-331-4315

GUAM

Agana:
Pacific News Building
238 O'Hara St., Rm. 902
  96910
472-7451

HAWAII

Honolulu (and other Hawaiian
  Islands and overseas):
Federal Building, Rm. 5316
300 Ala Moana Blvd., 96850
808-546-7108

IDAHO

(See Washington listing)

ILLINOIS

Chicago:
175 W. Jackson Blvd., Rm. 519
  60604
312-353-6192

INDIANA

Indianapolis:
Minton-Capehart
Federal Building
575 N. Pennsylvania Ave.
  46204
317-269-7161

IOWA

Des Moines:
210 Walnut St., Rm. 191, 50309
In Scott County
dial 312-353-5136
and in Pottawatomie County
dial 402-221-3815

KANSAS

Wichita:
One-Twenty Building, Rm. 101
120 S. Market St., 67202
316-269-6106
In Johnson, Leavenworth
and Wyandotte Counties
dial 816-374-5702

KENTUCKY

(See Ohio listing)

LOUISIANA

New Orleans:
F. Edward Hebert Building
610 S. Maestri Pl.,
Rm. 802, 70130
504-589-2764

MAINE

(See New Hampshire listing)

MARYLAND

Baltimore:
Garmatz Federal Building
101 W. Lombard Street 21202
301-962-3822

MASSACHUSETTS

Boston:
Boston Federal Office Building
10 Causeway St., 02222
617-565-5900

MICHIGAN

Detroit:
477 Michigan Ave.
Rm. 565, 48226
313-226-6950

MINNESOTA

Twin Cities:
Federal Building
Ft. Snelling, Twin Cities, 55111
612-725-4430

MISSISSIPPI

Jackson:
100 W. Capitol St.,
Suite 335, 39269
601-965-4585

MISSOURI

Kansas City:
Federal Building, Rm. 134
601 E. 12th St., 64106
816-374-5702

St. Louis:
Old Post Office, Rm. 400
815 Olive St., 63101
314-425-4285

MONTANA

(See Colorado listing)

NEBRASKA

Omaha:
U.S. Courthouse and
Post Office Building
Rm. 1010, 215 N. 17th St., 68102
402-221-3815

NEVADA

(See Sacramento, CA listing)

NEW HAMPSHIRE

Portsmouth:
Thomas J. McIntyre
Federal Bldg.
Rm. 104
80 Daniel Street, 03801
603-431-7115

NEW JERSEY

Newark:
Peter W. Rodino, Jr.,
Federal Building
970 Broad St., 07102
201-645-3673
In Camden, dial 215-597-7440

NEW MEXICO

Albuquerque:
Federal Building
421 Gold Ave., S.W., 87102
505-766-5583
In Dona Ana, Otero and El Paso
counties dial 505-766-1893

NEW YORK

New York City:
Jacob K. Javits Federal Building
26 Federal Plaza, 10278
212-264-0422

Syracuse:
James N. Hanley
Federal Building
100 S. Clinton St., 13260
315-423-5660

NORTH CAROLINA

Raleigh:
Federal Building
310 New Bern Ave.
P.O. Box 25069, 27611 (mailing
   address)
919-856-4361

NORTH DAKOTA

(See Colorado listing)

OHIO

Dayton:
Federal Building
200 W. 2nd St., 45402
513-225-2720

OKLAHOMA

Oklahoma City:
200 N.W. Fifth St.
Rm. 205, 73102
405-231-4948

OREGON

Portland:
Federal Building
1220 S.W. Third St., 97204
503-221-3141

PENNSYLVANIA

Harrisburg:
Federal Building, Rm. 168
P.O. Box 761, 17108
717-782-4494

Philadelphia:
Wm. J. Green, Jr.
Federal Building
600 Arch St., Rm. 1416, 19106
215-597-7440

Pittsburgh:
Federal Building
1000 Liberty Ave.
Rm. 119, 15222
412-644-2755

PUERTO RICO

San Juan:
Federico Degetau
Federal Building
Carlos E. Chardon St.
Hato Rey, 00918
809-753-4209

RHODE ISLAND

Providence:
John O. Pastore Federal Building
Rm. 310, Kennedy Plaza, 02903
401-528-5251

SOUTH CAROLINA

Charleston:
Federal Building
334 Meeting St., 29403
803-724-4328

SOUTH DAKOTA

(See Colorado listing)

TENNESSEE

Memphis:
100 N. Main Building
Suite 1312, 38103
901-521-3956

TEXAS

Dallas:
Rm. 6B4, 1100 Commerce St.
75242
214-767-8035

TEXAS (*cont.*)

Houston:
701 San Jacinto St.
4th Floor, 77002
713-226-2375

San Antonio:
643 E. Durango Blvd., 78206
512-229-6611 or 6600

UTAH

(See Colorado listing)

VERMONT

(See New Hampshire listing)

VIRGINIA

Norfolk:
Federal Building, Rm. 220
200 Granby Mall, 23510-1886
804-441-3355

WASHINGTON

Seattle:
Federal Building
915 Second Ave., 98174
206-442-4365

WEST VIRGINIA

Charleston:
Federal Building, Rm. 1017
500 Quarrier St., 25301
304-347-5174

WISCONSIN

Residents in counties of Grant, Iowa, Lafayette, Dane, Green, Rock, Jefferson, Walworth, Waukesha, Racine, Kenosha and Milwaukee should dial 312-353-6189 for job infor-

mation. All other Wisconsin residents should refer to the Minnesota listing for Federal Job Information in their area.

WYOMING

(See Colorado listing)

Appendix V
State Job Centers

Don't overlook the State Job Centers. They can refer you to state job openings as well as those with private companies. The state is the largest employment agency in the state.

Each state usually has its own procedures for hiring, and some states may have residency requirements. Each state also hires a diverse group of workers ranging from executives with professional and technical backgrounds to virtually any type of occupation you can name. Utilize this valuable resource.

Here is a list of the state administrators, including addresses, telephone and fax numbers.

STATE ADMINISTRATORS

ALABAMA

John G. Allen, Director
Dept. of Industrial Relations
649 Monroe Street
Montgomery, AL 36130
205-261-5386
Fax: 205-240-3070

ALASKA

Joseph M. Sitton, Director
Employment Security Division
Department of Labor
P.O. Box 3-7000
Juneau, AK 99802

ALASKA (*cont.*)

907-465-2712
Fax: 907-465-4537

ARIZONA

Linda Moore-Cannon, Director
Department of Economic
  Security
P.O. Box 6123
Phoenix, AZ 85005
602-542-5678

ARKANSAS

William Gaddy, Administrator
Employment Security Division
P.O. Box 2981
Little Rock, AR 72203-2981
501-682-2121
Fax: 501-682-3713

CALIFORNIA

Kaye R. Kiddoo, Director
Employment Development
  Department
P.O. Box 942880, MIC 83
Sacramento, CA 94280-0001
916-445-9212
Fax: 916-445-0764

COLORADO

John Donlon, Executive Director
Department of Labor &
  Employment
600 Grant Street, Suite 900
Denver, CO 80203-3528
303-837-3801
Fax: 303-837-3864

CONNECTICUT

Betty L. Tianti
Labor Commissioner
CT Labor Department
200 Folly Brook Boulevard
Wethersfield, CT 06109
203-566-4384
Fax: 203-566-1520

John C. Souchuns
Executive Director

CONNECTICUT (cont.)

Employment Security Division
CT Labor Department
200 Folly Brook Boulevard
Wethersfield, CT 06109
203-566-4280
Fax: 203-566-1520

DELAWARE

Ms. Jan Ewing Robinson
Secretary of labor
Department of Labor
820 N. French Street
Carvel State Building, 6th Fl.
Wilmington, DE 19801
302-571-2710
Fax: 302-571-2735

DISTRICT OF COLUMBIA

F. Alexis H. Roberson, Director
Department of Employment
  Services
500 C Street, N.W., Rm. 600
Washington, DC 20001
202-639-1000
Fax: 202-639-1016

FLORIDA

Hugo D. Menendez, Secretary
Dept. of Labor & Employment
  Security
The Berkeley Bldg., Suite 206
2590 Executive Center Circle,
  East
Tallahassee, FL 32399-2152
904-488-4398
Fax: 904-488-8930
DIV OF LABOR
904-488-7228

GEORGIA

Joseph D. Tanner,
  Commissioner
GA Department of Labor
Sussex Place
148 International Boulevard, N.E.
Atlanta, GA 30303
404-656-3011
Fax: 404-656-9377

HAWAII

Mario Ramil, Director
Dept. of Labor and Industrial
  Relations
830 Punchbowl Street
Honolulu, HI 96813
808-548-3150
Fax: 808-548-3285

IDAHO

Julie Kilgrow, Director
Department of Employment
317 Main Street
Boise, ID 83735
208-334-6110
Fax: 208-334-6430

ILLINOIS

Sally Jackson, Director
Department of Employment
  Security
401 South State Street, Rm. 615
Chicago, IL 60605
312-793-5700
Fax: 312-793-9306

INDIANA

Douglas Roof, Executive
  Director
Dept. of Employment & Training
  Services
10 North Senate Avenue,
  Rm. 331
Indianapolis, IN 46204
317-232-3270
Fax: 317-232-6950

IOWA

Cynthia Eisenhauer, Director
Dept. of Employment Services
1000 East Grand Avenue
Des Moines, IA 50319
515-281-5365
Fax: 515-242-5144

KANSAS

Ray Siehndel, Secretary
Department of Human
  Resources
401 Topeka Avenue
Topeka, KS 66603
913-296-7474
Fax: 913-296-4789

KENTUCKY

Darvin Allen, Commissioner
Department for Employment
  Services
275 E. Main Street
Frankfort, KY 40621
502-564-5331
Fax: 502-564-7452

LOUISIANA

Phyllis Mouton, Secretary of
  Labor
Department of Employment &
  Training
P.O. Box 94094
Baton Rouge, LA 70804-9094
504-342-3011
Fax: 504-342-3021

MAINE

John Fitzsimmons
Commissioner of Labor
Bureau of Employment Security
P.O. Box 309
Augusta, ME 04330
207-289-3788
Fax: 207-289-5292

Mary Lou Dyer, Executive
  Director
Bureau of Employment Security
P.O. Box 309
Augusta, ME 04330
207-289-2411

MARYLAND

Charles O. Middlebrooks, Jr.
Assistant Secretary for
  Employment and Training
Department of Economic and
  Employment Development
1100 North Eutaw Street
Baltimore, MD 21201
301-333-5070
Fax: 301-333-5304

MASSACHUSETTS

James F. French, Commissioner
Dept. of Employment & Training
Charles F. Hurley Building
Government Center
Boston, MA 02114
617-727-6600
Fax: 617-727-8014

MICHIGAN

Thomas Malek, Deputy Director
Employment Security
  Commission
7310 Woodward Avenue
Detroit, MI 48202
313-876-5500
Fax: 313-876-5072

MINNESOTA

Joseph Samargia,
  Commissioner
Department of Jobs & Training
390 North Robert Street
St. Paul, MN 55101
612-296-3711
Fax: 612-296-0994
SAMARGIA OFF
612-296-0994

MISSISSIPPI

Linda Ross Aldy
Executive Director
Employment Security
  Commission
P.O. Box 1699
Jackson, MS 39205
601-961-7400
Fax: 601-961-7405

MISSOURI

Tom Deuschle, Director
Division of Employment Security
Dept. of Labor & Industrial Rel.
421 East Dunklin Street
Jefferson City, MO 65101
314-751-3976
Fax: 314-751-7973

MONTANA

Mario (Mike) Micone
Commissioner
Department of Labor & Industry
State Capitol
Helena, MT 59624
406-444-3555
Fax: 406-444-2699

NEBRASKA

Virginia Yueill
Commissioner of Labor
Department of Labor
P.O. Box 94600
Lincoln, NE 68509-4600
402-471-3405
Fax: 402-471-2318

NEVADA

Stanley P. Jones, Director
Employment Security
  Department
500 East Third Street
Carson City, NV 89713
702-687-4635
Fax: 702-687-3903

NEW HAMPSHIRE

John J. Ratoff, Commissioner
Department of Employment
  Security
32 South Main Street
Concord, NH 03301
603-224-3311
Fax: 603-228-4145

NEW JERSEY

Raymond Bramucci
Commissioner
NJ Department of Labor
Labor & Industry Building
CN110
Trenton, NJ 08625-0110
609-292-2323
Fax: 609-393-7375

NEW MEXICO

Paul M. Garcia, Secretary
New Mexico Department of Labor
P.O. Box 1928
Albuquerque, NM 87103
505-841-8409
Fax: 505-841-8421

NEW YORK

Thomas F. Hartnett
Commissioner
NY State Department of Labor
Building 12, State Campus
Albany, NY 12240
518-457-2741
Fax: 518-457-0620

James Gutowski
Executive Deputy
  Commissioner
NY State Department of Labor
Building 12, State Campus
Albany, NY 12240
518-457-2270
Fax: 518-457-6908

NORTH CAROLINA

Betsy Y. Justus, Chairman
Employment Security
  Commission
P.O. Box 25903
Raleigh, NC 27611
919-733-7546
Fax: 919-733-9118

NORTH DAKOTA

Michael V. Deisz
Executive Director
Job Service North Dakota
P.O. Box 1537
Bismarck, ND 58502
701-224-2836
Fax: 701-224-3000

OHIO

Ellen O'Brien Saunders
  Administrator
Bureau of Employment Services
145 South Front Street
Columbus, OH 43215
614-466-2100
Fax: 614-466-5025

OKLAHOMA

Bob Funston, Executive Director
Employment Security
Commission
Will Rogers Memorial Office
Bldg.
Oklahoma City, OK 73105
405-557-7200
Fax: 405-557-7256

OREGON

Pamela Matson, Administrator
Employment Division
875 Union Street, N.E.
Salem, OR 97311
503-378-3211
Fax: 503-373-7460

PENNSYLVANIA

Franklin G. Mont, Deputy
  Secretary for Employment
  Security & Job Trng.
Dept. of Labor & Industry
Labor & Industry Building
Seventh & Forster Streets
Harrisburg, PA 17121
717-787-1745
Fax: 717-783-5787

Mr. Thomas Foley
Executive Deputy Secretary
Dept. of Labor & Industry
Labor & Industry Building
Seventh & Forster Streets
Rm. 1719
Harrisburg, PA 17121

PUERTO RICO

Antera Ortiz Garcia, Director
Bureau of Employment Security
505 Munoz Rivera Avenue
Hato Rey, PR 00918
809-753-9550
Fax: 809-754-5334

RHODE ISLAND

John S. Renza, Director
Department of Employment &
  Training
24 Mason Street
Providence, RI 02903
401-277-3732
Fax: 401-277-2731

SOUTH CAROLINA

Robert E. David
Executive Director
Employment Security
  Commission
P.O. Box 995
Columbia, SC 29202
803-737-2617
Fax: 803-737-2642

SOUTH DAKOTA

Pete F. de Hueck, Secretary
South Dakota Department of
  Labor
700 Governors Drive
Pierre, SD 57501
605-773-3101
Fax: 605-773-4211

TENNESSEE

Rayburn A. Traughber
Commissioner
Department of Employment
  Security
12th Floor—Volunteer Plaza
  Bldg.
500 James Robertson Parkway
Nashville, TN 37219
615-741-2131
Fax: 615-741-3203

TEXAS

William D. Grossenbacher
Administrator
Texas Employment Commission
638 TEC Building
15th & Congress Avenue
Austin, TX 78778
512-463-2652
Fax: 512-475-1133
JACKSONS OFF
512-463-2220

UTAH

Floyd G. Astin, Administrator
Department of Employment
  Security
174 Social Hall Ave.
P.O. Box 11249
Salt Lake City, UT 84147
801-533-2201
Fax: 801-533-2466

VERMONT

Patricia Thomas, Commissioner
Department of Employment &
　Trng.
P.O. Box 488
Montpelier, VT 05602
802-229-0311
Fax: 802-223-0750

VIRGINIA

Ralph G. Cantrell, Commissioner
Virginia Employment
　Commission
P.O. Box 1358
Richmond, VA 23211
804-786-3001
Fax: 804-225-3923

VIRGIN ISLANDS

Luis Llanos
Commissioner
Department of Labor
38 Queen Street, Christenstead
St. Croix, VI 00820
809-773-1994
Fax: 809-773-4780

Carol Burke, Assistant
　Commissioner for
Employment
　and Training
Department of Labor
22 Hospital Street
Christenstead
St. Croix, VI 00820
809-773-1994

WASHINGTON

Isiah Turner, Commissioner
Employment Security
　Department
212 Maple Park,
Mail Stop KG-11
Olympia, WA 98504
206-753-5114
Fax: 206-753-4851

WEST VIRGINIA

Andrew Richardson,
　Commissioner
West Virginia Division of
　Employment Security
112 California Avenue
Charleston, WV 25305-0112
304-348-2630
Fax: 304-348-8887

WISCONSIN

Gerald Whitburn, Secretary
Dept. of Industry,
Labor and Human Relations
P.O. Box 7946
Madison, WI 53707
608-266-7552
Fax: 608-267-4592

WYOMING

Dick Sadler
Executive Director
Employment Security
　Commission
P.O. Box 2760
Casper, WY 82602
307-235-3650
Fax: 307-235-3278

Appendix VI
Minority Business Development Agency
The Minority Business Development Agency provides assistance to minorities for starting or expanding a business, says Richard Stevens, chief of the research division. According to Stevens, the Minority Business Centers across the country assist minorities in putting together a business plan, help with market research, and provide technical assistance. They also help minorities get financial assistance from banks.

Stevens says one of the major problems minorities face is getting financing and preparing the necessary documents to go to a bank. He also notes that the motivation for going into business is often triggered when minorities don't get the corporate promotions they feel they deserve. He points out that minorities have to invest some of their money in the business they want to start.

Each agency is staffed by experienced professional advisers from the business world. Minority business agencies also provide grants ranging from $175,000 to $1 million to public and private organizations with the capability to provide business development services.

See Appendix VIII: Minority Resources.

Birmingham MBDC
Porter, White & Yardley
  Capital, Inc.
2100 16th Ave. South
Ste 203   Ash Place
Birmingham, AL 35205
205-930-9254

Mobile MBDC
Minact, Inc.
4321 Downtowner Loop North
  Ste D
Mobile, AL 36604
205-344-9650

Montgomery MBDC
Minact, Inc.
770 S. Mcdonough St., Ste 207
Montgomery, AL 36104
205-834-7598

Alaska MBDC
Community Enterprise Dev.
  Corp. of Alaska
1577 C St. Plaza, Ste 200
Anchorage, AK 99501
907-274-5400

Little Rock MBDC
Charles Cole Company
One Riverfront Place, Ste 415
North Little Rock, AR 72114
501-372-7312

Phoenix MBDC
Arizona Economic
  Development Corp.
1661 East Camelback, Ste 210
Phoenix, AZ 85016
602-248-7817

Arizona IBDC
Nat'l Ctr. for Amer. Indian
  Enterprise Devel.
2111 East Baseline Rd. Ste F-8
Tempe, AZ 85283
602-831-7524

Tucson MBDC
San Diego State University
  Foundation
181 W. Broadway
Tucson, AZ 85702
602-629-9744

Bakersfield MBDC
Neda San Joaquin Valley, Inc.
218 South H Street, Ste 103
Bakersfield, CA 93304
805-837-0291

California IBDC
Nat'l Ctr. for Amer. Indian
  Enterprise Devel.
9650 Flair Drive, Ste 303
El Monte, CA 91731
818-442-3701

Fresno MBDC
Neda San Joaquin Valley, Inc.
2010 N. Fine, Ste 103
Fresno, CA 93727
209-252-7551

Los Angeles 2 MBDC
Business Dev. Center of
  Southern California
3807 Wilshire Boulevard, Ste 700
Los Angeles, CA 90010
213-380-9541

Oxnard MBDC
Fontaine, Quintanilla &
  Associates
451 W. Fifth Street
Oxnard, CA 93030
805-483-1123

Sacramento MBDC
Neda San Joaquin Valley, Inc.
530 Bercut Drive, Ste C & D
Sacramento, CA 95814
916-443-0700

Salinas MBDC
Conwell Devereaux, Inc.
123 Capital Street, Ste B
Salinas, CA 93901
408-754-1061

San Diego MBDC
San Diego State University
  Foundation
6363 Alvarado Court, Ste 225
San Diego, CA 92120
619-594-3684

San Francisco MBDC
Grant-Thornton, Inc.
One California Street, Suite 2100
San Francisco, CA 94111
415-989-2920

San Jose MBDC
Grant-Thornton, Inc.
150 Almaden Boulevard,
PO Box 6779
San Jose, CA 95150
408-275-9000

Anaheim MBDC
Miranda, Strabala & Associates
856 North Rose Street, Ste 250
Santa Ana, CA 92701
714-542-2700

Santa Barbara MBDC
Fontaine, Quintanilla &
    Associates
4141 State St., Ste B-4
Santa Barbara, CA 93110
805-964-1136

Stockton MBDC
Technical Data Corporation
5361 No. Pershing Ave., Ste F
Stockton, CA 95207
209-477-2098

Washington, DC MBDC
Burgos & Associates, Inc.
1133 15th Street, N.W., Ste 1120
Washington, DC 20005
202-785-2886

Jacksonville MBDC
Boone, Young & Associates, Inc.
333 N. Laura Street, Ste 465
Jacksonville, FL 32202-3508
904-353-3826

Miami/Ft. Lauderdale MBDC
Kendall Square Consultants, Inc.
1200 N.W. 78th Ave., Suite 301
Miami, FL 33126
305-591-7355

Orlando MBDC
Boone, Young & Associates, Inc.
132 E. Colonial Dr., Ste 211
Orlando, FL 32801
407-422-6234

Tampa/St. Petersburg MBDC
Laventhol & Horwath
5020 W. Cypress, Ste 217
Tampa, FL 33607
813-228-7555

Atlanta MBDC
Minact, Inc.
75 Piedmont Ave., NE, Ste 256
Atlanta, GA 30303
404-586-0973

Augusta MBDC
CSRA Business League, Inc.
1208 Laney Walker Blvd.
Augusta, GA 30901-2796
404-722-0994

Columbus MBDC
Minority Assistance Corporation
1214 First Avenue, Suite 430
Columbus, GA 31902-1696
404-324-4253

Savannah, GA MBDC
Boone, Young & Associates, Inc.
31 W. Congress St., Ste 201
Savannah, GA 31401
912-236-6708

Honolulu MBDC
Grant-Thornton, Inc.
1001 Bishop Street,
2900 Pacific Tower
Honolulu, HI 96813
808-536-0066

Chicago 1 MBDC
Burgos & Associates, Inc.
35 East Wacker Drive, Ste 790
Chicago, IL 60601
312-977-9190

Chicago 2 MBDC
Grant-Thornton, Inc.
600 Prudential Plaza
Chicago, IL 60601
312-565-4710

Gary MBDC
Globetrotters Engineering
　Corporation
P.O. Box 9007, 567 Broadway
Gary, IN 46402
219-883-5802

Indianapolis MBDC
The Bennington Corp.
617 Indiana Avenue, Suite 319
Indianapolis, IN 46202
317-685-0055

Louisville MBDC
Brown & Robinson
　Computerized Acct. Services
835 W. Jefferson St., Ste 103
Louisville, KY 40202
502-589-7401

Baton Rouge MBDC
Wybirk & Associates, Inc.
2036 Woodale Blvd, Ste D
Baton Route, La 70806
504-924-0186

New Orleans MBDC
Montegut & Rabb, CPAS
1683 North Clayborne
New Orleans, LA 70116
504-947-1491

Shreveport MBDC
Wybirk & Associates, Inc.
202 North Thomas Dr., Ste 16
Shreveport, LA 71108
318-226-4931

Baltimore MBDC
Boone, Young & Associates, Inc.
2901 Druid Pk. Dr., Ste 201
Baltimore, MD 21215
301-383-2214

Boston MBDC
Council for Economic Action, Inc.
985 Commonwealth Ave.
Boston, MA 02215
617-353-7237

Detroit MBDC
Laventhol & Horwath
65 Cadillac Square, Ste 3701
Detroit, MI 48226-2822
313-961-2100

Minnesota IBDC
The Minnesota Chippewa Tribe
P.O. Box 217 (Facility Center,
　Tract 33)
Cass Lake, MN 56633
218-335-8583

Kansas City MBDC
Laventhol & Horwath
Comm Bank Bldg, Ste 1000,
　1000 Walnut St.
Kansas City, MO 64106
816-221-6504

Jackson MBDC
Minact, Inc.
1350 Livingston Lane, Ste A
Jackson, MS 39213
601-362-2260

Charlotte MBDC
Laventhol & Horwath
700 East Stonewall St., Ste 360
Charlotte, NC 28202
704-334-7522

Cherokee IBDC
Eastern Band of
Cherokee Indians
Alquoni Rd., Box 1200
Cherokee, NC 28719
704-497-9335

Ashton Pk Towers
165 French Broad Ave.
Ashville, NC 28801
704-252-2516

Fayetteville MBDC
Fayetteville Business &
  Professional League
P.O. Box 1387,
114½ Anderson Street
Fayetteville, NC 28302
919-483-7513

Raleigh/Durham MBDC
The Bennington Corp.
817 New Bern Ave., Ste 8
Raleigh, NC 27601
919-833-6122

North Dakota IBDC
United Tribes Educational
  Technical Center
3315 University Drive
Bismarck, ND 58501-7596
701-255-3225

New Brunswick MBDC
Boone, Young & Associates, Inc.
134 New Street, Rm 102
New Brunswick, NJ 08901
201-247-2000

Newark MBDC
Boone, Young & Associates, Inc.
60 Park Place, Ste 1404
Newark, NJ 07102
201-623-7712

Albuquerque MBDC
Neda
718 Central S.W.
Albuquerque, NM 87102
505-843-7114

New Mexico IBDC
All Indian Pueblo Council, Inc.
2401 Twelfth Street, N.W.
Albuquerque, NM 87197-6507
505-889-9092

Las Vegas MBDC
Nedco, Inc.
716 South Sixth Street
Las Vegas, NV 89101
702-384-3293

Bronx MBDC
Burgos & Associates, Inc.
349 E. 149th Street, Ste 702
Bronx, NY 10451
212-665-8583

Williamsburg MBDC
ODA Economic Development
  Corporation
12 Heyward Street
Brooklyn, NY 11211
718-522-5620

Brooklyn MBDC
Boone, Young & Associates, Inc.
16 Court Street, Rm 1903
Brooklyn, NY 11201
718-522-5880

Buffalo MBDC
Resource Planning
  Associates, Inc.
523 Delaware Avenue
Buffalo, NY 14202
716-885-0336

Queens MBDC
Murtha and Associates, Inc.
110-29 Horace Harding
  Expressway
Corona, NY 11368
718-699-2400

Nassau/Suffolk MBDC
Burgos & Associates, Inc.
150 Broad Hollow Road, Ste 304
Melville, NY 11747
516-549-5454

Manhattan MBDC
Interracial Council for Business
   Opportunity
51 Madison Ave., Ste 2212
New York, NY 10010
212-779-4360

Rochester MBDC
Darryl E. Green &
   Associates, CPA
111 East Avenue, Suite 215
Rochester, NY 14604
716-232-6120

Cincinnati/Dayton MBDC
Cincinnati Minority Business
   Assistance Corp.
113 West Fourth St., Ste 600
Cincinnati, OH 45202
513-381-4770

1116 West Stewart St., Ste 1
Dayton, OH 45408
513-228-8013

Cleveland MBDC
City of Cleveland-Office of
   Equal Opportunity
601 Lakeside, Ste 335
Cleveland, OH 44114
216-664-4150

Stark Tech. College
6200 Frank Rd., NW
Canton, OH 44720-7299
216-494-6170

Columbus, OH MBDC
Columbus Area
   Chamber of Commerce
37 North High Street
Columbus, OH 43215
614-225-6910

Oklahoma City MBDC
Oklahoma Business
   Development Centers, Inc.
1500 N.E. 4th Street, Ste 101
Oklahoma City, OK 73117
405-235-0430

Tulsa MBDC
Metropolitan Tulsa Urban
   League, Inc.
240 East Apache Street
Tulsa, OK 74106
918-592-1995

Oklahoma IBDC
T3RC Associates
5727 Garnett, Ste H
Tulsa, OK 74146
918-250-5950

Portland MBDC
Impact Business
   Consultants, Inc.
8959 S.W. Barbur Blvd.
Ste 102
Portland, OR 97219
503-245-9253

Philadelphia MBDC
John Milligan, Certified Public
   Accountant
801 Arch Street
Philadelphia, PA 19107
215-629-9841

Pittsburgh MBDC
The Bottom Line, Inc.
  Business Consultants
Nine Parkway Center Ste 250
Pittsburgh, PA 15220
412-921-1155

Mayaguez MBDC
Yolanda Velez De Garcia
  Consultants, Inc.
P.O. Box 3146 Marina Station
Mayaguez, PR 00709
809-833-7783

Ponce MBDC
M. L. Prats & Associates
19 Salud Street
Ponce, PR 00731
809-840-8100

San Juan MBDC
Asociacion Productos De
  Puerto Rico, Inc.
207 O'Neill St.
San Juan, PR 00936
809-753-8484

Charleston, SC MBDC
Minact, Inc.
701 E. Bay St., Ste I539
Charleston, SC 29403
803-724-3477

Columbia, SC MBDC
Technical Management
  Systems, Inc.
P.O. Box 5915,
2700 Middleburg Dr.
Columbia, SC 29204
803-256-0528

Greenville/Spartanburg MBDC
Minact, Inc.
300 University Ridge, Ste 200
Greenville, SC 29601
803-271-8753

Nashville Tennessee MBDC
Brown & Robinson
  Computerized Acct. Services
1380 Poplar Avenue
Memphis, TN 38104
901-725-4672

Memphis MBDC
Banks, Finley, White & Co.
5 North Third Street, Ste 2000
Memphis, TN 38103
901-527-2298

Austin MBDC
Grant-Thornton, Inc.
301 Congress Avenue, Ste 1020
Austin, TX 78701
512-476-9700

Beaumont MBDC
Boutee, Elmore & Company
  CPA'S
550 Fannin, Ste 106A
Beaumont, TX 77701
409-835-1377

Brownsville MBDC
Corporate America Research
  Assoc., Inc. (CARA)
2100 Boca Chica, Ste 301
Brownsville, TX 78521-2265
512-546-3400

Corpus Christi MBDC
Corporate America Research
  Assoc., Inc. (CARA)
Intl. Bank Tower, 3649 Leopard,
  Ste 514
Corpus Christi, TX 78404
512-887-7961

Laredo MBDC
Corporate America Research
  Assoc., Inc. (CARA)
P.O. Box 5011
Kingsville, TX 78364-5011
512-725-5177

Lubbock/Midland-Odessa MBDC
Corporate America Research
  Assoc., Inc. (CARA)
1220 Broadway, Ste 509
Lubbock, TX 79401
806-762-6232

McAllen MBDC
Corporate America Research
  Assoc., Inc. (CARA)
1701 W. Business Hwy 83,
  Ste 1108
McAllen, TX 78501
512-687-5224

San Antonio MBDC
University of Texas at
  San Antonio
Univ. of TX at SA,
Cntr for Econ Develop
San Antonio, TX 78285
512-224-1945

Salt Lake City MBDC
Impact Business
  Consultants, Inc.
350 East 500 South, #101
Salt Lake City, UT 84111
801-328-8181

Newport News MBDC
Myers & Myers, CPA
6060 Jefferson Ave., Ste 6016
Newport News, VA 23605
804-245-8743

Norfolk MBDC
Myers & Myers, CPA
355 Crawford Pkwy, Ste 608
Portsmouth, VA 23701
804-399-0888

Richmond MBDC
Rabb & Mitchel, CPA
2025 East Main St., Ste 212
Richmond, VA 23223
804-644-6501

Virgin Islands MBDC
Vitied, Inc.
P.O. Box 838
St. Thomas, VI 00801
809-774-7215

Seattle MBDC
Impact Business
  Consultants, Inc.
155 N.E. 100th Ave., Ste 401
Seattle, WA 98125
206-525-5617

Milwaukee MBDC
Globetrotters Engineering
  Corporation
3929 N. Humboldt Blvd.
Milwaukee, WI 53212
414-332-6268

Appendix VII
National Urban League Inc.

The National Urban League sponsors job training programs
in 113 cities throughout the United States for mature workers
55 years and older, according to Janet Zoebel, employment
director for the Seniors Program. Although the Urban League
deals mostly with job training for the underprivileged, it also

helps mature workers 55 and over who are seeking employment. Contact the Urban League office in your area for information and help.

NATIONAL URBAN LEAGUE, INC.
LOCAL AFFILIATES/CHIEF EXECUTIVE OFFICERS

AKRON, OHIO

Vernon L. Odom
Executive Director
Akron Community Service
   Center and Urban League
250 East Market Street
Akron, OH 44308
216-434-3101

ALBANY, GEORGIA

VACANT
President
Albany Urban League
1025-27 West Gordon Avenue
P.O. Box 383
Albany, GA 31707
912-883-1410

ALBANY, NEW YORK

Clarence E. Swanston
President
Albany Area Urban League
95 Livingston Avenue
Albany, NY 12207
518-463-3121

ALTON, ILLINOIS

Julia Tibbs
President
Madison County Urban League
210 Williams Street
Alton, IL 62002
618-463-1906

AMITYVILLE, NY

Rosemary Durant-Giles
President
Urban League of Long Island
221 Broadway, Suite 207
Amityville, NY 11701
516-691-7230

ANDERSON, INDIANA

Albert B. Simmons
President
Urban League of
   Madison County, Inc.
1210 West 10th Street
P.O. Box 271
Anderson, IN 46015
317-649-7126

ATLANTA, GEORGIA

Lyndon A. Wade
President
Atlanta Urban League
75 Piedmont Avenue, N.E.,
Suite 310
Atlanta, GA 30303
404-659-1150

AURORA, ILLINOIS

Peggy S. Hicks
President
Quad County Urban League
10 South Smith Street
Aurora, IL 60505
312-820-8030

AUSTIN, TEXAS

Linda Moore Smith
President
Austin Area Urban League
1825 East 38½ Street
Austin, TX 78722
512-478-7176

BALTIMORE, MARYLAND

Roger I. Lyons
President
Baltimore Urban League
1150 Mondawmin Concourse
Baltimore, MD 21215
301-523-8150

BATTLE CREEK, MICHIGAN

Joyce A. Brown
President
Battle Creek Area Urban League
Community Service Building
182 West Van Buren, Room 305
Battle Creek, MI 49017
616-962-5553

BINGHAMTON, NEW YORK

Laura C. Keeling
President
Broome County Urban League
43-45 Carroll Street
Binghamton, NY 13901
607-723-7303

BIRMINGHAM, ALABAMA

James C. Graham, Jr.
President
Birmingham Urban League
1717 4th Avenue, North
P.O. Box 11269
Birmingham, AL 35202-1269
205-326-0162

BOSTON, MASSACHUSETTS

Joan Wallace-Benjamin, Ph.D.
President
Urban League of
    Eastern Massachusetts
88 Warren Street
Roxbury, MA 02119
617-442-4519

BRIDGEPORT, CONNECTICUT

William K. Wolfe
President
Urban League of
  Greater Bridgeport
285 Golden Hill Street
Bridgeport, CT 06604
203-366-2737

BUFFALO, NEW YORK

LeRoy R. Coles, Jr.
President
Buffalo Urban League, Inc.
Buffalo Urban League Center
15 East Genesee Street
Buffalo, NY 14203
716-854-7625

CANTON, OHIO

Joseph N. Smith
Executive Director
Canton Urban League, Inc.
Community Center
1400 Sherrick Road, S.E.
Canton, OH 44707-3533
216-456-3479

CHAMPAIGN, ILLINOIS

Vernon L. Barkstall
President
Urban League of
  Champaign County
17 Taylor Street
Champaign, IL 61820
217-356-1364

CHARLOTTE, NORTH CAROLINA

Madine Hester Fails
President
Charlotte-Mecklenburg
  Urban League
A.M.E. Zion Building
401 East Second Street
Charlotte, NC 28202
704-376-9834

CHATTANOOGA, TENNESSEE

Jerome W. Page
President
Chattanooga Area Urban League
P.O. Box 1421
730 Martin Luther King Blvd.
Chattanooga, TN 37401
615-756-1762

CHICAGO, ILLINOIS

James W. Compton
President
Chicago Urban League
4510 South Michigan Avenue
Chicago, IL 60653
312-285-5800

CINCINNATI, OHIO

Dewey C. Fuller
Executive Director
Urban League of
  Greater Cincinnati
2400 Reading Road
Cincinnati, OH 45202
513-721-2237

CLEVELAND, OHIO

Calvin W. Humphrey
President
Urban League of
  Greater Cleveland
12001 Shaker Boulevard
Cleveland, OH 44120
216-421-0999

COLORADO SPRINGS, COLORADO

James E. Miller
President
Urban League of the
  Pikes Peak Region
324 North Nevada
Colorado Springs, CO 80903
719-634-1525

COLUMBIA, SOUTH CAROLINA

James T. McLawhorn, Jr.
President
Columbia Urban League, Inc.
2711 Middleburg Drive, Suite 316
P.O. Drawer "J"
Columbia, SC 29250
803-799-8150

COLUMBUS, GEORGIA

Jessie J. Taylor
Executive Director
Metro Columbus Urban League
802 First Avenue
Columbus, GA 31901
404-323-3687

COLUMBUS, OHIO

Samuel Gresham, Jr.
President
Columbus Urban League
700 Bryden Road—Suite 230
Columbus, OH 43215
614-221-0544

DALLAS, TEXAS

Roosevelt Johnson, Jr.
Executive Director
Dallas Urban League
2121 Main Street—4th Floor,
  Suite 410
Dallas, TX 75201
214-747-4734

DAYTON, OHIO

Willie F. Walker
President
Dayton Urban League
United Way Building, Rm. 200
184 Salem Avenue
Dayton, OH 45406
513-220-6650

DENVER, COLORADO

Lawrence H. Borom
President
Urban League of
  Metropolitan Denver
1525 Josephine Street
Denver, CO 80206
303-388-5861

DETROIT, MICHIGAN

N. Charles Anderson
President
Detroit Urban League
208 Mack Avenue
Detroit, MI 48201
313-832-4600

ELIZABETH, NEW JERSEY

Ella S. Teal
President
Urban League of Union County
272 North Broad Street
Elizabeth, NJ 07207
201-351-7200

ELYRIA, OHIO

Delbert L. Lancaster
President
Lorain County Urban League
401 Broad Street
Robinson Building
Suites 204 & 206
Elyria, OH 44035
216-323-3364/5

ENGLEWOOD, NEW JERSEY

William E. Brown
President
Urban League for Bergen County
106 West Palisade Avenue
Englewood, NJ 07631
201-568-4988

FLINT, MICHIGAN

Melvyn S. Brannon
President
Urban League of Flint
202 East Boulevard Dr. 2nd Floor
Flint, MI 48503
313-239-5111

FORT LAUDERDALE, FLORIDA

Jesse J. Payne
Executive Director
Urban League of Broward County
11 N.W. 36th Avenue
Fort Lauderdale, FL 33311
305-584-0777

FORT WAYNE, INDIANA

Rick C. Frazier
President
Fort Wayne Urban League
Foellinger Community Center
227 East Washington Blvd.
Fort Wayne, IN 46802
219-424-6326

GARY, INDIANA

Eloise Gentry
President
Urban League of
    Northwest Indiana, Inc.
3101 Broadway
Gary, IN 46408
219-887-9621

GRAND RAPIDS, MICHIGAN

Walter M. Brame, Ed.D.
President
Grand Rapids Urban League
745 Eastern Street, S.E.
Grand Rapids, MI 49503
616-245-2207

GREENVILLE, SOUTH CAROLINA

Myron F. Robinson
President
Greenville Urban League
15 Regency Hill Drive
P.O. Box 10161
Greenville, SC 29603
803-244-3862

HARRISBURG, PENNSYLVANIA

Kinneth W. Washington
President
Urban League of
    Metropolitan Harrisburg
28 North Second Street
Harrisburg, PA 17101
717-234-5925

HARTFORD, CONNECTICUT

Esther Bush
President
Urban League of
    Greater Hartford
1229 Albany Avenue, 3rd Floor
Hartford, CT 06112
203-527-0147

HOUSTON, TEXAS

Victor V. James, Ph.D.
President
Houston Area Urban League
5445 Almeda Street, Suite 400
Houston, TX 77004
713-526-5127

INDIANAPOLIS, INDIANA

Sam H. Jones
President
Indianapolis Urban League
850 Meridian Street
Indianapolis, IN 46204
317-639-9404

JACKSON, MISSISSIPPI

Maggie Tryman
Executive Director
Urban League of
    Greater Jackson
3405 Medgar Evers Boulevard
P.O. Box 11249
Jackson, MS 39213
601-981-4211

JACKSONVILLE, FLORIDA

Ronnie A. Ferguson
President
Jacksonville Urban League
101 East Union Street
Jacksonville, FL 32202
904-356-8336

JERSEY CITY, NEW JERSEY

VACANT
President
Urban League of Hudson County
779 Bergen Avenue
Jersey City, NJ 07306
201-451-8888

KANSAS CITY, MISSOURI

William H. Clark
President
Urban League of Kansas City
1710 Paseo
Kansas City, MO 64108
816-471-0550

KNOXVILLE, TENNESSEE

Mark Brown
President
Knoxville Area Urban League
2416 Magnolia Avenue
P.O. Box 1911
Knoxville, TN 37901
615-524-5511

LANCASTER, PENNSYLVANIA

Milton J. Bondurant
President
Urban League of
  Lancaster County
502 South Duke Street
Lancaster, PA 17602
717-394-1966

LANSING, MICHIGAN

Charles H. Mitchner
President
Greater Lansing Urban
  League, Inc.
809 Center Street
Lansing, MI 48906
517-487-3608

LEXINGTON, KENTUCKY

Porter G. Peeples
Executive Director
Urban League of
  Lexington-Fayette County
167 West Main Street, Room 406
Lexington, KY 40507
606-233-1561

LITTLE ROCK, ARKANSAS

Harold Barrett
Interim Administrator
Urban League of Arkansas
2200 Main Street
P.O. Box 164039
Little Rock, AR 72216
501-372-3037

LOS ANGELES, CALIFORNIA

John W. Mack
President
Los Angeles Urban League
3450 Mount Vernon Drive
Los Angeles, CA 90008
213-299-9660

LOUISVILLE, KENTUCKY

Benjamin K. Richmond
President
Louisville Urban League
Lyles Mall—Third Level
2600 West Broadway
Louisville, KY 40211
502-776-4622

MADISON, WISCONSIN

Betty A. Franklin-Hammonds
Executive Director
Madison Urban League
151 East Gorham
Madison, WI 53703
608-251-8550

MARION, INDIANA

Arthur N. Banks III
Executive Director
Marion Urban League, Inc.
1221 West Twelfth Street
Marion, IN 46953
317-664-3933

MASSILLON, OHIO

Joan Gillespie
Interim President
Massillon Urban League, Inc.
405 Massillon Building
Massillon, OH 44646
216-833-2804

MEMPHIS, TENNESSEE

Herman C. Ewing
President
Memphis Urban League
2279 Lamar Avenue
Memphis, TN 38114
901-327-3591

MIAMI, FLORIDA

T. Willard Fair
President
Urban League of Greater Miami
8500 N.W. 25th Avenue
Miami, FL 33132
305-696-4450

MILWAUKEE, WISCONSIN

Jacqueline J. Patterson
President
Milwaukee Urban League
2800 West Wright Street
Milwaukee, WI 53210
414-374-5850

MINNEAPOLIS, MINNESOTA

Gleason Glover
President
Minneapolis Urban League
2000 Plymouth Avenue, North
Minneapolis, MN 55411
612-521-1099

MORRISTOWN, NEW JERSEY

Janice S. Johnson
President
Morris County Urban League
27 Market Street
Morristown, NJ 07960
201-539-2121

MUSKEGON, MICHIGAN

VACANT
Urban League of
   Greater Muskegon
469 West Webster Avenue
Muskegon, MI 49440
616-722-3736

NASHVILLE, TENNESSEE

Joseph S. Carroll
Executive Director
Nashville Urban League
2701 Jefferson Street
Nashville, TN 37208
615-329-2575

NEWARK, NEW JERSEY

Lorna K. Johnson
President
Urban League of Essex County
3 William Street, Suite 300
Newark, NJ 07102
201-624-6660

NEW HAVEN, CONNECTICUT

Earl W. Fraser
President
Urban League of
  Greater New Haven
1184 Chapel Street
New Haven, CT 06511
203-624-4168

NEW ORLEANS, LOUISIANA

Clarence L. Barney
President
Urban League of
  Greater New Orleans
1929 Bienville Street
New Orleans, LA 70112
504-524-4667

NEW YORK, NEW YORK

Donald L. Polk
President
New York Urban League
218 West 40th Street
New York, NY 10018
212-730-5200

NORFOLK, VIRGINIA

Mary L. Redd
President
Urban League of
  Hampton Roads
147 Granby Street
Plume Center West
Norfolk, VA 23510
804-627-0864

OAKLAND, CALIFORNIA

Percy H. Steele, Jr.
President
Bay Area Urban League
Kaiser Center Mall
344 20th Street, Suite 211
Oakland, CA 94612
415-839-8011

OKLAHOMA CITY, OKLAHOMA

Leonard D. Benton
President
Urban League of
  Greater Oklahoma City
3017 Martin Luther King
  Avenue
Oklahoma City, OK 73111
405-424-5243

OMAHA, NEBRASKA

George H. Dillard
President
Urban League of Nebraska
3022-24 North 24th Street
Omaha, NE 68110
402-453-9730

ORLANDO, FLORIDA

Shirley J. Boykin
President
Metropolitan Orlando
Urban League
934 North Magnolia Avenue,
  Suite 333
Orlando, FL 32803
407-841-7654

PEORIA, ILLINOIS

Frank Campbell
Executive Director
Tri-County Urban League
317 South MacArthur Highway
Peoria, IL 61605-3892
309-673-7474

PHILADELPHIA, PENNSYLVANIA

Robert W. Sorrell
President
Urban League of Philadelphia
4601 Market Street—Suite 2S
Philadelphia, PA 19139
215-476-4040

PHOENIX, ARIZONA

Junius A. Bowman
President
Phoenix Urban League
1402 South Seventh Avenue
Phoenix, AZ 85007
602-254-5611

PITTSBURGH, PENNSYLVANIA

Leon L. Haley, Ph.D.
President
Urban League of Pittsburgh
200 Ross Street, 2nd Floor
Pittsburgh, PA 15219
412-261-1130

PONTIAC, MICHIGAN

Jacquelin E. Washington
President
Pontiac Area Urban League
50 Wayne Street, 2nd Floor
Pontiac, MI 48058
313-335-8730

PORTLAND, OREGON

Ernest C. Cooper
Interim Administrator
Urban League of Portland
Urban Plaza
10 North Russell
Portland, OR 97277
503-280-2600

PROVIDENCE, RHODE ISLAND

B. Jae Clanton
President
Urban League of Rhode Island
246 Prairie Avenue
Providence, RI 02905
401-351-5000

RACINE, WISCONSIN

Rodney Brooks
President
Urban League of Racine &
  Kenosha, Inc.
718-22 North Memorial Drive
Racine, WI 53404
414-637-8532

RICHMOND, VIRGINIA

Randolph C. Kendall, Jr.
President
Richmond Urban League
101 East Clay Street
Richmond, VA 23219
804-649-8407

ROCHESTER, NEW YORK

William A. Johnson, Jr.
President
Urban League of Rochester
177 North Clinton Avenue
Rochester, NY 14604
716-325-6530

SACRAMENTO, CALIFORNIA

George H. Dean
President
Sacramento Urban League
3501 Broadway
Sacramento, CA 95817
916-739-0627

ST. LOUIS, MISSOURI

James H. Buford
President
Urban League of
    Metropolitan St. Louis
3701 Grandel Square
St. Louis, MO 63108
314-371-0040

ST. PAUL, MINNESOTA

Willie Mae Wilson
President
St. Paul Urban League
401 Selby Avenue
St. Paul, MN 55102
612-224-5771

ST. PETERSBURG, FLORIDA

James O. Simmons
President
Pinellas County Urban League
333 31st Street, North
St. Petersburg, FL 33713
813-327-2081

SAN DIEGO, CALIFORNIA

C. Terry Whitesides
Interim Director
San Diego Urban League
4261 Market Street
San Diego, CA 92101
619-263-3115

SAN JOSE, CALIFORNIA

Dian J. Harrison
Executive Director
Santa Clara Valley
    Urban League, Inc.
753 North 9th Street, #131
San Jose, CA 95112
408-971-0117

SANTA ANA, CALIFORNIA

George L. Williams
President
Orange County Urban League
Old Lloyd's Bank Building
106 West 4th Street—Mez.
Santa Ana, CA 92701
714-558-7996

SEATTLE, WASHINGTON

Rossalind Y. Woodhouse, Ph.D.
President
Seattle Urban League
105 14th Avenue
Seattle, WA 98122
206-447-3792

SHARON, PENNSYLVANIA

Phillip E. Smith
President
Urban League of
  Shenango Valley
39 Chestnut Street
Sharon, PA 16146
412-981-5310

SOUTH BEND, INDIANA

Raymond Howard
President
Urban League of South Bend
  and St. Joseph County, Inc.
1708 High Street
P.O. Box 1476
South Bend, IN 46624
219-287-7261

SPRINGFIELD, ILLINOIS

Howard R. Veal
President
Springfield Urban League, Inc.
100 North 11th Street
P.O. Box 3865
Springfield, IL 62708
217-789-0830

SPRINGFIELD, MASSACHUSETTS

Henry M. Thomas III
President
Urban League of Springfield
756 State Street
Springfield, MA 01109
413-739-7211

SPRINGFIELD, OHIO

Charles E. Nesbitt, Ph.D.
President
Springfield Urban League
521 South Center Street
Springfield, OH 45506
513-323-4603

STAMFORD, CONNECTICUT

Curtiss E. Porter, Ph.D.
President
Urban League of Southwestern
  Fairfield County
231 Main Street
Stamford, CT 06901
203-327-5810

SYRACUSE, NEW YORK

Leon E. Modeste
President
Urban League of
  Onondaga County
505 East Fayette Street
Syracuse, NY 13202
315-472-6955

TACOMA, WASHINGTON

Thomas Dixon
President
Tacoma Urban League
2550 South Yakima Avenue
Tacoma, WA 98405
206-383-2006

TALLAHASSEE, FLORIDA

Reverend Ernest Ferrell
President
Tallahassee Urban League
923 Old Bainbridge Road
Tallahassee, FL 32301
904-222-6111

TAMPA, FLORIDA

Joanna N. Tokley
President
Greater Tampa Urban League
1405 Tampa Park Plaza
Tampa, FL 33604
813-229-8117

TRENTON, NEW JERSEY

Paul P. Pintella, Jr.
President
Urban League of
Metropolitan Trenton
209 Academy Street
Trenton, NJ 08618
609-393-1512

TUCSON, ARIZONA

Raymond Clarke
President
Tucson Urban League
2305 South Park Avenue
Tucson, AZ 85713
602-791-9522

TULSA, OKLAHOMA

Laverne Hill
Interim Director
Tulsa Urban League
240 East Apache Street
Tulsa, OK 74106
918-584-0001

WARREN, OHIO

Sydney Lancaster
Interim President
Warren/Trumbull Urban League
290 West Market Street
Warren, OH 44481
216-394-4316

WASHINGTON, D.C.

Betti S. Whaley
President
Washington Urban League
3501 14th Street, N.W.
Washington, D.C. 20010
202-265-8200

WAUKEGAN, ILLINOIS

Lorraine Hale-Bryant
Interim Director
Lake County Urban League
122 Madison Street
Waukegan, IL 60085
312-249-3770

WEST PALM BEACH, FLORIDA

Percy H. Lee
President
Urban League of
  Palm Beach County, Inc.
1700 Australian Avenue
West Palm Beach, FL 33407
407-833-1461

WHITE PLAINS, NEW YORK

Ernest S. Prince
President
Urban League of
  Westchester County
61 Mitchell Place
White Plains, NY 10601
914-428-6300

WICHITA, KANSAS

Otis G. Milton
President
Urban League of Wichita, Inc.
1405 North Minneapolis
Wichita, KS 67214
316-262-2463

WINSTON-SALEM, NORTH CAROLINA

Delores Smith
President
Winston-Salem Urban League
201 West 5th Street
Winston-Salem, NC 27101
919-725-5614

YOUNGSTOWN, OHIO

Stephen Pressley, Jr.
President
Youngstown Area Urban League
2516 Market Street
Youngstown, OH 44507
216-788-6533

NATIONAL URBAN LEAGUE, INC.

WASHINGTON OPERATIONS

Billy J. Tidwell, Ph.D.
Director, Research

Robert McAlpine
Director
Public Policy and
Government Relations

Washington Operations
National Urban League, Inc.
1111 14th Street, N.W.,
   6th Floor
Washington, DC 20005
202-898-1604

NATIONAL HEADQUARTERS

John E. Jacob
President and Chief
Executive Officer
National Urban League, Inc.
500 East 62nd Street
New York, NY 10021
212-310-9000

Appendix VIII
Minority Resources
The organizations listed below can be contacted for advice and job information.

Association on American Indian
  Affairs
95 Madison Avenue
New York, NY 10016

Black Business Alliance
2713 Classen Avenue
Baltimore, MD 21215

Hispanic Organization of
  Professionals & Executives
87 Catotin Court
Silver Spring, MD 20906

National Association for the
  Advancement of Colored
  People (NAACP)
4805 Mt. Hope Drive
Baltimore, MD 21215

National Black MBA Association
111 East Wacker Drive
Suite 600
Chicago, IL 60601

U.S. Hispanic Chamber of
  Commerce
Board of Trade Center
4900 Main, Suite 700
P.O. Box 30177
Kansas City, MO 64112

GLOSSARY

Lexicon of Temporary-Help Terms

To improve understanding of the temporary-help business and to help distinguish it from fundamentally different businesses such as employment agency business and employee leasing, the National Association of Temporary Services has prepared this lexicon of terms.

APPLICANT   An individual seeking temporary employment with a temporary help company. In the employment agency business, "applicant" means a person seeking to be permanently placed.

ASSIGN   The act of sending a temporary employee to work on the premises of a customer of the temporary help company. "Assign" is different from a "referral" which describes the employment agency practice of sending an applicant to a prospective employer for an interview. "Refer" or "referral" does not apply to the act of assigning temporary employees.

ASSIGNMENT   The period of time during which a temporary employee is working on a customer's premises.

COMMINGLING   See Joint Operations

COORDINATOR   The staff employee of a temporary help company who assigns temporary employees to work on the customer's premises.

COUNSELOR   An employment agency employee who refers or places applicants for employment with employers. The term does not apply to a staff employee of a temporary help company. Many state employment agency laws require that counselors be licensed.

CUSTOMER   The person, organization or business that uses the services of a temporary help company.

DISPATCH   This term is generally used to refer to the act of assigning industrial temporary employees to report for work on customers' premises.

EMPLOYEE LEASING   An arrangement whereby a business transfers its employees to the payroll of a "leasing organization" after which the employees are leased back to their original employer where they continue working in the same capacity as before in an *ongoing, permanent* relationship.

EMPLOYMENT AGENCY   A business whose purpose is to bring a job seeker and a prospective employer together for the purpose of effecting a permanent employment relationship.

FEE   The amount charged by an employment agency for placing job seekers in permanent positions. The term does not refer to a temporary help company's gross profit or liquidated damages charge. (See Liquidated Damages)

GENERAL EMPLOYER   An employer who has the right to hire and fire an employee, is responsible for the employee's wages and benefits, and exercises ultimate supervision, discipline and control over the employee. Temporary help companies are the general employees of their temporary employees. (See Special Employer)

IN-HOUSE TEMPORARY An individual hired directly by a non-temporary help company as a permanent employee to perform various temporary assignments within that company.

INDEPENDENT CONTRACTOR A person, not an employee, who performs work for another. Unlike employees, independent contractors: (1) are not subject to the control and supervision of the person using the services regarding the details of how the work is to be performed, (2) generally have specialized training or education, and (3) supply all necessary tools, supplies or equipment necessary to perform the work.

JOB ORDER See Work Order

JOB SHOP A colloquial term generally used to refer to businesses that supply longer-term temporary employees on a contract basis in technical or specialized areas such as engineering, drafting, etc.

JOINT OPERATIONS The operation of both a temporary help company and an employment agency by the same firm. Problems arise when these fundamentally different operations are conducted with the same personnel, forms and procedures so that the two businesses are not easily distinguished by job applicants and customers. Such "commingling" leads to public confusion about the nature of the temporary help business and could subject the industry to employment agency regulation. To avoid confusion, NATS has developed guidelines to help NATS members keep the two businesses separate.

LIQUIDATED DAMAGES Liquidated damages are monies paid by temporary help customers under agreements in which the customer agrees not to hire the temporary employee within some specified period of time and to pay damages for breach of that promise in the agreed-upon (i.e., "liquidated") amount.

PART-TIME A work period less than the full work day or full work week. "Part-time" employees are not "temporary employees" because, unlike temporary employees, they work a regular schedule for their employer on an ongoing, indefinite basis. (See Temporary Employee)

PAYROLLING   A colloquial term in the temporary help industry that describes a situation whereby the customer, rather than the temporary help company, recruits an individual and asks the temporary help company to consider employing the individual and assigning him to the customer on a temporary basis. Once hired by the temporary help company, the "payrolled" employee's employment relationship with the temporary help company is the same as any other temporary employee.

PLACEMENT   An employment agency term describing the act of successfully placing a job seeker in a permanent position with an employer.

SPECIAL EMPLOYER   A term referring to a customer's legal relationship to the temporary employees assigned to them. The relationship is based on the customer's right to direct and control the specific details of the work to be performed. As "special employers," customers have certain legal rights and obligations regarding temporary employees. For example, because worker's compensation insurance (which temporary help companies provide for their employees) is the exclusive relief available to employees against "employers" for work related injuries, a temporary employee generally cannot sue his "special employer" (the customer) for negligence. Hence, the customer's special employer status insulates it from such liability. On the other hand, as special employers, customers may also have certain obligations to temporary employees, e.g., not to discriminate against them in violation of the civil rights laws. (See General Employer)

SUPPLEMENTAL STAFFING   The term is generally used to refer to the practice of supplementing the permanent staff of hospitals and nursing homes with nurses and other health care personnel employed by temporary help companies.

TEMP-TO-PERM (Also referred to as "Try before you hire") The practice of sending temporary employees on an assignment for the express purpose of ultimately placing them in a permanent position with the customer. This is an employment agency activity which may subject a temporary help company to regulation under state employment agency laws.

"Temp-to-perm" practices include but are not limited to:

Advertising "temp-to-perm" positions to attract workers seeking permanent jobs.

Suggesting or *recommending* to customers that they use temporary employees on a "temp-to-perm" basis.

Agreeing to customers' requests to send temporary employees to the customer on a "temp-to-perm" basis.

Sending temporary employees to customers to be interviewed for the purpose of determining who will be assigned to the customer on a "temp-to-perm" basis.

TEMPORARY EMPLOYEE An employee who does not make a commitment to an employer to work on a regular, ongoing basis but instead is free to accept (or reject) assignments at such times and for such lengths of time as the employee may choose. A temporary employee is obligated only to complete a particular assignment once one is accepted, but has no obligation to accept further assignments. (See Part-Time Employee)

TEMPORARY HELP COMPANY An organization engaged in the business service of furnishing its own employees ("temporaries") to handle customers' temporary staffing needs and special projects.

TRY BEFORE YOU HIRE   See Temp-To-Perm

WORK ORDER   An order received from a customer for a temporary help company's services. In the employment agency industry, the term "Job Order" refers to a request from a prospective employer authorizing the employment agency to find an appropriate prospective employee.

Bibliography

Books

Birch, David. *Job Creation in America: How the Smallest Companies Put the Most People to Work.* New York: Free Press, 1987.

Bolles, Richard. *What Color Is Your Parachute?* Berkeley: Ten Speed Press, 1991.

Dickens, Floyd. *The Black Manager: Making It in the Corporate World.* New York: AMACOM, 1982.

Half, Robert. *How to Get a Better Job in This Crazy World.* New York: Crown, 1990.

Irish, Richard. *Go Hire Yourself an Employer.* New York: Doubleday/Anchor, 1987.

Jackson, Tom. *Guerrilla Tactics in the New Job Market.* New York: Bantam, 1991.

Kennedy, Joyce Lain, and Darryl Laramore. *Joyce Lain Kennedy's Career Book.* Lincolnwood, NE: VGM Career Horizons, 1988.

Krannich, L. Ronald. *Careering and Recareering for the 1990s.* Manassas, VA: Impact Publications, 1989.

Parker, Yaba. *The Damn Good Resume Guide.* Berkeley: Ten Speed Press, 1989.

Schmidt, Peggy. *The 90-Minute Resume*. Princeton, NJ: Peterson's Guides, 1990.

Software

Career Design. Crystal-Barkley Corporation, 111 East 31st Street, New York, NY 10016.

Career Management Partner. Scientific Systems, 5 Science Park, New Haven, CT 06511.

Career Navigator. Drake Beam Morin, 100 Park Avenue, New York, NY 10017.

The Perfect Resume Computer Kit. Permex Systems, Inc., 5008 Gordon Avenue, Madison, WI 53716.

Resume and Letters for Your Resume. North American InfoNet, P.O. Box 750008, Petaluma, CA 94975-0008.

Resume Kit. Spinnaker Software, 1 Kendall Square, Cambridge, MA 02139.

ResumeWriter. Bootware, 28024 Dorothy Drive, Agoura Hills, CA 91301.

Index